D1209838

A Communication Universe

LEXINGTON STUDIES IN
POLITICAL COMMUNICATION

Series Editor: Robert E. Denton, Jr.,
Virginia Polytechnic Institute and State University

This series encourages focused work examining the role and function of communication in the realm of politics including campaigns and elections, media, and political institutions.

RECENT TITLES IN THE SERIES:

Making a Difference: A Comparative View of the Role of the Internet in Election Politics,
Edited by Stephen Ward, Diana Owen, Richard Davis, and David Taras
Seen and Heard: The Women of Television News, By Nichola D. Gutgold
Nuclear Legacies: Communication, Controversy, and the U. S. Nuclear Weapons Complex,
Edited by Bryan C. Taylor, William J. Kinsella, Stephen P. Depoe, Maribeth S. Metzler
Conditional Press Influence in Politics, By Adam J. Schiffer
Telling Political Lives: The Rhetorical Autobiographies of Women Leaders in the United States, Edited by Brenda DeVore Marshall and Molly A. Mayhead
Media Bias? A Comparative Study of Time, Newsweek, the National Review, and the Progressive, 1975–2000, By Tawnya J. Adkins Covert and Philo C. Wasburn
Navigating the Post–Cold War World: President Clinton's Foreign Policy Rhetoric,
By Jason A. Edwards
The Rhetoric of Pope John Paul II, Edited by Joseph R. Blaney and Joseph P. Zompetti
Stagecraft and Statecraft: Advance and Media Events in Political Communication,
By Dan Schill
Rhetorical Criticism: Perspectives in Action, Edited by Jim A. Kuypers
Almost Madam President: Why Hillary Clinton "Won" in 2008, By Nichola D. Gutgold
Cracked But Not Shattered: Hillary Rodham Clinton's Unsuccessful Run for the Presidency, Edited by Theodore F. Sheckels
Gender and Political Communication in America: Rhetoric, Representation, and Display,
Edited by Janis L. Edwards
Communicator-in-Chief: How Barack Obama Used New Media Technology to Win the White House, Edited by John Allen Hendricks and Robert E. Denton, Jr.
Centrist Rhetoric: The Production of Political Transcendence in the Clinton Presidency,
By Antonio de Velasco
Studies of Identity in the 2008 Presidential Campaign, Edited by Robert E. Denton, Jr.
Campaign Finance Reform: The Political Shell Game, By Melissa M. Smith, Glenda C. Williams, Larry Powell, and Gary A. Copeland
Us against Them: The Political Culture of Talk Radio, By Randy Bobbitt
Internet Policy in China: A Field Study of Internet Cafés, By Helen Sun
A Communication Universe: Manifestations of Meaning, Stagings of Significance,
By Igor E. Klyukanov

302.2 K719

A Communication Universe

Manifestations of Meaning,
Stagings of Significance

Igor E. Klyukanov

Nyack College - Bailey Library
One South Blvd.
Nyack, NY 10960

LEXINGTON BOOKS
A division of
ROWMAN & LITTLEFIELD PUBLISHERS, INC.
Lanham • Boulder • New York • Toronto • Plymouth, UK

Published by Lexington Books
A division of Rowman & Littlefield Publishers, Inc.
A wholly owned subsidary of The Rowman & Littlefield Publishing Group, Inc.
4501 Forbes Boulevard, Suite 200, Lanham, Maryland 20706
http://www.lexingtonbooks.com

Estover Road, Plymouth PL6 7PY, United Kingdom

Copyright © 2010 by Igor E. Klyukanov

All rights reserved. No part of this book may be reproduced in any form or by any
electronic or mechanical means, including information storage and retrieval systems,
without written permission from the publisher, except by a reviewer who may quote
passages in a review.

British Library Cataloguing in Publication Information Available

Library of Congress Cataloging-in-Publication Data

Klyukanov, Igor.
 A communication universe : manifestations of meaning, stagings of significance / Igor
E. Klyukanov.
     p. cm. — (Lexington studies in political communication)
 Includes bibliographical references and index.
 ISBN 978-0-7391-3723-9 (cloth : alk. paper)—ISBN 978-0-7391-3724-6 (pbk. : alk.
paper)—ISBN 978-0-7391-3725-3 (electronic)
 1. Communication—Philosophy. I. Title.
 P90.K557 2010
 302.2—dc22   2010019619

⊗ ™ The paper used in this publication meets the minimum requirements of
American National Standard for Information Sciences—Permanence of Paper for
Printed Library Materials, ANSI/NISO Z39.48-1992.

Printed in the United States of America

#613311533

To Galya and Anya with love,
everywhere and everywhen

~

Contents

Acknowledgments

This book would never have seen the light of day—literally—were it not for my parents, Lyudmila A. Klyukanova and Engel N. Loitsker. I owe them a debt of gratitude for steering me toward philology: I was brought up to love the word—and I still do.

This book might never have seen the light of day without many other people, and I thank them all for helping me in one way or another.

I thank those teachers and friends whom I will never see again, not in this life anyway: Roman R. Gel'gardt, Il'ya N. Gorelov, Yuriy A. Sorokin, and Tom Puckett. As I would lead my slate-pencil to where my voice will tell me, I couldn't help hearing their voices—gentle, stern, pensive, arguing, and always encouraging.

I thank my students—both in the United States and Russia—for their interest in what I had to say, or lack of it. I thank my colleagues, who fortunately did show an interest in what I had to say: Juan José Padial Benticuaga, Mara B. Borisova, Donal Carbaugh, Pedro J. Chamizo Domínguez, Patricia Chantrill, David Demers, Deborah Eicher-Catt, William Graves III, Boris Gubman, Sergei Klyagin, Mikhail Makarov, Antonina A. Khar'kovskaya, Gary Krug, Vera A. Pichal'nikova, Peter Shields, Evgeniy F. Tarasov, Yuriy Varzonin and Alexandra A. Zalevskaya. They all generously shared their expertise in those areas where mine was lacking. Often, we simply talked about communication, and they didn't know that their remarks would make it into my book; at many such points in time and space, neither did I.

I am grateful to those who read the initial drafts of the manuscript and provided helpful feedback: Richard Lanigan, Isaac Catt, John D. Peters, Evgeniy Kluev, Vyacheslav V. Ivanov, and Mikhail N. Epshtein. I have always found inspiration in their work.

I am particularly grateful to Andrew Smith for his numerous and insightful comments on the draft of this book. He was a careful and constructive critic of my work, always making his suggestions in a dialogical spirit. I found our conversations—if only via email—extremely helpful and stimulating.

I am especially grateful to Anthony Flinn for his advice on the overall structure of the book as well as many conceptual and stylistic issues—and for his good humor. I thank him for being such a perceptive reader who had a genuine interest in my work.

I wish to thank Matthew R. McAdam for getting me onboard with Lexington Press, Rebecca McCary, who took over as the acquisitions editor, for her patient and constant support, and Michael Wiles, who as assistant editor carefully oversaw the production of the book.

I thank Judy McMillan for creating a beautiful image that you see on the cover of this book.

This book is dedicated to my wife who may well be the closest reader this book will ever have, and to our daughter who I hope one day will read this book.

PART I

THE FUTURE BEHIND US: PERSPECTIVES ON COMMUNICATION

CHAPTER ONE

~

Toward the Nature
of Communication: Unforgetting

Communication Unfolding

"Communication(s) Revolution": this phrase has recently been used with increasing frequency (cp. Behringer 2006; Farman 2005; Giddens 2004; Mansell 2002; McChesney 2007; Schuller 2008; Vasilik 2006; Wersing 1985). In general, "promises of a communication revolution have a long history" (Flichy 2007, 1), each communication revolution usually associated with a new technological medium. For example, the invention of the printing press in the fifteenth century is considered to have been a revolutionary event, leading to innovations in science, politics, and religion (Covington 2002). Today, of course, we are said to live in the midst of a digital communication revolution, made possible by new electronic media. As new digital technologies become more pervasive, revolutionary changes are said to affect all aspects of our lives—from (inter)personal to global. Sometimes, a communication(s) revolution is presented as a result of a new pattern of technical and social interaction, cf. such article titles as "Facebook Creates a Communication Revolution" (Walber 2008), "Instant Messenger and the Communication Revolution" (Morris 2007), or "PODCAST: Social Media Leads Communication Revolution" (Kleinsasser 2009).

The modern Communications Revolution as a separate phenomenon is often traced back to the period around 1500, permanently changing the communications systems; its significance is considered "as fundamental as that of the Scientific Revolution, the Industrial Revolution and the revolutions in politics that took place in the same period" (Behringer 2006, 373).

The concept of the communication(s) revolution, therefore, refers to radical changes in the structure of communication, caused by new media and forms of technologies, and their profound effects on various aspects of people's lives.

The concept of a communication revolution is used not only in relation to how the process of communication takes place, but also how this process is theorized. In communication theory, too, revolutionary ideas seem to be abundant. For example, C. Shannon's ideas are often considered to form one of the first truly revolutionary theories of communication (Brittain 1984). Similarly, it is noted that the ideas developed by J. Habermas made a revolution in communication theory (Farman 2005, 257). Cf. also such article titles as "The Cognitive Revolution in Public Opinion and Communication Research" (Beniger and Gusek 1995), "A Revolutionary View of Communication: Cheris Kramarae's Theory of Muted Groups" (Harris 1999) or "High-Speed Management: A Revolution in Organizational Communication in the 1990s" (Gushman 1994).

One can see a clear isomorphism between everyday and scientific views on communication. Both these views reflect a craving for, and hope of, radical innovations in the form of new gadgets or ideas; it seems as if all problems of communication will be solved, and the nature of communication will be discovered. For example, while discussing the notion of the electronic revolution, J. Carey (1995, 115) speaks about those who

> have cast themselves in the role of secular theologians composing theodicies for electricity and its technological progeny. Despite the diversity of their backgrounds and positions on other questions, there is within their rhetorical descriptions of the electronic revolution a common set of ideas. They all convey an impression that electrical technology is the great benefactor of mankind. Simultaneously, they hail electrical techniques as the motive force of desired social change, the key to the re-creation of a humane community, the means for returning to a cherished naturalistic bliss.

The key question raised in the revolution discourse is "how communication can be tailored to ameliorate social problems or promote positive options" (Hornsey 2008, 749). The twentieth century and beginning of the twentieth-first century especially seem to be characterized by such hopes and cravings, having witnessed a number of violent and bloody failures to communicate. At the same time, new electronic technologies, exemplified by the Internet, seem to promise profound transformations of the existing conditions. Most recently, the potential of such promises as well as the necessity of translating that potential into action were articulated by R. McChesney in his book titled (not surprisingly) "Communication Revolution" with the subtitle "Critical Junctures and the Future of Media" (2008). R. McChesney considers communication to be central to democratic theory and practice, the society's "central nervous system" formed by the new technologies previously unimaginable. He believes that people today have an unprecedented opportunity to create a more sustainable and self-governing society; this critical juncture, however, calls for immediate public involvement and social reform because it won't remain open for long. In other words, we cannot afford to waste the potential offered by the present communication revolution, for its success (or failure) will be "critical."

It must be noted that, in spite of—or perhaps because of—its ubiquity, many publications (both popular and academic) often make "more or less unreflective use of the term 'communication revolution'" (Behringer 2006, 336). Indeed, "the idea of 'revolutions' has been trivialized" (Bauman 2008, 64); it seems as if each day "the advent of the next 'historic' or 'revolutionary' event is announced, with bated breath, by TV-anchor-people and splashed all over the front pages of the tabloids, only to be wiped away shortly afterwards from the drifting attention of the public by another batch of 'sensational' and 'unprecedented' events" (Bauman 2008, 63). In a similar vein, it is noted that the "Information Revolution" is "largely an illusion, a rhetorical gambit and an expression of technological ignorance" (Winston 1998, 2).

What most often appears to be meant by the term "revolution" is a supposedly sudden and momentous change with profound implications. The revolutionary slogan is "Time, Forward!" for every revolution spurs the time in the hopes of bringing about a certain condition as quickly as possible. And, in so doing, a revolution is often viewed as a complete break with the past. It is not surprising, for example, that T. Kuhn's theory of scientific revolutions is based on the notion of the incommensurability of different paradigms (Kuhn 1962); all new paradigms, brought about by scientific revolutions, replace the old ones and are incommensurable with them. Such paradigms are not necessarily "truer" than the old ones; they are simply revolutionary—different, new. Perhaps it is no accident that T. Kuhn's ideas especially appealed to those in social sciences and humanities who may have been envious of the successes of the physical and biological sciences known for their revolutionary discoveries; some guilt and narcissism of those in the "soft" sciences might have also played their part. It should be remembered that "Kuhn is primarily concerned with the incommensurability of *scientific* paradigms. But the very idea of incommensurability became so fertile and suggestive that it was soon generalized and extended to problems and contexts far beyond Kuhn's original concern to analyze scientific inquiry" (Bernstein 1992, 61). In the same vein, "Kuhn's slippery and ambiguous term 'paradigm'" (Bernstein 1992, 24) was uncritically accepted (see: Bostrom 2003), focusing on "paradigm shifts" instead of describing the development of scientific knowledge in terms of, for example, gradualism (Cohen 1985).

A revolutionary spirit does not really possess the virtue of patience, which would require looking as far into the past as possible as well as a hermeneutically sensitive self-inquiry. Unfortunately, "today we lack the patience to dig too far, or perhaps we lack the patience to unravel the implications of discoveries into the past" (Jacoby 2008, B6). Because we want an instant solution to every problem and a quick answer to every question, we often "triumphantly treat the effect as the cause" (Jacoby 2008, B6), and such treatment is not the result of the art of deconstruction (cf. Peters 2005, 26). Of course, such an approach can be justified as a practical measure, but "it avoids a deeper search," leading to the "domestication" of great thinkers, for instance, turning Marx into a cinema theorist, Freud—an interpreter of texts and Hegel—a philosopher of art (Jacoby 2008, B6). Today *docta ignorantia* for many is nothing but a curious artifact, covered up with the dust of centuries, unused for centuries—and for a reason.

A revolutionary view presents communication in the form of (discontinuous) momentous moments; each such moment is viewed as "distinct" and each juncture as "critical." However, on close reading, one can discern in the discourse of "communication revolution" elements of continuity, consciously downplayed or present as "blind spots." For example, according to R. Albion who is believed to have developed the concept back in 1932, the "communication revolution" was "a distinct development with its own separate phenomena and quantities. . . . The change in communications has knit the world closer together. It has widened the horizons of every community. . . . It has made possible far greater centralization in commerce and in government" (Albion 1932, 718). The view of the revolutionary changes in communication here is clearly comparative in nature; cf. "closer," "widened," and "greater." Similarly, it is stated that "the communications revolution . . . began in the early modern era, and is still ongoing" (Behringer 2006, 374).

In this light, T. Kuhn's position on paradigms can be seen as refutation of its own premises. If rival paradigms cannot be compared or communicate in a common language, in what sense are they rivals? With no common subject matter, there is nothing for them to disagree about (Doppelt 2006). Besides, "revolutionary paradigms" in T. Kuhn's theory, which appear "all of a sudden" as a Gestalt-switch change, actually go through several stages such as pre-paradigmatic, normal, anomaly, etc., thus forming a continuous pattern. In spite of T. Kuhn's later efforts to refine his concept of incommensurability by emphasizing the comparability and translatability of taxonomies (Chen 1997), his ideas—not surprisingly—were criticized from the perspective of evolutionary epistemology (Cartmill 1999; Radnitzky and Bartley 1987). In this light, it is impossible to discuss communication only in terms of "meaningful digits" (revolutions) without emphasizing any comparison and continuity between them. According to Ch. S. Peirce, continuity "is by far the most difficult for Philosophy to handle" (Peirce 1992, 37). It is noted that "the notion of continuity, along with the notions of chance, as really operative in the universe, and love, as 'the great evolutionary agency of the universe,' are the three key doctrines of Peirce's comprehensive evolutionary cosmology" (Nubiola 1994, 365).

A revolution, to use G. Bateson's definition of the elementary unit of information (Bateson 2000, 457–459), can be seen as a difference which makes a meaningful difference. At the same time, a different state of affairs is always different from something else; in other words, a difference can be conceptualized only as *more or less* meaningful. In this respect, it can be stated that a revolution can be understood only at the background of evolution and vice versa. From this point of view, communication appears as both a discontinuous (revolutionary) and a continuous (evolutionary) process.

In this connection, the way T. Kuhn drew a parallel between his account of revolutions and Darwin's account of evolution is quite surprising. It is especially surprising that he saw revolutionary transitions rather than normal scientific developments as evolutionary. Examined on a minute time scale, "normal science also involves a more constrained variation and selection process, as scientific practitioners search for ways to articulate the paradigm. Examined from afar, revolutions are simply the more noteworthy episodes in the evolution of the sciences. Examined up close, they . . . have a detailed structure that is evolutionary, even something as revolutionary as the quantum theory" (*Stanford Encyclopedia of Philosophy*). Thus, one can speak about revolutions "only retrospectively—when, looking back, we realize that enough small and apparently insignificant changes have accumulated to produce a qualitative, not just an incremental transformation in the human condition" (Bauman 2008, 64). Used in the study of cosmos, for example, looking back follows "the Doppler effect—waves moving away from a fixed observer are stretched into greater lengths (and thus lower frequencies)— light from distant sources in space is shifted toward the red (lower frequency) part of the spectrum. . . . The farther we see into space, the earlier we look into time, and the redder the light is the farther we look. The universe is inside out: its distant edges constitute its youngest parts. (But they are oldest to us)" (Peters 2008, 26–27). The same interpretive strategy of "looking back" should be used in the study of communication if we want to come closer to its nature, which gets "younger and younger" with each of our "discoveries."

Although normal scientific developments can reveal distinct episodes of revolutionary variation and development, the way to new paradigms lies through resolving anomalies by which we come to be puzzled. It is at this stage that wonder comes to play a crucial role in the pursuit of knowledge. According to Aristotle, our search for meaning is driven by something that raises our curiosity and by which we are perplexed. Thus we move from wonder to certainty, from *aporia* to *theoria*; we escape from wonder by theorizing the cause. Once the cause is theorized, a paradigm changes and normal science sets in; this new view is accepted by all and so becomes no longer wonderful. However, there is another way to look at wonder, as A. Nightingale reminds us in her *Spectacle of Truth in Classical Greek Philosophy* (Nightingale 2006). This different conception of wonder is Platonic wonder, which does not occur only at the beginning of our quest, but is present simultaneously with how we experience the world and ourselves; "it is more like awe or reverence than perplexity or curiosity" (Nightingale 2006, 257). Only this way can any object be perceived as kindred to us—beautiful, divine, and wonderful. And only this way can we feel not only puzzlement, but also a reverence for—and kinship with—any object. From this perspective, communication can be conceptualized as "a wondrous vision" that persists, a thing of beauty (and wonder) that is "a joy forever"; "An endless fountain of immortal drink/ Pouring unto us from the heaven's brink" (John Keats).

The first view, based on Aristotle's ideas, requires that the viewer act upon the world trying to change it; the second view, based on Plato's ideas, requires that we, similar to the Greek theoretical philosophers returning from their journeys to sacred sites, seek to change ourselves rather than the world around us (cf. Nightingale 2006, 10).

So, an evolutionary approach allows us to understand how communication evolves by searching continuity between its different concepts. It must be remembered that "every concept . . . invents its ancestors" (Peters 2005, 11). In other words, no communication concept, including the concept of communication itself, can be fully understood if we forget—or rather fail to remember—its ancestry. Even history in general "viewed reflexively, is communication history," and in this respect "we have much work left to do" (Peters 2008, 32). The evolutionary slogan is "Back to the Future!" Unfortunately, few today seem to hear this call and fewer still (are willing—or able—to) respond to it. In fact, more and more often, instead of looking for kinship, the opposite seems to be the case, and the Latin expression *Pereant qui ante nos nostra dixerunt* ("May they perish who have expressed our bright ideas before us") still sounds as true as ever.

It is no wonder, then, that wonder is less and less often a part of the spectrum of our feelings otherwise so broad and diverse. Also, it is no wonder that the phrase "communication(s) revolution" has recently been used with increasing frequency. In communication theory, such revolutions take the form of numerous "turns." For example, in just one article on philosophical aspects of communication we read about the "turn toward a social epistemology" (Anderson and Baym 2004, 604), "the turn toward a feminist or standpoint epistemology" (Anderson and Baym 2004, 605), "the turn toward epistemic multiplicity" (Anderson and Baym 2004, 606), and "the postmodern turn" (Anderson and Baym 2004, 608). Other examples include "an interpretive turn" (Anderson 1996), "a critical turn" (Craig 1999), "a cultural turn" (Biernacki and Bonnell et al. 1999), and "a reflexive turn" (Myers 2001). One also comes across "the probabilistic turn in communication theory," "the linguistic turn in the theory of communication systems" (Leydesdorff 2002; cf. Rorty 1992), "the discursive turn" (Angus 1998), "a naturalistic turn" (Russill 2005), and "iconic, visual and perceptive turns" (Kudryashova 2008, 174).

One's head just spins, and we feel as if the ground were slipping away from under our feet. It is not surprising, therefore, that some communication scholars get "a distinct impression that the discipline is experiencing a high degree of 'methodological schizophrenia'" (Hanna 1982, 43), while others admit that "the field increasingly suffers from epistemological erosion" (Donsbach 2006, 444). Interestingly, one reason for such erosion might be too short a distance between communication, as an object of study, and those who study it. As a result, "the closeness of its object to everybody's reality and experience makes everybody a self-proclaimed 'expert.' People say, 'Because I watch a lot of television (be it a politician, a spokesperson, spin-doctor, or just a parent), I have at least as much to say as a researcher in this field'" (Donsbach 2006, 445).

In this light, no research can be proclaimed "groundbreaking" by simply staying on the ground, i.e., too close to the object of one's study. On must soar above the ground, so to speak, and look—without constantly turning one's head—at the "big picture" of communication; only this way can a certain event be proclaimed "revolutionary" while still being a part of the overall evolutionary process. Today history is often broken down into constant "turns," "revolutions," and "paradigms," while its development must also be viewed as leading not only to another revolution, but to "a success of evolution" (Stepanov 2005, 49). Ironically, the study of communication at present may be experiencing "methodological schizophrenia" precisely because of too many and too zealous attempts of understanding its nature. While a profusion of theories and methods in the study of communication can certainly be viewed as a sign of its vibrancy and vigor, it should be noted that, when one tries too hard to solve a problem or find an answer to a question too quickly, nothing is successfully achieved, and one has to start anew. Perhaps we should slow down and look further back; then, given more time and space, we might understand the nature of communication more fully. Perhaps we should ask more questions and become more hermeneutically involved in the process of communication, letting our prejudices come to the fore (cf. H.-G. Gadamer). Maybe, such a gradual approach, more time- (and space-) consuming, will in the long run allow the study of communication to make a grade, i.e., more successfully overcome its "epistemological erosion." Let us not forget that any study is a matter of degree (including academic degrees such as Bachelor's or Master's).

In short, communication should be viewed in more evolutionary—and less revolutionary—terms. While revolutions are "made," communication as an evolutionary process simply takes place (and time), i.e., goes on naturally. From an evolutionary point of view, instead of acting on the world, we can only act in/with the world; in this sense, we can only be part of, and subject to, the process of communication. The closer our kinship with its objects, the more successful—and wonderful—communication appears. By the same token, the study of communication should have a less revolutionary and thus more evolutionary character. We should study communication the way we communicate, in which wonder is present simultaneously with our experiences. Only this way can lead to "a success of evolution" when communication as an object opens up and unfolds, revealing its nature. Such a feeling of discovery will then appear only natural. The highest praise for a scholarly work should be someone exclaiming: "What an evolutionary study!" It should be noted that many scholars deserve such praise, especially those focusing on everyday communication as they approach it, for example, from intercultural, critical rhetoric, or performance studies perspectives.

Thus, it is important to think about communication not only in terms of "explosions" (cf. the revolutionary if not military connotations of this term), but also continuous, gradual changes. The following words by Yuriy Lotman about culture can be applied very well to the study of communication: "The progression from thinking oriented toward explosions to an evolutionary consciousness now takes on a special significance" (Lotman 1992, 265).

Let us see, then, how the study of communication can be conducted from a more evolutionary perspective. To that end, it is necessary to take a look at the history of communication study, identifying the main problems that the study of communication faces. Also, a way must be found to address such problems so that the study of communication can develop further.

The Identity (Crisis) of Communication Study

Thus, it is important—although not easy—to think about communication in evolutionary terms given the long and diverse history of its study (Delia 1987; Harper 1979; Meadow 2002; Rogers 1994; Schramm 1997). Communication theory "has a long and . . . illustrious history" (Harper 1979, 1). The nature of communication has been the focus of theoretical study for at least 2,000 years (Liska and Cronkhite 1995, 75–100; Ruben and Stewart 2006, 35–53; Rogers 1994; Schiller 1996).

The beginnings of this study in the West are usually traced back to ancient Greece and Rome, Aristotle's "Rhetoric" was considered one of the main sources. In this respect, it is common to speak about "different roots of the communication paradigms, political in the West and philosophical in the East" (Bryant and Miron 2007, 407). The Western paradigm has been very influential, and today the study of communication is "still entrenched in Eurocentrism or Americanism" (Jia 2002, xv) and it is stated that the "mainstream communication theory is limited by Eurocentric cultural assumptions" (Craig 2007, 256). It must be noted, though, that "the relationship of American communication research to European communication studies" has been "uneasy" and "has been highlighted by a number of commentators over the years" (Renckstorf 2004, 69–70).

Besides, even within Europe one finds differences in the study of communication. For example, as S. Averbeck (2008) notes in her article "Comparative History of Communication Studies: France and Germany," communication studies in Germany are rooted in journalism studies and mass communication research while the study of communication in France is grounded in semio-pragmatics and social constructivism. She labels the discipline in both countries as relatively "old," tracing the German tradition to the beginning and the French one to the middle of the last century. However, the study of communication today is still at its core commonly perceived to be "an almost exclusively American enterprise" (Vroons 2005, 496). For example, authors and editors from the United States dominate most "major international" communication journals, cf. "Overall, the most visible countries in communication journals are English-speaking ones, the U.S. in particular" (Lauf 2005, 148). However, it is noted that there are certain areas of inquiry "that have been insufficiently treated within the mainstream discourse of American communication theory: (1) the 'relational' self, (2) human 'feeling' and the human 'body,' (3) 'nature,' and 'spirit,' and (4) 'communal' conceptions of the core term 'communication'" (Gordon 2007, 89–90).

Not surprisingly, attempts are made to look at communication from other cultural perspectives (Jia et al. 2002; Kim 2002; Monge 1998). Asian scholars, for instance, challenge the theoretical bias in Western communication research limited to the social scientific methods, which exclude alternative ways of knowledge production, and argue that the linguistic, religious-philosophical, and historical dimensions should be more prominent in the study of communication. The Arab-Islamic view is presented as diverging from "American-dominated views of communication as a rational, cognizant, and goal-oriented act" (Ayish 2003, 91). Such a view, derived from secular sociocultural traditions and values as well as religious Islamic attitudes embodied in scriptures, works of jurisprudence, philosophy, and literature is best understood "in the context of four dichotomous themes: individualism-conformity, transcendentalism-existentialism, rationality-intuition, and egalitariamism-hierarchy" (Ayish 2003, 85). At the same time, it should be noted that, alongside the traditionalists valorizing revelatory knowledge, one finds in the Islamic study of communication "the rationalists, those who subscribed to rational opinion, *ra'y*" and who argue "that where there is no clear guidance from the Quran or tradition," one can make one's "own rational judgments on moral and ethical questions" (Mowlana 2007, 27). In general, however, instead of the more rational roots of communication study in the West with its focus on acting upon the external world, the study of communication in the East is considered to have originated from less transactional premises, emphasizing its transcendental and interpretative aspects. It is noted, for example, that

> the primary goal of communication in Taoism and Buddhism was knowledge of the self and of the essence of the world, rather than informing and influencing others or manipulating the external world. As a consequence, communication took a "transcendental" form geared toward the eternal reality assumed to underlie all temporary events, including one's own individual existence. Such a form of communication was radically different from the transactional European type of communication. The method of transcendental communication involved intuitive interpretation (distinct from the rational conceptualization practiced around the Mediterranean). (Bryant and Miron 2006, 405)

At the same time, it should be remembered that the theoretical contemplation practiced in ancient Greece, as mentioned earlier, required that, upon one's returning from the journey to a sacred site, one would seek to change oneself rather than the world around, pointing to the introspective and interpretive side of making one's communicative experience meaningful.

The study of communication in Russia has been centered on the concepts of language, culture, and thought. These three concepts have appeared—in various combinations—in the titles of numerous Russian books, collections of articles, conference proceedings, etc. Out of these three it is perhaps linguistics that could lay—and has laid—claims as the foundational framework for the study of communication. Linguistics here should be understood in a broad philological sense as the study of language in its relation to society, culture and thought, cf. such subfields as sociolinguistics, ethno-linguistics and psycholinguistics. Incidentally, the latter in Russia has traditionally had a broad scope, going beyond the study of the psychological and neurobiological factors that enable humans to acquire, use, comprehend, and produce language, which seems to be more of the case in the West. In this, psycholinguistics can be viewed as a close ally of communication studies; not for nothing one of the earliest centers of the study of communication in Russia is the Sector of Psycholinguistics and Theory of Communication at the Institute of Language Study at the Russian Academy of Sciences, Moscow. The interest of the Russian study of communication in language is similar to that in Europe, especially in the UK, where communication studies traditionally include prominent emphases on language, especially from a semiotic perspective. For example, *The Communication Theory Reader* (Cobley 1996) features sections on linguistic and visual meaning, sign users and speech acts, readers and reading.

The study of culture in Russia has taken shape mostly under the aegis of Culturology that deals with various aspects of cultural dynamics, identity, and history. Loose parallels are usually drawn between Culturology and the discipline of Cultural Studies in the West. Finally, thought as a cornerstone of human communicative experience has been studied either as a psychological or a philosophical phenomenon. From a philosophical perspective (for more see: Epstein 1996) one can mention N. Berdiaev with his concepts of "nothingness" and "creativity" as part of human existence; P. Chaadaev whose ideas gave rise to the continuing debate between Westernizers and Slavophiles; N. Fedorov, the founder of Russian "cosmism" and the doctrine of the "resurrection of the dead"; V. Soloviev, one of the most systematic of all Russian philosophers promoting the concept of "all-unity"; and P. Florensky, a most original philosopher of Orthodox rituals and universal symbolism. Many of these names and ideas can and should be related to the study of communication more directly. From a psychological perspective, besides the work of L. Vygotsky and A. Luria, already well-known in the West, one can mention the research by B. Lomov and his colleagues into cognition and communication. In the 1970s B. Lomov and his colleagues started a comprehensive program of studies into how people interact by making use of various psychological qualities, functions, and states. The results of these studies have been published in four volumes put out by the Institute of Psychology of the Russian Academy of Sciences. The latest—*Communication and Cognition*—came out in 2007 (see: Kharitonov 2008). Such studies are very close in nature to what is known as the socio-psychological tradition in the United States.

It is worth noting that in Russian "communication" can be expressed by two words—"*obchenie*" understood as interaction, based on shared values, and "*kommunikatsiya*," typically associated with a transfer of information. In all three foundational frameworks of the study of communication in Russia—linguistic, cultural, and philosophical—the key term commonly used until recently has been "*obchenie*," which is usually assigned more positive connotations than the word "*kommunikatsiya*" ("communication") (Peshkov 1998, 143; Shaikhitdinova 2004, 166; Vasilik 2006, 25–26). The so-called Language and Social Interaction (LSI) studies can be viewed as close in meaning to the study of communication as interaction in Russia with its attention to various factors of discourse, conversation, narration, etc., that constitute human life.

Ironically, the ideology of a new social order in the USSR was being built under the name of communism ("*kommunizm*," in Russian) while the word "*obchina*" ("*commune*"), more native to the Russian ear, suffered in the aftermath of the October Revolution of 1917. Had, perhaps, the idea for a new society been expressed by a different name, capturing the roots of the Russian language and soul and thus more native to the Russian ear, the country's development might have been more evolutionary. Today, however, the term "*kommunikatsiya*" seems to be gaining ground, and its derivatives are found in the names of the candidates for the discipline, e.g., "*kommunikativistika*" ("communicativistics") or "*kommunikologiya*" ("communicology"). One reason for that might be found in the usage and morphological structure of Russian: the terms derived from "*kommunikatsiya*"—"*kommunikativistika*" and "*kommunikologiya*"—are more grammatically well-formed than those that could be derived from "*obchenie*," cf. * "*obchenievistika*" and * "*obchenielogiya*." More importantly, "obchenie" produces lacunas for such modifiers as "*kommunikativnyi*" ("communicative") and "*kommunikatsionnyi*" ("communicational").

So, scholars are invited "to reflect on culturally based assumptions that characterize current theories of communication and to imagine how our field might be enriched or perhaps even fundamentally transformed by concepts derived from different cultural traditions" (Craig 2007, 256).

Thus, the history of communication study is quite long and (getting even more) culturally diverse. At the same time, after numerous attempts to explain and understand the nature of communication, its study still has no clear identity, and those studying communication openly admit that "this identity crisis has been with us for as long as we have existed in academia" (Donsbach 2006, 439). It is noted that "the field has been in a perpetual identity crisis—or rather legitimation crisis" (Peters 1993, 133). It should also be noted that this perpetual identity crisis seems to be perceived (and maintained) primarily from within the study of communication, as such. Just, for example, as "the biggest critics of cultural works today are not the hard-core positivists, but the cultural theorists themselves" (Demers 2000, 1), the biggest critics of the field of communication seem to be the communication scholars themselves. From the outside, communication is usually recognized as a discipline, cf. "Communication as a discipline has the additional responsibility of understanding communication in its entirety" (Hornsey et al. 2008, 752).

In general, "communication theorists have . . . long been caught between the need to conceptualize communication as a materially social phenomenon on one hand, and its historic subservience to individualism on the other" (Shepherd 1999, 158). That is why any conceptualization of the nature of communication can be viewed as "an attempt to account for the multiplicity and diversity of this field . . . historically caught in the tension between material and immaterial networks" (Mattelart and Mattelart 1998, 1). The former view called for understanding communication as the (ideally mechanically engineered) transfer of information while the latter view emphasized the need to look at communication as an exchange—and ideal fusion—of internally held thoughts and emotions. In these two views, one can discern the two prototypes for the two main paradigms in the study of communication—scientific and humanistic—that will be discussed in more detail later in this book. At this point, it is important to note that, from the first perspective, communication must be studied primarily within the social sciences while, from the second perspective, communication clearly appears to be part of the humanities if not their "core" (cf. Emauel 2007). However, when one starts to look at communication as a material phenomenon, one is inevitably tempted to go beyond the traditional social sciences. Overall, anything, including sound waves and the nature of light and sight can be viewed as a social achievement (cf. Rasch 2000, 79). For example, it is stated that "a material theory of communication includes not only verbal exchanges, but virtually all others, including those at the molecular level, where the odor of freshly baked foods communicates in much the same way as speech" (Jordan 2002, 380).

Similarly, citing the effect of humidity on suicide rate, it is argued that the ban on non-phenomenological research is unhealthy because not all aspects of communication are in an individual's awareness (Bowers and Bradac 1982, 15). Along the same lines the question is raised whether "the narrative itself" is "a posited physical object, . . . a series of triggerings and firings of the very sense receptors it posits in order to describe itself" (Rasch 2000, 16). Let us not forget, too, that communication processes cannot be studied separately from biology, cf. the so-called communibiological approach, which although not widely accepted should not be ignored (Beatty et al. 2001; Beatty and McCroskey 2000; Beatty, McCroskey, and Floyd 2009); after all, humans are social *animals*. Of course, it can be argued that, due to their biological make-up, people have no control over their behavior and that our communicative behavior cannot be changed. However, the proponents of the communibio-logical approach are the first ones to draw everybody's attention to how it can be misconstrued, cf. the deterministic and immutability fallacies just mentioned (Floyd, Mikkelson, and Hesse 2008, 6–7); in other words, humans are still *social* animals.

To capture both individualistic and social aspects, the study of commu-nication casts its net extremely widely. In fact, calls are made to study com-munication by using the potential of the social, natural, technical disciplines as well as the humanities (Vasilik 2006, 17). It is noted that "communication theory has most typically drawn upon the humanities and the social sci-ences, with occasional forays into the natural sciences (mostly in the hunt for metaphors), but the natural sciences, medicine, and engineering are full of consideration of time, space, signals, distance, contact—central concerns and topics of communication theory" (Peters 2003, 398–399).

To a significant degree "the incoherence of communication theory as a field can be explained by communication theory's multidisciplinary origins" (Craig 1999, 120). It must be remembered that the field of communication theory "resulted from the merger of at least four lines of inquiry . . . : (a) the rhetorical tradition, (b) propaganda and media effects, (c) transmission and reception of information, as well as (d) group dynamics and interpersonal relationship development. Academic disciplines such as social psychology, sociology, and anthropology have also contributed valuable insights" (Heath and Bryant 2000, 55). At one point, it seemed as if "the close partnership be-tween sociology, psychology, philosophy, history, and even economics created a uniquely favorable situation for a well-rounded approach to human commu-nication" (Bryant and Miron 2007, 421). This list of "theoretical partners" is, of course, not exhaustive and, as just mentioned, can be easily expanded to include anything from rhetoric to biology. And yet today, according to a more somber assessment, we can at best talk about *psychology-based* or *sociology-based* communication research; in other words, it is difficult to claim that all research could not have been conducted outside of the so-called communication study, as such (Donsbach 2006, 439–442). It may be hard to admit, but "research on psychological deformations as an effect of violent media content is still psychology and research on the causes of media concentration is still economics . . . not communication" (Donsbach 2006, 439–439). And, if one looks at the newest developments in neurological research, the concept of "free will" appears to be nothing but a fiction (Donsbach 2006, 439–444). So, bright as the prospects for the integration of communication study might appear, such attempts in reality do not turn out to be very successful; for example, this is reflected in the make-up of the departments where communication is studied. As R. McChesney observes, "communication departments often have some variety of quantitative scholars, psychologists, sociologists, cultural theorists, historians, legal and policy experts, political economists, and so on. They tend to keep to themselves, so the whole is less than the sum of the parts" (McChesney 2007, 21). The identity crisis of communication study is this search for "the whole," which proves elusive. However, this search continues as scholars are trying to identify distinctive qualities in communication research (Buzzanell and Carbaugh 2009).

So, too, continue critical attacks against the study of communication as a (supposedly) distinct science. For example, critics see communication study as a "motley assortment of guerrilla bands that raid other disciplines for tools and texts" (Simonson 2001, 20) or compare it to a no-host party at an academic convention (LeBaron 2003, 10). The self-critical admit a lack of unity in the development of communication study (Harper 1979, 1), noting that it seems to be "held together not by paradigmatic coherence, but by tenuous administrative arrangements" (Anderson and Baym 2004, 603). It is openly admitted that "we have no clear identity" and that in the study of communication "there is no common object" (Donsbach 2006, 439). In the UK, for instance, communication research is sometimes called by its opponents "Mickey Mouse studies" (Nordestreng 2007, 211). According to this label, communication study appears as something popular and adorable, yet fictitious. Herein is the key problem: Is it possible to state that communication research exists as a real science, i.e., one integral whole with a distinct object of study? Or, perhaps, "communication can be seen merely as camouflage distracting attention from more fundamental levels such as economics or socio-political power structures" (Nordestreng 2007, 219). As is clear from a brief overview above, the history of communication study can be viewed as "largely a story of struggle with a legacy" (Shepherd 1999, 156). Has the study of communication been fighting a losing battle? Have we been making "new clothes for the emperor"? Will it take but a small child to cry out, "But he has nothing on!" for the whole project of "communication studies/science" to collapse?

Even if its identity crisis is resolved and the study of communication is accepted as a (real) distinct science with its own object, the question remains whether it is a separate discipline or simply a field. Those who favor communication study as a discipline traditionally place it within the humanities (cf. Apel 1972; Emauel 2007) or social sciences (Hornsey et al. 2008; Vroons 2005). Often, communication study is assigned to both and viewed as a social-human science (Grant 2003a). As noted by R. Craig who has made great efforts toward the acceptance of communication study as a discipline, "communication is warranted as a practical discipline insofar as it effectively marshals its available institutional and intellectual resources to address 'problems of communication' in society, thereby growing in all three dimensions of disciplinary authority (intellectual, institutional, and sociocultural)" (2008, 16). Although contributions of communication study to knowledge as well as its evolving institutional forms are important, R. Craig states that the sociocultural context of disciplinarity plays a primary role. At the same time, he admits that the study of communication "is not yet well entrenched institutionally and its intellectual contributions, while hardly negligible, are not yet of such weight as to explain its apparent emergence toward disciplinary status" (2008, 17). Other scholars are more categorical. G. Shepherd speaks of "the undisciplinary nature of the field of communication" (1993, 84). S. Hall believes that constituting communication as a self-sustaining, disciplinary speciality is "the altogether misguided attempt" (Hall 1989, 43). While noting that the disciplinary identity always has been problematic for the study of communication, D. Swanson states: "It is not a discipline, at least not in any traditional sense, and it will be helpful to discard the contrary view once and for all. . . . Communication is an interdisciplinary field" (Swanson 1993, 169). These views are echoed by P. Simonson: "If there is a canon in communication studies, it is one that is disputed, argued for, and periodically reinvented. The field is not a discipline in any narrow sense of the word. . . . If communication studies is a discipline, it should periodically discipline itself to visit old texts with new eyes" (Simonson 2001, 20). Most recently K. Nordestreng stated his opinion on this issue in very clear terms: "Today my answer to the discipline/field question is that it remains rather a field than a discipline" (Nordestreng 2007, 212; cf. Korn et al. 2000).

Thus, the integrity of communication study as a science and its acceptance as a discipline or a field appear problematic. We continue searching for answers to the following critical question: "How can one make sense of what we are doing?" (Powers 1995, 213). This search is not based on mere prestige but is vital as it will have intellectual, institutional, and sociocultural ramifications. In the meantime, the study of communication goes under many different names, including "communication," "communications," "communication studies," "speech communication," "communications science," "communication arts," etc. One name for the study of communication would probably put an end to the situation where different approaches to communication in academia "occupy the same space only by administrative convenience" (Anderson and Baym 2004, 590). Clearly, much support is needed "for the unity and coherence of communication as a concept and as a field of research, a goal that is acknowledged by many communication theorists as important and pressing" (Dresner 2006, 170). It is also clear that the identity crisis of communication study, reflected in its "epistemological erosion," has ontological roots. "It is the forwarding of a unique foundational ontology that grants fields of study their disciplinary status. Correspondingly, it is communication's failure to articulate a unique, foundational ontology that has kept it from achieving the status of a discipline" (Shepherd 1993, 84). To really understand what the matter *with* the study of communication is requires, first of all, that we understand what the matter *of* the study of communication is. The first step in this direction is to articulate the key concept of communication study, i.e., the concept of communication itself.

The (De)Fault of Ontological Assumptions

Thus, the "disciplinary identity always has been problematic for communication, and speculation about the field's future must recognize the importance of long-standing identity issues" (Swanson 1993, 163). These "long-standing identity issues" of communication study have ontological roots. The main reason for "the ragged state" (Myers 2001, 218) of the study of communication is its "inability to define core concepts" (Myers 2001, 218). Paradoxically, in spite of a long and diverse history of its study, communication scholars admit that "communication is itself so weakly defined" (Donsbach 2006, 440). The fact is, scholars tend not to discuss "the fundamental nature of human communication" because they "assume rather than problematize communication" (Burleson 1992, 80). It is noted that, while the need to use ontology as a criterion "for the advancement of a philosophy of communication has been stated before, . . . it has only been declared as an option, it has not been seriously considered" (Nastasia and Rakow 2004, 13).

Without understanding the nature of communication we can never answer the repeated calls for "a reformulation of communication theory"

(Leydesdorff 2002, 130) and "new ways of schematizing the field" (Craig 1999, 139). Clearly, in the study of communication today, more emphasis must be placed "not so much upon verification and replication but upon generativity. It is not that we need to 'build' tightly formulated dense theoretical structures at this stage, but rather to 'flower' far-reaching visions. We need to playfully explore our central topic, 'communication,' looking from fresh directions" (Gordon 2007, 101).

So, the nature of the object is the "unavoidable starting point for any effort to gain or construct knowledge" (Anderson and Baym 2004, 601). To put it simply, we cannot study communication unless we know what it is that we study. In this respect, "'ontologizing' communication . . . is the challenge that must be met" (Shepherd 1993, 91; cf. Bowers and Bradac 1982, 15) in developing the coherent study of communication—whether as a discipline or a field. The present book is an attempt at meeting this challenge. This attempt is guided by the general premise that ontology is "the scaffolding upon which structures of scholarship are crafted" (Anderson and Baym 2004, 603).

In the study of communication "ontological positions undergird most thought systems, even when not specifically acknowledged as doing so" (Babe 2000, 11). In other words, "all communication theories have their ontologies, whether these are explicit or not; and conversely, all ontologies are based on a theory of communication, even if this theory is not explicitly articulated" (Petrilli 2008, 195). Thus, it must be remembered that every scholar must deal with ontological issues "either intentionally or by default" (Anderson 1996, 17). In the study of human communication ontological issues seem to be treated more often by default, i.e., assuming we all know what is being discussed. In the field of computer-mediated communication, however, an intentionally open discussion of ontology of communication is required; ontology there is typically defined as *explicit* formal specifications of the terms in the domain and relations among them (Gruber 1993) or understood as an agreed upon vocabulary of common terms and meanings (Roche 2002). The first step in the development of a program for the Web is made by addressing its ontology, cf. the following very indicative title: "Let's Talk about Our 'Being': A Linguistic-Based Ontology Framework for Coordinating Agents" (Pazienza et al. 2007). It is assumed that all problems of understanding our being (without the quotes) are solved, and now the main objective is to focus on communication in terms of applied programs such as the FIPA Ontolgy Service Specification, which is a linguistically aware methodology describing a wide-scope framework for multiagent systems design, discussed in the article. Perhaps the concept of ontological commitment as an agreement to use the shared vocabulary in a coherent and consistent manner should be expanded and applied to the study of communication, in general. Then, a commitment to a common ontology, intentionally and explicitly articulated, would act as a guarantee of consistency, but not necessarily completeness, which fits well into the contingent nature of communication.

It is noted that researchers working within different cultural traditions are more or less likely to make an ontological commitment. For example, communication researchers in the United States are said to "avoid specifying an ontological stance" (Braman 1994, 93), while relatively greater attention is "being paid to ontology in Canadian versus U.S. communication studies" (Babe 2000, 30). The Russian tradition, for example, due to its strong philosophical foundations, displays a strong interest in ontological issues of communication (Kalmykov 2007; Kostina 2004; Tiupa 1998; Zhuravlev 2006).

In general, today the interest to ontological aspects of communication is clearly growing. It is stated that "communication should be considered in terms of being" (Petrilli and Ponzio 2006, 521). Attempts are made to conceptualize the relationship between communication and being, cf. "If we wanted to venture into the territory of general ontology, we could risk formulae such as these: being = communication: false; communicating = being: true" (Petrilli and Ponzio 2006, 522). It is argued that only by turning attention to the ontological dimension of communication does it become possible to understand its nature (Kostina 2008, 130; Limonova 2006, 2; Tiupa 1998, 10). The need to turn our attention to the ontology of communication cannot be questioned, and "the inevitable connection between ontology and communication theory" (Petrilli 2008, 196) raises a number of important questions such as:

Is "reality" simply a product of the human mind, or does it exist apart from human knowers? Do humans make real choices, or are all actions determined, in principle, by prior causes? To what extent is existence individual, and to what extent is it collective or social? Is ultimate reality material and mechanical, in which case events may well proceed from prior causes, or is it immaterial and mental, in which case events may tend toward final purpose? Or is reality chaotic, in which case the order we think we discern is really a gross simplification, indeed an imposition of our imaginations onto infinite complexity? (Babe 2000, 11)

These questions address the most important ontological concerns in the study of communication, including the question of the existence of abstract and/or particular entities. However, one question stands apart and must be answered, in the first place: "What is communication?"

To summarize, several points need to be emphasized. First, it is shown how the study of communication suffers from the identity crisis, which is manifest in its "epistemological erosion." Second, it is argued that the roots of this identity crisis are ontological in nature and so the goal of ontologizing communication is formulated. And, third, it is emphasized that this goal can be achieved more successfully through a more evolutionary approach to communication, looking for continuity. This approach would require stepping back and taking a longer look at communication in order to let it remind us what constitutes its nature; in this sense, the present book can be viewed as "an exercise in anamnesis—unforgetting" (Peters 2005, 27). We need to go back in space and time in order to move forward.

CHAPTER TWO

~

Communication Theorizing:
Being-(on)-the-Way

An Impressive Disarray

Let us identify and briefly discuss the main ways of studying communication by looking at the numerous attempts that have been made to explain and understand its nature.

The study of communication is conducted, first of all, in terms of individual theories. Each theory is an attempt to look at communication based on certain assumptions; for instance, one of the assumptions underlying uncertainty reduction theory (Berger 1987) is that similarities between persons reduce uncertainty while dissimilarities produce increases in uncertainty.

The diverse historical nature of communication study "led to the development of a whole host of communication theories" (Neuliep 1996, 10). The number of communication theories varies from publication to publication: one is introduced to over twenty communication theories (Stone et al. 1999); one finds over thirty communication theories (Griffin 2002); one is exposed to forty-two communication theories (Cragan and Shields 1998, 5); or one learns that there are two hundred and forty-nine theories of communication (Craig 1999, 143). The list of the theories that are mentioned in most publications includes information theory, symbolic interactionism, systems theory, rhetorical theory, dramaturgical theory, constructivist theory, standpoint theory, to mention but a few.

In addition to these "usual suspects," new attempts to explain and understand the nature of communication are made, which is part of "a greater focus on theory development and on using theory to guide our research endeavors" (Kalbfleisch 2002, 6). For example, the new communibiological theory, mentioned earlier, has been actively debated (Babrow 2005). Or, the following five communication-based theories, recently proposed and briefly discussed below, are considered to be original contributions to communication theory (see Kalbfleisch 2002). Interaction appearance theory focuses on how perceptions of physical attractiveness can be changed through skilled social interaction; "hypertext in the key of G" theory uses the Internet analogy of hypertext and describes how the history of relationships influences the structure and flow of interaction; communication in mentoring relationships theory describes how mentors and their protégés develop and maintain their relationships through communication; communication in family relationships theory focuses on how family relationships are affected by various schematic perceptions; and theory of relationship awareness focuses on the role of the attention we give to our relationships through thinking and talking about relationships.

In short, there are a large number of theories that attempt to explain and understand communication based on various assumptions about its nature. Herein, however, lies the central problem of communication theory—"a proliferation of distinct communication theories and no consensus among them" (Myers 2001, 218). That is why theorists look for assumptions about communication that they might share. As the authors of various theories find out they view communication from a similar angle, communication theories are grouped into approaches. Thus, "rather than discussing every assumption of every theory, communication scholars often find that certain sets of assumptions go together" (Baldwin et al. 2004, 25).

The most common theoretical way to approach communication is by what is usually referred to as "contexts." Understanding contexts as environments in which communication takes place, one finds theories grouped into such approaches as intrapersonal, interpersonal, relational, small group, organizational, public/rhetorical, mass, intercultural, international, family, health, or political (Baldwin et al. 2006; Cragan and Shields 1998; Heath and Bryant 2000; Infante et al. 2003; West and Turner 2004). For example, the five original theories, described above, can all be considered relational communication theories.

Sometimes, the broadly defined contextual approach is replaced by a more refined approach to communication phenomena according to levels or situations of their use. For example, "among the criteria used for dividing communication levels from one another are (a) the number of people involved, (b) the agent controlling the communication event, (c) the degree of formality expected during the event, and (d) the degree of personal information exchanged between the communicators" (Powers 1995, 209). Thus, such approaches as interpersonal, small group, and mass communication are considered levels-based, while such approaches as health, family, and legal communication are considered situation-based for they study events that take place in "the recurrent social situations" (Powers 1995, 210).

Some other ways to approach communication include classifying theories into micro-theories and midrange theories (Bryant and Miron 2007, 424–427); trait, persuasion, verbal behavior, and nonverbal behavior theories (Infante et al. 2003, 75); rhetorical, causal process, human action, and systems-interactional theories (Neuliep 1996); or symbolic activity, performance, constructivism, interpersonal dynamics, evolution of relationships, and communication communities theories (Wood 2004). Some theoretical approaches to communication are quite idiosyncratic. For example, J. Cragan and D. Shields (1998) group communication theories (a) on the basis of classifying elements into general, contextual, micro, special, and symbiotic; (b) on the basis of anatomical elements—into origin, roots, and assumptions; communicative force and paradigm; theoretical technical concepts; modeling and relating concepts; and (c) on the basis of evaluative elements—into power and scope; heuristic and isomorphic theories.

It is noted that, overall, communication theories can be classified based on (a) their chronology, i.e., according to their development in time; (b) domain of origin, i.e., according to their relationship with a certain discipline in the sciences or humanities; (c) subfield of study, i.e., according to the agreed upon parts of the field; and (d) component of the communication process (Nastasia and Rakow 2004).

New ways of approaching communication are also being developed. In G. Shepherd et al. (2006), twenty-seven different metaphorical views on communication are grouped into five approaches; respectively, communication is discussed as making, materializing, contextualizing, politicizing, and questioning. The approach to communication as making is built around theories that view it in terms of relationality, ritual, transcendence, construction, and practice; the approach to communication as materializing is built around theories that view it in terms of collective memory, vision, embodiment, raced, social identity, and techné; the approach to communication as contextualizing is built around theories that view it in terms of dialogue, auto-ethnography, storytelling, complex organizing, and structuring; the approach to communication as politicizing is built around theories that view it in terms of political participation, deliberation, diffusion, social influence, rational argument, and counterpublic; and, finally, the approach to communication as questioning is built around theories that view it in terms of dissemination, articulation, translation, communicability, and failure.

While many theoretical approaches to communication are at various stages of fermentation, another way to view communication—in terms of traditions—is more accepted.

By a communication tradition is meant "a general way of thinking that has been shared in common by a community of scholars" (Klein and White 1996, 10). Based on individual communication theories and common approaches, traditions are broad attempts to conceptualize communication in a more meta-theoretical way.

One of the most well-known and productive conceptualizations is R. Craig's attempt to present communication theory as "a theoretical metadiscourse engaged in dialogue with the practical metadiscourse of everyday life" (Craig 1999, 127). In his view, "a field of communication becomes possible because all theories of communication, whatever their substantive claims or underlying assumptions, however contradictory or even incommensurable with each other they may be in other respects, can still be regarded as different ways of constituting communication for practical purposes" (Craig 2001, 234). Thus, the field of communication theory is presented in terms of seven traditions—rhetorical, semiotic, phenomenological, cybernetic, sociopsychological, sociocultural, and critical—that appeal to certain metadiscursive commonplaces. The rhetorical tradition conceptualizes communication as a practical art of discourse; the semiotic tradition—as intersubjective mediation by signs; the phenomenological tradition—as the experience of otherness; the cybernetic tradition—as information processing; the sociopsychological tradition—as expression, interaction, and influence; the sociocultural tradition—as the (re)production of social order; and the critical tradition conceptualizes communication as discursive reflection. These seven traditions were presented by R. Craig as "alternative vocabularies for theorizing communication as a social practice" (Craig 1999, 120).

Later R. Craig has elaborated on his framework, discussing the pervasiveness of metadiscourse in private, public, and academic realms. He emphasized the fact that various traditions of communication theory can be used to describe and analyze different assumptions about communication, contributing to new ways of talking about talk for practical purposes (Craig 2005). Craig's model has been taken as the foundation for the new introduction to communication theory built around the main traditions developed in his work (Craig and Muller 2007).

Although his ideas are widely accepted and used, R. Craig's constitutive model of communication as the meta-theory is sometimes questioned. For ex-

ample, it is noted that in this model "communication theories having rhetoric as a field of provenience are not all based on the same conceptual assumptions, communication positions derived from sociology differ or even oppose
[one another], communication views developed from sciences do not offer
a unitary picture, and communication conceptualizations with linguistic-
literary origins criticize one another" (Nastasia and Rakow 2004). Also, D.
Myers (2001) challenges the significance of R. Craig's meta-model and wonders how it is different from any first-order constitutive model of communication. Also, he fails to find in R. Craig's model any criterion for adjudicating
among competing theories. In responding to this criticism, R. Craig does not
claim his model to be the meta-theory; on the contrary, he acknowledges
and deconstructs what he considers the reflexive paradox of his theorizing,
cf.: "If the constitutive model is uniquely true, then communication exists
only as constituted in communication. Communication, however, can be
constituted in communication in many different ways, hence there can be
no uniquely true way of constituting communication, hence the constitutive
model is not uniquely true" (Craig 2001, 234). Also, he argues that he does
not propose the single criterion for adjudicating among competing theories;
instead, his constitutive meta-model simply "holds that different theoretical
vocabularies constitute (or model) communication differently for practical
purposes" (Craig 2001, 231). As a result, R. Craig sees the ability to carry out
argumentation across traditions as the main value of his meta-model.

This willingness to carry on such a theoretical conversation generates
attempts to propose new traditions in communication theory. For example,
it is noted that in R. Craig's work "only cursory and uninspiring mention
of a genuinely pragmatist tradition is made" (Russill 2005, 296). Thus, the
following question is raised, "Why have we not more fully reconstructed
pragmatism as a tradition of thinking about communication?" (Russill 2005,
p. 296; cf., however, Langsdorf and Smith 1995). So, arguments about traditions that make up communication theory continue. Where we find less
argument about how to conceptualize communication is in the area of communication theory paradigms.

The broadest and most accepted way of viewing communication is in
terms of paradigms. Paradigms share the same idea of serving as "a world-
view, a set of presupposed beliefs that pervasively shapes one's perceptions
of and orientation toward the world" (Feldman 2005, 297). In most current
writing, paradigms as worldviews are equated with "general ways of viewing
human communication" (West and Turner 2004, 48) or "'grand models'
or sets of theoretical assumptions shared by many theorists" (Infante et al.
2003, 49). Communication paradigms are usually built around ontology and

epistemology, focusing on how we understand reality that is constructed in communication and how knowledge of such understanding is achieved (Anderson and Baym 2004). The number of communication paradigms also varies from publication to publication. Besides, communication paradigms are discussed under different labels, e.g., dimensions, perspectives, meta-theories, orientations, views, or epistemologies. Moreover, understood loosely, it becomes tempting to present any more or less general view of communication as a paradigm. For example, one reads that communication researchers today are guided by such paradigms as feminist, constructivist, or Marxist (West and Turner 2004, 48–49). In addition, attempts are made to establish new communication paradigms such as critical theory and cultural studies (Heath and Bryant 2000, 36) or narrative (Fisher 1989; Roberts 2004) paradigms.

In some cases, four communication paradigms are isolated. It is noted, for instance, that, to understand communication, "researchers have examined four meta-theories: Scientific laws meta-theory, rules meta-theory, systems meta-theory, and covering law meta-theory" (Heath and Bryant 2000, 29). Elsewhere, four social science paradigms—positivist, systems, interpretive, and critical—are discussed (Baxter and Babbie 2004). In J. Liska and G. Cronkhite (1995, 93–94), four different perspectives or epistemologies are identified—mechanistic, human action (symbolic interactionaism), systems, and semiotic. In D. Infante et al. (2003), the following four paradigms are identified: the covering laws paradigm, the communicobiological paradigm, the human action paradigm, and the systems paradigm.

In some cases, three communication paradigms are isolated. For example, one reads that three "dimensions"—scientific, humanistic, and critical—are "commonly accepted . . . in our discipline today" (Baldwin et al. 2004, 32). In one publication, attention is focused on systems, rules, and laws paradigms (Stacks et al. 1991, 13), and in another publication (Cragan and Shields 1998), three different paradigms—rational, relational, and symbolic—are identified, based on ontological assumptions. Elsewhere, under the name of "meta-theory" as a theory about theories, the following three paradigms are discussed: covering laws, rules, and systems (West and Turner 2004).

Most often, however, two main communication paradigms are isolated. For example, it is emphasized that, to understand communication theory, one needs "to first grasp the crucial difference between the objective and interpretive approaches to communication" (Griffin 2002, 6). It is noted that most textbooks "highlight the difference between specific theories by describing the two fundamental paradigmatic assumptions that govern the field: humanistic (interpretive/qualitative research) and positivistic (objective/

quantitative research)" (Heisler and Discenna 2005, 44). Sometimes, the two paradigms are called empiricist and interpretive (Bostrom 2003). In another publication, two paradigms are identified with the following two main views of communication: the positivist (Cartesian) view, which presupposes an objective researcher, single truth and predictability, and the phenomenological view, which presupposes an operative intentionality and is always dynamic (Smith 1997, 330).

Broadly conceptualized, it is possible to say that the first (scientific or objective) paradigm focuses on the explanation of communication, while the second (humanistic or subjective) paradigm focuses on its understanding. This distinction parallels the split between the empirical-inductive methodologies based on observation used by natural sciences, and those of a more speculative-deductive character, which are more common in the humanities (Bryant and Miron 2007, 412).

The first paradigm can be metaphorically seen as Ptolemaic in nature wherein people strove to ground themselves, as it were, in a system of meanings in order to establish their identity. That was done by finding such meanings in predictable movements of the stars, so the "transcendental signified" was taken literally from the sky. (According to one hypothesis, writing was created based on the imitation of celestial bodies and constellations—see: Epshtein 2004, 197). In other words, people had to depend upon the material composed by nature, cf. the focus on imitation in ancient rhetoric (Crowley and Hawhee 1999, 291). In a manner of speaking, the objective paradigm, found in classical science, brought the skies down to the earth (cf. Prigogine and Stengers 1984); as a result, regular meaningful patterns were identified and so one's identity was established. The best example of such translation of the empirical data into a language of meaningful patterns is found in logical positivism, which viewed the world as "an elegant machine, rather like a very complicated clock" (Cronen 2001, 16). This view, however, aimed at grounding meaning, left the door open for metaphysical readings of the world; cf. the (specially gifted) augurs who could see in the flight of birds the heavenly bodies not visible to ordinary mortals.

The second paradigm can be—again metaphorically—seen as Copernican in nature, indicating a shift from the epistêmê of representation to the "epistêmê of man" (M. Foucault) when humans had to invent themselves, as it were, by focusing on their differences from the "original" transcendental signified. This view challenged any authority and required a radical change in the philosophical conception of the universe. In this sense, Hamlet with his "We defy augury" can be seen as a grammatologist. In a manner of speaking, the subjective paradigm, found in non-classical science, reversed the situation and lifted the earth up to the skies (cf. Prigogine and Stengers 1984). As a result, objectivity was found to be nothing but the illusion that reality could be observed without an observer (Krippendorff 1994, 49). It turned out that there is no longer any master-clock: "each clock signified the individual and that clock coordination came to stand in for a logic of linkage among people and peoples" (Galison 2000, 358). Hence the modern person experienced freedom as well as an acute identity crisis for, in J. Ortega-y-Gassett's words, the modern person no longer knew by what clock to live (Chertkova 2005, 115).

As we see, communication is a very complex phenomenon, especially if understood "from a wider viewpoint, encompassing the multiple circuits of exchange and circulation of goods, people, and messages. This definition simultaneously covers avenues of communication, networks of long distance transmission, and the means of symbolic exchange, such as world fairs, high culture, religion, language, and of course the media" (Mattelart 1996, xiv). A short overview of the attempts to conceptualize communication, presented above, reveals "a relative abundance of communication theory today—and its equally impressive disarray" (Craig 1993, 27). Communication is studied in terms of individual theories, shared approaches, established traditions, and broad paradigms. Moving from theories to paradigms, the view of communication becomes more general and more accepted. Communication theorizing can be visualized as a cone-shaped process driven by a vanishing point that can never be reached for, in communication, a gap exists that can never be bridged, epistemologically reflected in the two main paradigms, discussed above. This gap can be presented in various terms, for example, between the observer and the observed, being and appearance, original and translation, Self and Other, or Self and Self. Communication theorizing is a process of explaining and understanding how this gap is (attempted to be) bridged.

The diversity of views in the study of communication should not be underestimated; however, "the effects of such diversity are unknown and whether theoretical pluralism advances or hinders progress remains to be seen" (Neuliep 1996, 20). What is clear is that the study of communication "requires an attitude we might call theoretical cosmopolitanism . . . a willingness and ability to participate in more than one theoretical conversation" (Craig 2001, 235–236). Only this way can we learn to live tenaciously in terrains of various gaps and transitions (Pollock et al. 2002, 4). To develop such an attitude is not easy, though; it is much easier to break communication into small parts, so to speak, and study each part as if the rest did not exist.

A Pathway to/of Communication

Theorizing the nature of communication can be viewed as a journey, cf. the traditional practice of *theoria* in ancient Greece when a *theoros* made a "pilgrimage abroad for the purpose of witnessing certain events or spectacles" (Nightingale 2006, 3), publicizing all findings upon return (unless the *theoros* was an individual answerable only to oneself). As mentioned earlier, such a quest was characterized by wonder present simultaneously with how the world was experienced.

At the center of such a journey was contemplation, which presupposed looking at any object in its cosmic beauty and order and which thus required transcending one's particularity.

> To look upon the universe in its beauty and order (we get the word cosmetic from *kosmos*) was to abandon oneself to something greater, and *theoria* may originally have suggested out-of-body experiences practiced in the mystery cults that sought to glimpse the place beyond the heavens Plato mentioned in the *Phaedrus*. . . . To view the cosmos, the self had to be purged. Part of this vision persists in the idea that science is an activity to which partisan interests are indifferent (i.e., objectivity). But the moral or aesthetic notion—that theory reveals the good and the beautiful as well as the true—has gone underground today. (Peters 2005, 23)

In the present book, we will try to look at the universe of communication in all its beauty and order; also, we will highlight its moral underpinnings.

It is important to remember that theory cannot be viewed as something detached from its object—as idle contemplation or useless knowledge. Theorizing is a practical activity with all epistemological and ethical implications. The way to understanding an object is not simply a stretch lying between the starting point and the goal. Emphasizing a distinction between the "road" and the "path," M. Heidegger writes:

> The ordinary Greek word for "way" [path] is ἡ ὁδός, from which derives ἡ μέυοδος [literally: "with(in)-a-path"], our borrowed word "method." But ἡ μέυοδος is to be-on-the-way [path], namely on a way [path] not thought of a "method" man devises but a way that already exists, arising from the very things themselves, as they show themselves through and through. The Greek μέυοδος does not refer to the "procedure" [*Verfahren*] of an inquiry but rather is this inquiry itself as remaining-on-the-way. (Heidegger 2005, 60)

In this sense, it seems that "we are not only always 'on-the-way' traveling the path but we are intrinsically that pathway itself" (Heidegger 2005, 62). Thus, no object can be made to say anything that we want it to say, and neither does it ever lie (Prigogine and Stengers 1984, 5); it simply reveals itself to those who ideally become one with it, not so much being-on-the-way as being-the-way-itself.

It is easy to see how this understanding of a method fits the constitutive view of communication when meaning is "defined from *within* the processes being defined" (Krippendorff 1994, 86). Theorizing, therefore, should be treated both in terms of "theories of," focusing on representation, and "theories for," highlighting their reentry into the social fabric theorized and thus enabling further practices. In other words, all theories must be treated as "social inventions that intervene with, transform, create, or maintain the realities we experience" (Krippendorff 1994, 102). Theorizing with a tacit preference of sight over sound is sometimes criticized as the "spectator theory of knowledge"; it is argued that such theorizing supports "conceptual imperialism" with its "urge to oversee, predict, control, and govern expanding territories" (Krippendorff 2009, 104). The method as-being (on)-the-way should safeguard us against such "imperialistic impulses" as long as communication is viewed as (a-path-being-traveled-by-) us.

So, theorizing in the present book takes the form of a journey within which communication is looked at (contemplated) in all its cosmic order and beauty.

Theoretical pluralism does not automatically translate into an adequate view of communication. As R. Craig notes, students of communication "come for something comprehensible, and we offer them fragments of a subject no one can comprehend—up to 249 theories and still counting" (Craig 1999, 143). Many who teach communication theory can relate to his words, cf. "In a communication theory course, many students are uncomfortable; they feel they have been unable to grasp the 'big picture'" (Infante et al. 2003, 334). As a result, one never understands the overall nature of communication, and a genuine argumentative dialogue within the study of communication never takes place, replaced instead by a simple comparison of various conceptualizations. While each of these theoretical attempts, in and of itself, has an undeniable value, a unified, coherent, and comprehensive understanding of communication is not achieved.

The view of communication wherein each theoretical attempt of looking at its nature "serves at best as a fuzzy snapshot" (Baldwin et al. 2006, 17), is oversimplified and suffers from at least two significant limitations.

First, the snapshot view "reduces to a still picture what actually is a dynamic, ever-changing entity" (Baldwin et al. 2006, 17), thus reifying communication. The desire to capture communication and represent it as a clear-cut object is understandable. This desire is viewed as consistent with the political agenda of the transmission conception of communication, related to control and domination rather that participation (Dresner

2006, 160). However, the clarity obtained by the cutting of the dynamic world into supposedly frozen objects that are given names and can be easily controlled "may be only a false security. . . . By using artificial linguistic divisions . . . , *students of communication risk removing themselves from the very process they seek to understand*" (Anderson and Ross 2002, 58; emphasis mine). As a result, theorizing becomes limited only to "theories of," and we fail to understand communication as a process in which we ourselves participate, cf. "theories for." Unfortunately, it is quite often that communication is "talked about as if it were some physical entity or 'thing' that could be held in the palm of one's hand" (Neuliep 1996, 3). It is important to remember that communication "is impossible to slow down or stop. There aren't snapshots or instant replays of communication, then, because when it's frozen . . . , it ceases to be living communication" (Anderson and Ross 2002, 57). One of the main negative consequences of reification is that communication, instead of an organic—living, orderly and beautiful—phenomenon that it is, appears in the form of static and rigid categories. In this respect, one can recall the Marxist critique of reification by G. Lukács ("*Verdinglichung*"—literally "thingification"); for example, in the capitalist society "properties and abilities are no longer bound to the organic unity of the person, but rather appear as 'things,' which man possesses and disposes of" (quoted by: Peters 2005, 261).

The social scientific approach to culture, for example, views it "by abstracting the value of a cultural element, necessarily removes that element from its native context" (Rogers 2006, 488). As a result, one fails to understand culture as a living phenomenon. Ironically, the harder we try to approach culture by using this approach, the more difficult it becomes to identify its (inter)subjectivity, its very spirit. The study of culture can be diagnosed with a form of psychosis, signified by the repression of certain possibilities of culture's existence, such as its fluidity and fragmentation, its "always already" nature, its indeterminacy and ambiguity, and its situated particularity. Such crucial aspects of culture cannot be fully explained within the social scientific approach where "the phenomenological aspect of existence is sublimated" and where "our discursive freedom to constitute a more enabling . . . subjectivity . . . is denied" (Eicher-Catt 2001, 111). Similarly, according to such an approach, communication as something dynamic and flowing is fixed and frozen (cf. Adams and Markus 2004, 337). This way, one can claim to "understand" a plant by looking at its herbarium. And yet, communication is often understood exactly this way, as if made up of numerous snapshots that "come in varying sizes and shapes" (Cragan and Shields 1998, 5). It must be noted here that reification as a problem of communication theorizing must not be equated with the devaluation of things themselves;

as will be shown later in the book, there is "something blessed about things" (Peters 2005, 262).

Second, the snapshot view promotes essentialism by treating fixed and rigid categories as inherent to communication (cf. Adams and Markus 2004, 340). Such a view reduces the essence of communication to a set of categories while leaving out "what is not within the frame of the camera's lens" (Baldwin et al. 2006, 17). Naturally, in this view, the essence of anything, e.g., communication, can sooner or later be "discovered."

Not surprisingly, understanding communication in terms of isolated theoretical snapshots is considered a daunting task and even might appear insurmountable; it seems as if "incompatible ontological starting points . . . render cross-continuum conversations and partnerships all but impossible" (Anderson and Baym 2004, 603). With this danger in mind, we are warned not to underestimate "the difficulty of integrating definitions derived eclectically from disciplines with incommensurable intellectual agendas" (Craig 1999, 121). To overcome this danger means overcoming the limitations of reification and essentialism, outlined above. To that end, it is necessary, first, to conceptualize communication not as an entity but rather as an orderly and rhythmic process where all parts are dynamically interconnected, and, second, to show how this living being is not reduced to a set of properties but rather is open to new meanings with something significant always left outside the "camera's lens."

Communication as a Moving Experience

Two main questions must be raised in order to overcome the limitations of reification and essentialism, thus presenting a more complex model of communication. First, if communication is constitutive of all relations—political, economic, technological, etc. (Hall 1989, 43), what constitutes the nature of communication itself? In other words, we need to find out what makes communication such a dynamic force. Meanwhile, we seem to know more about how or why communication takes place rather than what it really is. And, second, since the concept of a model is derived from the Latin word "modus," meaning "measure," "rhythm," or "harmony" (Morris 1982, 843), the second question is what a possible measure of communication may be. If we identify a measure of communication dynamics, we will be able to see communication as an organic, cosmic phenomenon in all its orderly beauty or beautiful order. However, when one looks at communication in terms of hundreds of theories, dozens of approaches and traditions, or several paradigms, one fails to find any measure of communication as a moving—in every sense of the word—phenomenon.

Let us turn to the first question, i.e., what constitutes the nature of communication? In the present book, communication is conceptualized as experience becoming meaningful to those involved in it, cf. "the needed new definition is communication as experience" (Shepherd 2001, 248–249). To communicate is to let someone know about something meaningful to oneself thus aiming at common experience. It must be noted right away that experience should not be identified only with accumulating cognitive knowledge; rather, it is a dangerous search for something meaningful—for example, truth, freedom, or Self—that is participated in or lived through, cf. the root "per" in the word "experience," which carries connotations of danger, trial, or fear (Morris 1982, 1534). In this light, we all are experienced communicators because we all constantly try to find meaning in whatever we participate or through whatever we live; communication as experience is a process of trial and error rather than a jigsaw puzzle that eventually can be "done."

Experience is an apt way to characterize the nature of communication because of several important characteristics. First, the concept of experience is neutral and all-inclusive: it can be applied to any object that can be apprehended through the senses or mind. Second, experience can be viewed both as a physical reality and a psychical phenomenon, cf. a thought experiment. Third, experience is clearly dynamic in nature for it presupposes one's active participation in something. And, fourth, experience is evolutionary because, through it, meaning unfolds. Thus, it is experience that constitutes the nature of communication wherein something is constantly tried and let known, i.e., communicated. They say that knowledge is power, and indeed, it is knowledge as common meaningful experience that makes communication such a powerful force.

Let us emphasize once again that experience and knowledge here are taken in a very broad sense, combining both representational and non-discursive elements of meaning. An attempt to approach communication from both such perspectives is made, for example, by communicology as a complex and rigorous framework for the study of human discourse in all of its semiotic and phenomenological manifestations. Over the past several decades, communicology as a field of study has been gathering strength. In a nutshell, "communicology is a human science grounded in consciousness and its reflexive condition, experience" (Lanigan 2000, 102; see also: Lanigan 2008). In this light, communicology is positioned as "perhaps, the most interdisciplinary of all disciplines" (Catt 2006, 36). R. Jakobson is reported to have spoken in a similar vein about the science of communication and exchanges in human society as the broadest theoretical framework (see: Ivanov 1999, 776).

Let us now turn to the second question posed above, i.e., what a possible measure for communication as meaningful experience might be. In the study of communication, "researchers must agree on what is being studied—the object of the study" (Heath and Bryant 2000, 89). In other words, in spite of many different views of communication, there must be something that all conceptualizations have in common. The most general treatment of communication is found in what is known as "core" communication theories that "provide insight into processes that operate whenever communication takes place" (Littlejohn 2002, 15). Core theories tell us something about the development of messages, address interpretation and the generation of meaning, discuss message structure, address interactional dynamics, and help us to understand institutional and societal dynamics (Littlejohn 2002, 15). However, at the core of all core theories, so to speak, we find the treatment of communication as a process; cf. "perhaps the most widely held truism about the nature of communication is that it is a process" (Neuliep 1996, 3), or "perhaps the most widespread point of convergence in definitions of communication is the notion that communication is a process" (Miller 2002, 5), or communication is conceptualized as "a symbolic process whereby reality is produced, maintained, repaired, and transformed" (Carey 1992, 23).

So, "communication is a process. This is a nearly sacred statement that begins most communication textbooks. And then, like magic, any mention of process disappears. The remaining material is about constructing and sending messages" (Salem 2009, 1). This is because a process is typically understood only as an interconnected series of steps leading toward a goal (Anderson and Ross 2002, 57). However, a process is first of all a dynamic of meaningful change in experiences; in this sense, communication "can be viewed as motion instead of action" (Heath and Bryant 2000, 52). In other words, communication is motion—a moving experience. Although as early as Aristotle motion was seen as the key to understanding the Universe (Feldman 2005, 2), it is easy to underestimate or completely ignore motion because of its ubiquitous character; in this respect, motion is similar to breathing. Yet, our very survival depends on our ability to detect motion (Vyvyan 2003, 202), and detecting motion is a matter of marking a meaningful change in experiences.

Thus, a process is not simply a series of interconnected steps, but also—and more importantly—"a course or passage of time" (Morris 1982, 1043).

Therefore, "to understand communication as a process, researchers must treat it as ever changing. . . . It is time dependent because no two communication events are the same" (Heath and Bryant 2000, 53). Communication as a process must be conceptualized as "an activity that has many separate but interrelated steps that occur over time" (Ruben and Stewart 2006, 15) or unfold "over time" (Miller 2002, 5).

Time has always had a special significance due to its mysterious nature (TenHouten 2005, 1). It is well known that time played a special role in the works of many thinkers such as I. Kant, M. Heidegger, M. Bakhtin, etc. Due to its special status, "the conceptualization of time is much more demanding on the attempts to explicate a theory of communication . . . , perhaps more demanding than any other single factor" (Fisher 1978, 222). However, A. Fisher's next words from more than thirty years ago still ring true today: "The full implications of the increased complexity of time are not yet fully comprehended in the performance of contemporary communication research" (Fisher 1978, 222). To be sure, it is not easy to study time and comprehend its implications for communication research because of the nature of time, as such, cf.: "in a sense, time 'is' nothing else but the ontological difference. Yet strictly speaking time 'is' not, because it is not a being among beings; it *temporalizes itself* as the ontological difference" (Chernakov 2002, 3).

The "special character of time" (Leydesdorff 1994, 42) is overshadowed by treating it as a mere extension of space, which is reflected in language. It is noted that time is typically lexicalized in terms of space as we routinely think of time that way, e.g., it flows, it has arrived (Vyvyan 2003, 14). It is emphasized that "the spatial terms are not only the sources of temporal concepts, but also lurk behind other complex notions such as logical exclusion. The flow from space to time is thus only one part of a much more far-reaching drift, from space to many other abstract domains" (Deutscher 2005, 136). It is important to remember, however, that "calling time the fourth dimension gives it an air of mystery. One might think that time can now be conceived as a kind of space and try in vain to add visually a fourth dimension to the three dimensions of space. It is essential to guard against such a misunderstanding of mathematical concepts" (Reichenbach 1958, 110). It must be remembered that the tendency to spatialize time is "consonant with the idea of classical determination" (Čapek 1961, 163); in a way, this tendency can be viewed as an attempt to eliminate time, cf. "the elimination of time and its spatialization are closely related" (Čapek 1961, 161–162). Spatial experience tries to repress yet cannot completely annihilate temporality. Moreover, as it constantly escapes spatialization, time makes it possible for space itself to exist, cf. "it cannot be denied that space . . . *still endures through time*" (Čapek 1961, 50). It must also be noted that

> since the trace is the ultimate relation of the living present with its outside . . . , the temporalization of sense is, from the outset, a "spacing." As soon as we admit spacing both as "interval" or difference and as openness upon the outside, there can no longer be any absolute inside, for the "outside" has insinuated itself into the movement by which the inside of the nonspatial, which is called "time," appears, is constituted, is "presented." Space is "in" time; it is time's pure leaving-itself; it is the "outside-itself" as the self-relation of time. The externality of space, externality as space, does not overtake time; rather, it opens as pure "outside" "within" the movement of temporalization. (Derrida 1973, 86)

Thus, the importance of spatial perspective in communication (e.g., Shome 2003) cannot be emphasized without understanding the role that time plays in it. The interplay of space and time should be more accurately characterized as a spatialization of time or "a *temporalization* or *dynamization* of space" (Čapek 1961, 161). So, "motion . . . implies both space and time" (Čapek 1961, 67). That is why time, which is commonly taken as the metric of motion, presupposes space, as well. Communication, therefore, as "a codependently emergent, self-organizing whole" (Merrell 2000, 139) is a continuous process of spatiotemporal meaningful experience.

In a word, communication is both space and time. Defined separately, time can be conceptualized as a "series of succession" and space as a "series of simultaneities" (Latour 2004, 39); in other words, time can be identified with the duration of things while space can be identified with the arrangement of things. It is easy to see that space, conceptualized as simultaneity, is defined through time, i.e., as something happening/existing at the same time; by the same token, time, conceptualized as sequence, is defined through space, i.e., as a following of one thing after another. Clearly, time and space cannot be understood in isolation from each other, cf. "the only thing that is real is the whole of spacetime" (Greene 2004, 131). This is why perhaps, applied to communication, space and time, sometimes receive diametrically opposing treatments when taken separately. In some cases, space is identified with immanence and time with transcendence (Massey 1992); in other cases—the other way around. For example, H. Innis associated time with stability and space with change (Innis 1991; cf. Angus 1998; Babe 2000). In this sense, he identified temporal and spatial biases in communication media as follows: "Media that emphasize time are those that are durable in character, such as parchment, clay, and stone. Media that emphasize space are apt to be less durable and light in character, such as papyrus and paper" (Innis 1950, 7).

These ideas gave rise to the two well-known views of communication developed by J. Carey—ritual and transmission. The "ritual view of communication is directed not toward the extension of messages in space but toward the maintenance of society in time; not the act of imparting information but the representation of shared beliefs" while the transmission view conceptualizes communication as "the extension of messages across geography for the purpose of control" (Carey 1989, 18). It must be emphasized once again, though, that communication is a process that occurs in space and time (in spacetime), made clear by A. Einstein's theory of relativity, which can be seen as "a theory of communication, more specifically, of the universe's difficulty of communicating with itself" (Peters 2003, 407). Thus, instead of treating the spatial and the temporal as two separate realms, it makes more sense to follow in the footsteps of those who, like M. McLuhan, "under the influence of contemporary theories of physics, and particularly Einstein's theory of relativity, sought to interface space and time" (Cavell 1999, 352). It should be remembered that communication must be conceptualized as a process in which "time is necessary for the bringing forth the space, in a manner of speaking, *and vice versa*" (Merrell 2000, 83; emphasis mine). So, in the present book, communication is viewed as a spatiotemporal experience of meaning that is constantly changing.

By emphasizing the process of communication as motion of a space-time continuum of meaning, we begin to understand its truly dynamic nature. The fact is that "communication theory has most typically drawn upon the humanities and the social sciences, with occasional forays into the natural sciences (mostly in the hunt for metaphors), but the natural sciences, medicine, and engineering are full of consideration of time, space, signals, distance, contact—central concerns and topics of communication theory" (Peters 2003, 398–399). The extension of such concepts "to non-physical realms may sound at first like positivism, but this is not positivism" (Leydesdorff 1994, 44). Understanding communication in such terms as motion, space, and time opens up a lot of possibilities. These possibilities have already been probed from the perspectives of general philosophy (Gebser 1985), general systems theory (Leydesdorff 1994), general semantics (Korzybski 1994), semiotics (Bruneau 2007; Merrell 1996), literary criticism (Bakhtin 1981, 1986), linguistics (Deutscher 2005), intercultural communication (Scollon and Scollon 2004), etc. And yet, a comprehensive analysis of the nature of communication in terms of time-space relations is clearly still in the future. Thirty years ago, A. Giddens challenged social theory to "situate time action in *time* and *space* as a continuous flow of conduct" (Giddens 1979, 3). Much later, however, it was admitted that "social theorists have responded to that challenge in a minimalist way . . . or ignore it altogether" (Adam 2000, 125–126). The same words could be repeated for communication theory. In fact, even calls for communication theory to make time and space the focus of attention are extremely rare; instead, one comes across somewhat tentative pronouncements, cf. "the ways in which communication has come to be viewed . . . might also be understood in terms of time and space" (Pinchevski 2005, 29). A notable exception can be found in J. Peter's consistent efforts to bring time and space to the center of theoretical discussion of communication. He explicitly states that "to study space and time . . . is to get a clearer fix on what is at stake for communication theory" (Peters 2003, 399) and that, in this respect, a "lifetime of work (fortunately) remains" (Peters 2003, 398–399; cf. Klaygin 2008). Part of such work is undertaken in the present book. Making time and space the focus of communication is one way to respond to the question best phrased by J. Carey, cf.: "where does one turn, even provisionally, for the resources with which to get a fresh perspective on communication" (Carey 1992, 23). Perhaps time and space as the key resources with which to look at communication in a new light have been mostly overlooked or given very little attention because of their ubiquitous character.

So, communication is a process wherein meaning continuously moves as spatiotemporal experience. It is common to conceptualize meaning as something contained or developed in a message. However, it is more appropriate to view meaning as a mark, created in and by a message. In this sense, a message can only mean what it will have said at the moment whose time is always to come, interpretation remaining forever open (Chang 1996, 201). In other words, meaning is (in) a constant process of becoming, always but a trace; meaning never is, it always becomes. We can be conscious of future communication only when it is already becoming present, and as it is becoming present, communication is already passing away into the becoming past. Therefore, communication is no more than a process of constant becoming (unfolding and enfolding) of meaning.

In the present book, experience is considered meaningful when a change in the interplay of space and time (in spacetime) is marked. In other words, a meaning(ful experience) originates as "a splitting of the temporal and spatial dimensions in the very act of signification" (Bhabha 1994, 182). Any meaningful experience is but a clearance in the spatiotemporal continuum that is (attempted to be) bridged by those participating in the process of communication. Experience becomes meaningful in the gap between space and time. It is interesting to note that in medieval Europe changes in the sun's shadow cast on a sundial were observed as "hora," cf. the English word *hour* derived from the Latin and Greek *hora*, which in turn originated from the ancient Egyptian *hor*, meaning the *sun's path*, named from their "god of the dawn" *Horus* (see: Stepanov 2004, 242). Therefore, *hora* here is not simply a period of duration, but also a stroke; in this sense, one can say that experience becomes meaningful when time is literally cut into space. Moreover, one can see in such collective practice totemic traces; according to O. Friedenberg (see: Perlina 1992), the originary totem is found in dividing up a killed animal by a tribe. In this sense, a killed animal as one of the first meaningful experiences in human life represents something pulled out of the spatiotemporal continuum—literally a captured meaning.

So, communication "is dependent on an appreciation of a proper balance between the concepts of space and time" (Innis 1991, 64). When (and where) a meaning is "captured," experience is considered "completely" meaningful, and the gap between space and time seems to disappear; hence it seems as if motion stops. At this point, a balance between space and time is—or rather seems to be—found, i.e., space and time are found to be one (and the same). In reality, of course, life goes on and our experiences continue as new gaps open up waiting to be filled.

All a Matter of Perspective

It is important to highlight the transformative nature of motion. Moreover, "as the classical concept of motion is indissolubly tied with the visual images of spatial displacement, it would be less misleading not to use this term at all and to replace it by some more general and less visual term like *change, modification, or transformation*" (Čapek 1961, 267). It is through transformation that "time becomes 'spatialized,' but at the same time—a 'same time' that is dynamic time, so there is no sameness, you cannot dive into the same time twice—space is 'temporalized'" (Merrell 2000, 139). Thus, communication is (trans)formed in/as the dynamics of space and time.

In the present book, communication as a continuous process of meaningful spatiotemporal experience—a circle of 360 degrees—is theorized as rotating four times in 90-degree transformations. The fourfold approach to symbolic phenomena "is associated with equality, reliability, fairness, firmness, and solidity" (Schneider 1995, 65) and has a long-standing tradition from Aristotle's square of oppositions to the semiotic square of A. Greimas and J. Courtés (1982) to the four-tiered structure of human communication research proposed by J. Powers (1995) to the four philosophical domains of communication theory identified by J. Anderson and G. Baym (2004).

Based on this approach, as a result of the meaningful transformations of spatiotemporal experience, five fundamental perspectives on communication are identified, each presenting a certain view of its nature. Each perspective highlights a certain "'zone of lucidity,' while attempting to tackle questions pertaining to the status of communication within wider contexts, its various manifestations, and its proper form and operation" (Pinchevski, 2005, 28). In other words, each perspective provides a view of communication as "an order according to which things within the elucidated zone appear to operate" (Pinchevski 2005, 27).

In general, "illuminated by the power of our consciousness" (Greene 2004, 139), communication in the present book is conceptualized as a dynamic interplay of space and time. Each perspective presents a certain staging of communication whereby some of its meaningful characteristics are manifest. Overall, in the present book, communication is discussed as a dynamic phenomenon undergoing several transformations, moving from stable and observable structures, which exist in—supposedly pure—space, to ever-changing semiotic relationships, which exist in—supposedly pure— time, and finally to their "ideal" unification. Respectively, several perspectives are identified; "each perspective is . . . an epistemology that guides our theorizing, our inquiry, our thinking about the process of human communication" (Fisher 1978, 322).When (and where) communication comes full circle, a universe of communication is (trans)formed as space and time (seem to) become one, with "the identity of experience instantaneously present to itself" (Derrida 1973, 60). Thus, "in the essential history the beginning comes last" (Heidegger 2005, 63), and we walk, as S. Kierkegaard says, backwards into the future (see: Peters 2003, 409). Overall, communication is viewed as a continuous attempt of creating and bridging the gap between space and time.

So, in the present book, the nature of communication is conceptualized as a universe. The word "universe" is derived from the Greek "ūniversus," meaning "whole," "entire," or "turned into one" (Morris 1982, 1402). It is in this meaning that communication is presented as a process of meaningful experience undergoing spatiotemporal transformations and (continuously attempted to be) turned into one. Communication is a moving, constantly transformative and transformed, experience. Regardless of its goal, level, participants, etc., the motive of communication is always the same—motion; it must be noted that the word "motive" is derived from Latin *movēre*, "to move" (Morris 1982, 857). It is through motion that experience is (trans)formed, becoming meaningful.

Thus, communication in the present book is put in perspective(s). The word "perspective" means, first of all, "a view" (Morris 1982, 979); at each staging, different aspects of communication come into view (unfold). The word "perspective" also means "relative significance of something" (Morris 1982, 979). In this respect, different theoretical views of communication "are not mutually exclusive but offer limited, complementary perspectives" (Craig 1999, 123). The approach to communication in the present book, therefore, emphasizes its holographic nature: the whole nature of communication can be brought to light starting at any point, i.e., viewed in terms of any of its stagings. The significance of each perspective discussed in the following chapters is relative to how we look at communication or from which angle the process of communication is illuminated by theoretical thought. All the theoretical perspectives, to be discussed in detail in the following chapters, must be seen as equally important. Only together do they present a holistic and dynamic view of communication as a universe manifest in its main stagings.

To summarize, communication theorizing is characterized by an abundance of views and an equally impressive disarray; numerous attempts have been made to explain and understand its nature. Methodologically, theorizing can take the form of a journey within which communication must be looked at (contemplated) in all its cosmic order and beauty. Such a methodological journey must overcome the obstacles of reification and essentialism and be consistent with the evolution of communication study "from source- and message-centered to receiver- and meaning-centered; from one-way to interactive and transactional; from event- to process-oriented; from an exclusive emphasis on information transmission to an emphasis on interpretation and relationships, as well as information transmission" (Ruben and Stewart 2006, 50). To that end, the nature of communication in the present book is identified with the motion of meaningful experience, and its measure with the interplay of space and time.

Communication thus is presented as a continuously moving process in which meaningful experience unfolds and enfolds in space and time or, rather, as spacetime. As soon as motion is introduced in discussion, communication comes to life, as it were, and a truly dynamic conceptualization of communication becomes possible. In this sense, our knowledge claims about communication match its transformations, moving from those resting on (as if in space) empirically obtained and verifiable facts to those based on seemingly nothing but an intersubjective agreement reached over time. This conceptualizationl is consistent with the open nature of communication and can generate "new and potentially unforeseen ways of knowing" (Anderson and Baym 2004, 605). Meanwhile, let us focus on the first staging of communication and see what comes into view.

PART II

THE STAGING(S)
OF COMMUNICATION

~

CHAPTER THREE

Up in the Air:
Communication as Invocation

The Call of Communication

The first human condition one experiences is that of total disorder and confusion. Any object—a stone, rain, gusts of wind—appear to undergo continuous metamorphosis and can magically turn into any other object. "In fact, the very notion of stable object or stable being is not present" (Bińczyk 2007, 104). The only way of "fixing" such experiences is to call up an object by giving it a name. This way, meaning is captured in/as a syncretic form: at this staging, names, reality, and actions are all glued together, and names are seen as a part of the invoked objects. Here objects are united not by anything pertaining to the objects themselves. What takes place at this staging of communication can be viewed in terms of L. Vygotsky's notion of "syncretic conglomeration" (see: Gillett and McMillan 2001, 39). Anything that stimulates one's senses is on its way to becoming a meaningful experience. In other words, at this staging, objects are organized under words, but "in order to grasp this notion, we must accept that there is no general, abstract, or public basis for the . . . grouping of objects under that term, and that objects placed in such categories are inherently unrelated. . . . Thus the grouping under the term is both arbitrary and idiosyncratic. For this reason syncretic conglomerations are not adequate for meaning and understanding" (Gillett and McMillan 2001, 39).

It must be emphasized that, at this staging, "the distance between words and things is not present, words exert a direct and immediate influence on reality" (Bińczyk 2007, 105). In the same light, it is possible to say that, at this staging, "the subject of knowledge, as a kind of independent, reflexive instance, is not present" (Bińczyk 2007, 104). The subject here is similar to a child who is not self-aware and in whose mind "everything is connected with everything else, everything can be justified by means of unforeseen allusions and implications" (Piaget 2002, 227). Such connections are made or "justified" by way of invocation, and the entire essence of an object turns out to be captured in its name.

Thus, at this staging, "the universe cannot be distinguished from how we act upon it. . . . A universe comes into being when a space is severed or taken apart. . . . The act is itself already remembered, *even if unconsciously*, as our first attempt to distinguish different things in a world where, in the first place, the boundaries can be drawn anywhere we please" (Spencer-Brown 1979, xxix; emphasis mine). The first act of space being severed is one of invocation—often desperate and quick; this way, the distance between words and things (read: the subject and the world) appears overcome and therefore not present. Whatever grabs one's attention is itself grabbed out of chaos, so to speak, and put in a name; thus it becomes possible to perceive and "fix" (the arrangement of) objects existing (as if) simultaneously in space.

The "name" by which an object is conjured up at this staging of communication is not so much a symbolic means as a signal directly connecting the subject and the object. In this sense, communication is similar in function to that of *Appell* proposed by K. Bühler whereby language is "a *signal* by virtue of its appeal to the hearer, whose inner and outer behavior it directs" (Bühler 1990, 35). It should be noted, though, that K. Bühler's concept of appeal is more complex and can even be viewed as "*an open-ended communicative sign*" (Grant 2003a, 103). In other words, here the object is signaled rather than signified. In this respect, the distinction between reference and sense can be viewed as a result of the narrow understanding of the object as an entity that exists only in space (Uemov 1975, 459). On the one hand, such an understanding of the object can be considered an advantage of the so-called philosophy of the name because the object is treated as a "timeless" entity (cf. Stepanov 1985, 23) and so can be invoked—with the same result—over and over again. On the other hand, this understanding is still limited (to space) and overlooks the fact that objects live (and may die) in time, as well, as will be discussed in more detail later in the book.

At this staging of communication, meaning is apprehended, i.e., mentally seized, which nicely expresses both uneasiness and a limited understanding of the object. Communication as invocation is an attempt to arrest the object by putting it in a name. It is an attempt to "fix" meaning (in space) from a distance and without any real contact with the object, as it were. It is interesting to note that the term "invocation" is often used in (the study of) computer-mediated communication or technical processes of information transfer (Thelwall 2002), where it is conceptualized as a remote method of information retrieval (Aderounmu et al. 2006). In this sense, invocation can be viewed as a means of reaching the object without any real contact; it seems as if objects can obey by simply being called out. In a manner of speaking, the subject is not yet ready "to go the distance"; it seems as if the distance here magically disappears once the right word is used.

It is noted that an invocation by early pagan priests was recited in an unintelligible tongue (Ivanov 1999, 624). It could have been any tongue as long as it was other than one's own or sounded differently. In this light, invocation can be viewed as a precursor to intercultural communication except for, at this point, the culturally different Other is not really present, but rather anticipated. Or, one might say that the Other is present through its absence. It will take time for other characteristics of communication to unfold. Here a communication universe is only beginning to come into being, with the attention focused on the materiality of objects, which can be perceived through senses.

In this connection, one can think of Aristotle's "mysterious faculty, *nous*" (Aydede 1998, 5). This faculty is said to have a non-discursive nature, grasping the first principles intuitively from sensible particulars. Considered to be the starting point in acquiring knowledge, *nous* is identified by Aristotle with perception. It highlights the material role of the process of communication, "by operating on some form of primitive perceptual data" (Taylor 1990, 137). In this respect, it is noted that "it should be seen rather as a sort of perception than as any form of apprehension of general truth" (Taylor 1990, 137).

In his reading of Book 6 of *Nicomachean Ethics*, M. Heidegger identifies *nous* with "pure beholding," which "produced *everything* as [a kind of] being-able-to-have-at-one's-disposal" (Heidegger 1992, 380). This reading is consistent with the nature of communication as invocation when the subject (be)holds the object at one's disposal (or vice versa).

Aristotle's *nous* is concerned with variable facts that "are the starting-points for the apprehension of the end" (Aristotle 1143a, 35). The states of apprehension reached this way "are thought to be natural endowments" (Aristotle 1143b, 5). When Aristotle speaks about *nous*, he says that for this kind of apprehension, "*nature is the cause. [Hence intuitive reason is both beginning and end . . .]*" (Aristotle 1143b, 5; emphasis mine). It will be shown later how communication comes back to where it started, its end becoming a new beginning. Right now, it must be emphasized that the first staging of communication is its first beginning on its way to the end, which is to become another beginning, etc.

At this staging, then, communication can be conceptualized as invocation or bringing forth objects with the help of various signals. Invocation is a customary procedure, a rite. The word "rite" is derived from Latin "rītus"; its root "ar"—"to fit together" (Morris 1982, 1121, 1506)—expresses the essence of invocation very well. Through invocation, different objects are fit together, making it convenient for the subject to deal with them. In this respect, one can recall *convenientia* as one of four similitudes, discussed by M. Foucault, which refers to the universal convenience of things and is connected with space. To be more precise, "this word denote the adjacency of places more strongly than it does similitude. Those things are 'convenient' which come sufficiently close to one another to be in juxtaposition, their edges touch, their fringes intermingle, the extremities of the one also denote the beginning of the other. . . . So that in this hinge between two things a resemblance appears" (Foucault 1970, 20). One can say that such a resemblance appears between the subject and the object, invoked by the subject; in other words, the object comes to resemble the subject for it was the subject that conjured up the object by giving it a name, in the first place. In other words, the subject and the object as "two things" do not simply happen to find themselves in a convenient proximity of each other.

The rite of invocation is a procedure with a goal (if not fully conscious) of bringing forth the object viewed by the subject as a high power. This power is invoked and thereby recognized by the subject not so much to be venerated; rather, the subject appeals to it for assistance; at this point, of course, such an appeal cannot be viewed as a Habermasian rationally discursive process. Simply put, the subject needs to overcome one's own fear of objects (cf. Prigogine and Stengers 1984). As was mentioned earlier, communicative experience is a dangerous search for meaning—a process participated in or lived through, cf. the root "per" in the word "experience" with its connotations of danger, trial, and fear (Morris 1982, 1534). At this staging, the elements of fear are especially present in communication. It is here that the origins of the so-called communication apprehension are to be found. The term "apprehension" is usually applied to the "sender" (the subject) rather than the "receiver" (the object) of communication. The subject's apprehension originates from the fear—although one is not fully aware of it at this point—of a possible failure to invoke the object and arrest its meaning. Only by arresting or apprehending meaning can chaos be kept at bay, apprehension overcome, and a connection established between the subject and the object, thus bridging a gaping gap between them and making it seem as if the distance between them, just as the distance between words and things, were not present.

As mentioned earlier, the term "invocation" is often used in (the study of) computer-mediated communication where it is associated with the execution of programs made up of formalized objects (Evered et al. 1995). In this connection, communication at this staging can be viewed as an attempt by the subject to execute objects, not so much putting them into effect, but, as it were, depriving them of their own life, i.e., their meaning ("executing them"). Even more interestingly, objects can be "saved" only by the subject as if it were simply a matter of pressing the button "save." In other words, the subject is perceived to be a powerful agent acting on (executing and saving) the world. In real (not computer-mediated) reality, of course, understanding the living being of communication is not so simple.

Thus, at this staging of communication, objects are brought into existence by the subject giving them names. The intention of the subject here is not really to venerate objects, but use them toward one's own end. Of course, intention here is not a conscious aim guiding one's action; rather, it is more like an impulse, a gust of air experienced by the subject. By giving it a name, the subject does not really submit to the object as a high power; rather, the object is subjugated by the subject. Now the subject can carry out any action in the name of the object. It can be argued, therefore, that invocation "attempts to initiate a circular process which will be advantageous to the speaker" (Greene 2005, 46). It can also be argued that carrying an action out in someone else's name is easier than taking responsibility for one's own actions. Here, one's response to objects is mostly devoid of ethical underpinnings. That is why, perhaps, one's actions may turn into what K. Burke calls "the mania of the One" (Crusius 1999, 133); the One, naturally (pun intended), being the subject. Mania is an inordinately intense ("crazy") behavior because the subject who is a maniac fails to adequately understand reality, not bothering to let its objects reveal their true meaning and thus passing them by, as it were, cf. the root "mei'" in the word "mania," meaning, among other things, "to go," "to pass," and "to miss" (Morris 1982, 1528). It is worth noting that the same root is found in the Latin word "mūnus," which means, among other things, "service performed for the community" and "gift" (Morris 1982, 1528). It will take time—in the form of several transformations of meaningful experience—for communication to overcome its maniacal nature and reveal its nature as a gift. Right now it must be emphasized that a name as a sacred part of the object is only one part of a communication being because communication is sacred overall. As will be shown, the object ("the receiver") is also part of the subject ("the sender"), and vice versa. In other words, they are parts of each other—and also participants in this wondrous process of communication, constantly striving and yet failing—or failing and yet striving—to bridge the gap between them and arrive at that point where and when space and time are one.

Thus, we (as subjects) make objects "part of a 'reality' that we alone invent, denying their creativity by usurping the right to create, . . . and make them subservient to ourselves" (Wagner 1981, 16). In a manner of speaking, the subject's communicative behavior with respect to the object is "disrespectful." In other words, the true voice of the object is not yet heard at this staging; every object here is taken as a given, something that exists in an open space. The object's motion is limited (by the subject) to predictable movements from one position to another, i.e., conquered. An example of such communication can be found in Tz. Todorov's *Conquest of America: The Question of the Other* (1984), which describes Spanish colonials' "discovery" of the Americas and their contact with the native peoples. In this connection, "according to Todorov, Columbus's goal in his interactions was only to reaffirm his idea of the world, classifying his findings like specimen in a prearranged table. . . . Columbus addressed his language, accordingly, *directly to nature*, to the referent. To him, words and things were tied together, *circumventing the dimension of intersubjectivity*. . . . In Columbus's view, there was no human subject on the other side" (Pinchevski 2005, 144; emphasis mine). Clearly, at this staging of communication, "the question of the Other" is not really addressed in all its complexity.

The object can be brought into existence by invocation as well as evocation. In the latter case, what is summoned or called out serves one's needs yet coexists with the subject, cf. childhood memories or curiosity. Both invocation and evocation are attempts to answer the call of communication, with the subject trying to find one's voice, i.e., how to respond to one's experiences. Evocation gives objects more space, as it were, while invocation is an attempt by the subject to control every object. However, through invocation, the subject also exposes one's intimacy to objects, implicitly—though not yet consciously—treating every object as the Other. In this sense, "the voice cuts both ways: as an authority over the Other and as an exposure to the Other, an appeal, a plea, an attempt to bend the Other" (Dolar 2006, 80).

Not only are objects invoked (by the subject) at this staging of communication, but the subject's courage is also summoned up. This way, the subject can overcome communication apprehension and start making steps toward (one)Self and even further—to an end without an end, eternal return, which cannot yet be seen from this point (in space). At this staging, the existence of the subject is postulated (positioned) by the virtue of invocating objects. Here the subject—not yet Self and therefore not yet completely aware of the Other—could say: "I summon, therefore, I am." Of course, the subject cannot really say it or understand what is truly said because communication here is still not yet a truly symbolic (inter)action let alone a self-reflective act. Communication as invocation, then, is an attempt of the subject to bring (one)Self into existence.

Thus, at this staging of communication, the focus is on the effect brought about by a certain instrumental action. The subject here tries to explain objects and predict their response to a summons. Understanding communication is not yet an issue: no question is raised (and discussed) about the correspondence between ideas and reality. At this staging, it is more appropriate to speak about (in)effective rather than (un)successful communication. Communication can be considered effective once something is brought into effect, i.e., once a gap between the subject and the object is bridged or rather not perceived to be present. Then, one can use the same procedure again and again, with the same effect. What happens "along the way" of that procedure is not as important as the effect itself.

The Medium Is Not the Message

There are a number of theories that view communication as an (ideally) supposedly instantaneous procedure of sending a message from one end to the other, cf. information theory, classical rhetorical theory, and technological determinism. A message, conceptualized as an entity, has a stable "meaning" and is supposed to generate the same response regardless of context. The word "meaning" is put in quotes here because C. Shannon defined information as a probability function, "repeatedly stressing that information theory concerned only the efficient transmission of messages through communication channels, not what those messages mean" (Hayles 1999, 54). Thus, "it is important to remember that Shannon's theory of communication is explicitly concerned with statistical structures. Questions of meaning are not, therefore, considered relevant" (Grant 2003a, 102). The classical Western rhetoric does not, of course, directly equate a message with a probability function, focusing more on its meaning (without quotes). At the same time, from the classical rhetorical point of view, communication can still be viewed as moving "in a linear way, . . . from preexisting situation to text to audience effect" (Combs 2005, 11). In other words, "rhetoric remains defined by a linear, cause-and-effect model in which an object receives some unintended, meaningful action" (Vivian 2004, 59). It is pointed out that "rhetoric is *regulatory* rather than *constitutive*, i.e., it modulates a meaning which is already there, rather than creating it anew"

(Sonesson 1996/1997, 50). In this light, rhetoric is sometimes seen as a "managerial art" (Fisher 1989, 8); hence a rhetor is but a communication manager. It is argued that the linear understanding of communication can be traced back to Aristotle, whose ideas were based on absolute and classifying categories instead of relative and relational categories. In this connection, it is stated that

> rhetors possessed of a storehouse of available means of persuasion like the one Aristotle compiles will lack means of choosing and ordering them unless they can respond to the questions posed to them and select among those means with knowledge of what their auditors already know, believe, or hold dear. They cannot decide what to say just by knowing what might be said; they must also know what has just been said by others and what goes without saying for their audiences. (Bialostosky 2004, 406)

In the same vein, "reception studies, which in their most outraged version divide the different parts of communications processes totally from each other and thus unable to explain the co-relationship between communicative agents qua media offers, also appear on this background as a reductive perspective" (Langer 1999, 80).

It is interesting to note that the roots of modern day political propaganda are sometimes traced back to rhetoric; for example, the systematic use of communication media during wars is seen as "taking the ancient art of 'manufacturing consent' to a new level" (Pinchevski 2005, 30). In this light, a direct parallel can be drawn between the classical works of Western rhetoric and the well-known propaganda model advanced by E. Herman and N. Chomsky (Herman and Chomsky 1988); in both cases, messages are viewed as propagated or transmitted from point A to point B. From this perspective, effective communication does not involve any constitutive interplay between participants; rather, it depends on a rhetor's artistry. In this respect, it is possible to argue that traditional rhetoric "functions as an extension of subjective intentions, which, in turn, depend upon the notion of a concept or meaning independent of language" (Vivian 2004, 77). It is claimed that such a view, grounded in speech and associated with truth and transparency, "preserves an intellectually conservative and rigidly moral interpretation of pedagogy, communication and civic conduct" (Vivian 2004, 74–75). It is also argued that speech instruction from a classical rhetorical perspective reaches back to the colonial period (Bryant and Miron 2007, 415). In this context, one can even view the Western communication research as an example of the transmission of knowledge rather than from the positions of a more invitational rhetoric (Foss and Griffin 1995). Perhaps it is for this reason that the study of communication today is still commonly perceived to be "an almost exclusively American enterprise" (Vroons 2005, 496) or "limited by Eurocentric cultural assumptions" (Craig 2007, 256).

Thus, the classical Western rhetoric may be interpreted as placing emphasis on the sender and treating those on the receiving end as objects taken for granted. Incidentally, a distinction is sometimes made between rhetorical theory and communication theory. Rhetorical theory is said to focus on situations in which intentions are stipulated or taken for granted, while communication theory focuses on situations where no such stipulation exists and which therefore call for interpretation. In this sense, communication theory "would be the body of generalizations resulting from studies of the *development* and *assigning* (or *attribution*) of meanings" while rhetorical theory "would be the body of generalizations resulting from studies of the *management* of meanings" (Bowers and Bradac 1982, 10). In the present book, rhetorical studies in the sense just described are treated as a part of communication theory overall, cf. the rhetorical tradition as one of the seven traditions discussed in the previous chapter.

Similar to information theory and classical rhetorical theory, technological determinism views those on the receiving end, i.e., a society as such, determined by something inherent on the sending end, i.e., a technology as such. Unlike the first two theories, though, here one cannot really talk about a message designed or transmitted from point to point. In this light, it is possible to argue "that Shannon-Weaver was a *transportation* model of communication, whereas what he [McLuhan] was interested in was a *transformation* model" (Cavell 1999, 348). It is noted that, "contrary to the Shannon-Weaver model of communication devised in the late 1940s for application to information theory and machines, McLuhan's interpretation was that in communication there is no transportation of information (concepts or 'content') from a source to target, but a transformation of the source and target *simultaneously*" (De Kerckhove 1981, 8; emphasis mine). In the same vein, it is argued that, unlike, for example, E. Hall's spatial theory, "McLuhan's spaces were much more the product of dynamic interrelationships" (Cavell 1999, 357). However, it must also be noted that "all of McLuhan's reasoning is dominated by a series of equivocations very troubling to a theoretician of communication, because the differences between the *channel* of communication, the *code*, and the *message* are not established" (Eco 1986, 234). Besides, in this view of communication, the distance between the sending and receiving ends is not really present as there really is no message separate from a medium; as the famous phrase puts it, "the medium is the message." It is a medium that leaves a society no choice but to respond to it in a certain way. Thus a society overall, as the object with all its meanings, is brought into effect (invoked) by a technology.

In this respect, one can recall that M. McLuhan played upon the words "utter" and "outer," using them interchangeably, when he presented media as "The Extensions of Man"—"our uttered or outered senses" (McLuhan 1994, 57). To him, communication is first of all a spatial process of the subject ("The Man") reaching out toward, and thereby determining, a destination. Although supposedly concerned with the transformations in the relationship between message and context, M. McLuhan must still be treated as a spatial theorist of communication (cf. Cavell 1999).

Thus, it is possible to view any transmission of a message as a spatial process. This way, for example, the expansion of empires takes place (cf. Innis 1950). However, this expansion is not a simple process of conquering space and establishing new and newer borders; interactions over time play in this process an equally important role, identified only by a close reading of history of empires. For instance, "the time-honored image of Muscovite Russia as a harshly hierarchical society, one where power flowed only from the top down, needs to be treated with caution; *there is much evidence of dialogue and compromise,* and we should not accept at face value, unexamined, the rhetorical self-image of the autocratic regime" (Martin 2008, 486; emphasis mine).

Just as communication is not simply a process of spatial expansion, a destination is not simply a place toward which something is directed and what can be invoked at one's will. A destination is more of a destiny with which one must come to terms; significantly, the word "fate," as a synonym of "destinty," is derived from Latin "fārī," meaning "to speak" (Morris 1982, 478). Therefore, the destiny of/in/as communication is in messages uttered, not simply "outered." Communication is more about "message Dasein" than "message design." In communication, the medium is *not* the message, "not" suggesting a gap that must exist between the message and the medium and so must be (re-)created all the time; this creative aspect of human agency does not find any place in technological determinism. Why does communication continue if everything is predetermined? Why do people create meaning even—or perhaps especially—in the face of Fate?

There exists, then, a gap between messages uttered and "outered," "Dasein-ed" and designed; if no such gap is discerned (marked), it must be created. Communication is a constant effort to create and fill up this gap, and such an effort involves not only spatiality, but temporality, as well. Just as time is enfolded at this staging of communication, it is implicitly present in M. McLuhan's views, as well as those expressed within the frameworks of information theory and rhetorical theory. Communication will reveal its temporal nature more fully as its other meaningful characteristics become manifest, and so different theories, to be discussed later, will present communication as a more dynamic, creative, and contingent process.

The linear theories, discussed above, view communication not so much as a process of extension of "The Man," but rather as its projection onto the object selected as its destination, its "aim." At this staging of communication, the subject is a dimensionless point; it simply thrusts oneself outward, as it were, and reaches, point by point, a destination. In a way, all the so-called linear theories, discussed above, are projective communication theories, and so the object is nothing but a projection of the subject. From this perspective, communication is similar to the so-called projective identification, discussed by psychoanalysts, when "an individual projects parts of the self onto another person, and then identifies with that other person. To maintain the fit, the person upon whom the attributes are projected is pressured by subtle or not-so-subtle means to act in a manner consistent with the projected qualities" (Wexler 2006, 129).This kind of identification, it can be argued, is different from the identification which results in consubstantiality (in K. Burke's sense), to be discussed in the next chapter. In a similar vein, the doctrine of the Eucharist affirms that Christ's body and blood *substantially coexist* with the consecrated bread and wine. Unlike the "projective identification," identification as consubstantiality is an act performed by one *with* the other (cf. "con" meaning "with")—an act in which both essences are present while being shared.

The subject that projects parts of the self onto (another as) the object can be seen as someone on a mission to reach a certain goal. From this perspective, communication is an act of sending or dispatching a message that contains a certain meaning (creed or doctrine); the missionary, as the messenger, is but a means toward this end, whose goal is to convert, not to be converted. Missionaries are supposed to change others, not themselves. It seems only natural that no mission can reach its goal without love, and yet, as Tz. Todorov writes, "can we really love someone if we know little or nothing of his identity, if we see, in place of that identity, a projection of ourselves or ideals. . . . How much is such love worth?" (Todorov 1984, 168).

Significantly, the theories that share their views on the nature of this staging of communication do not directly address the concept of love, cf. information theory and technological determinism or else predominantly treat it as a form of pathos to be used as an emotional appeal, cf. classical rhetorical theory. This concept finds a place in the conceptualization of communication only as a means to an end; if one cannot appeal to and invoke an audience as the object by using love, what good is it for? In other words, love must be meaningful only as long as one knows how much it is worth. In this respect, one can learn (or teach) how to (use) love. However, one can never really learn (or teach) how to love. Love matters not because it can help one to reach one's goal; it matters because one cannot help it and so it has no reason other than itself. In *Two Gentlemen of Verona*, Lucetta puts it very well as she responds to Julia's question "Your reason?" speaking not only for women, but for all people: "I have no other, but a woman's reason; I think him so because I think him so." To put it another way, love is so because love is so. When another staging of communication is discussed later in the book, it will become clear why love cannot be worth more or less and why love is all there is, moving "the sun and the other stars" (Dante Alighieri), i.e., the entire universe.

It must be emphasized that, at this staging of communication, as discussed in the present book, the subject cannot yet be viewed as the true Self, that the Other is still viewed as the object, and so they cannot (inter)act in the true sense of the word. It must also be noted that here any message that is sent by the subject is, in effect, a "Note to Self." However, communication must undergo several transformations before the subject can understand the real meaning of that "Note," i.e., before it truly makes sense.

While analyzing Plato's *Phaedrus*, J. Peters notes: "Because writing can live on far beyond the situation of utterance, it can mean many things for many people. The clients of sophists such as Lysias are at best transmitters, ignorant of the messages they bear" (Peters 1999, 47). It can be argued that communication overall, not just writing, can live on in time "far beyond the situation of utterance." More importantly, it can be argued that not only "the clients of sophists," as the objects of rhetorical artistry, are transmitters of the message that they are unaware of. The sophists themselves, as the subjects of the message, can never be completely sure of its meaning until it comes back to them. Communication is a contingent process, and anything can happen "beyond the situation of utterance."

So, communication here can be seen as transmission of a message from the subject to the object, which then responds to it in a precise and stable manner. In a way, communication appears as a process of transmitting a message that "can pass continuously from one frame of reference to the other. In this way, change in perspective is contained, subsumed within the changeless continuity that is space" (Rosen 2004, 14). A message, thus, moves from the subject to the object as its destination, from point to point to point. It is as if an arrow, instead of being shot and hitting (or not!) the target, is taken by hand and stuck to its center. Nothing (it seems) can sway it on its way to the target. This staging of communication can be seen as *pointctuality*, i.e., making a mark. Both "point" and "punctual" are derived from the same Latin word "pungere," meaning "to pierce" (Morris 1982, 1012, 1060). Punctuality will become more important in communication with more of its meaningful characteristics becoming manifest; for example, the concept of "punctum," proposed by R. Barthes and discussed later in this book, cannot be conceptualized as a purely spatial phenomenon, i.e., a "pointed" process wherein a message is sent across space, cf. the meaning of "trans" as "across" in "transmission." At another staging, the nature of communication will reveal its "appointed," temporal character more fully; as successful communication will involve an action taking place at the appointed time, communication will be conceptualized as a process of going "beyond space," cf. another meaning of the prefix "trans-" as "beyond." Moreover, communication will be viewed as a process of one coming to terms with one's fate. It will be shown later in the book how, in a metaphorical sense, communication can be seen as a process of "overcoming death," cf. the meaning of the Greek word "nek-tar" ("overcoming death") related to "ter," which gives rise to "trans-" (Morris 1982, 1546). In other words, one's lot is sweet no matter what; according to the Russian saying, even death is beautiful (sweet) if you are not alone ("На миру и смерть красна").

So, communication at this staging is conceptualized as a message moving— or rather moved—along a series of discrete points; it is worth mentioning that space can also be understood as a set of objects conventionally known as points (Stewart 2001, 135). At each point, the same content of a message can be captured in its entirety as a spatially conceptualized meaning— "meaning in crisp simultaneity," to use M. McLuhan's words (quoted by: Cavell 2002, 67). Naturally, communication viewed in the form of discrete objects can be easily visualized and presented graphically; it is such linear models that are found, first of all, in most communication theory textbooks (Kashkin 2007; Berlo 1960; Wood 2004). This view of communication is exemplified by the transmission model, derived from the human desire to increase the speed and effect of messages as they travel in space, and focused on signals sent over distance (Carey 1992; Innis 1991). Without a question, this view of communication is valuable as it draws our attention to its instrumental character (Craig 1999; Leydesdorff 2002, 131; Pinchevski 2005, 39). In addition,

> we may find, moreover, upon critical reflection, that there are often good reasons for using a transmission model: that it can be useful to distinguish pragmatically between communication sources and receivers, to map the flow of information through systems, or to think of messages as containers of meaning or of communication as an intentional act performed in order to achieve some anticipated outcome. (Craig 1999, 137)

However, we should not forget about the ritual view, which is focused on the representation of shared beliefs rather than the act of imparting information and directed more toward the maintenance of society in time rather than the extension of messages in space (Carey 1992). It is argued that "[Carey's account of] the ritual view of communication was about correcting the 'spatial bias' of U.S. communication research and policy through an awareness and analysis of (cultural) history" (Hay 2006, 31). Furthermore, it is stated that "Carey's emphasis on time and history—and on culture as community and fellowship—also carried a nostalgic charge" (Hay 2006, 35). Such a romantic attitude to the concept of communication may not be very widespread in U.S. research; people in North America tend to look forward, treating nostalgia as a peculiar (and rare) psychological state. Still, there are noteworthy efforts such as the science of communicology, striving to study the cultural and social conditions of communicative praxis by establishing a historic link between the philosophy of American pragmatism and the European phenomenological tradition that is now being rediscovered (Catt & Eicher-Catt 2010; Lanigan 2008). In other words, more attention is being paid to time. Still, it must be reminded that communication can be conceptualized most productively not in terms of either space or time, but in terms of "a more dynamic model of space-time" (Cavell 2002, 10), as discussed in the previous chapter.

The Noise of Time

Not surprisingly, linear models of communication treat any obstacle on the way from the subject to the object as noise, which is to be eliminated or manipulated by the subject. Respectively, the attitude of such models towards uncertainty is clearly negative (cf. Anderson 1996, 206). For example, M. Serres uses the information theory in his analysis of the Platonic dialogue and argues that Self and the Other have a common enemy—"a third man," i.e., noise as the "empirical portion of the message" (Serres 1982, 70). M. Serres states: "A successful communication is the exclusion of the third man" (quoted by: Serres 1982, xxvi). Thus, "the parasitic third party called 'noise'" clearly has no place in the process of communication "visualized in terms of *discretely discriminated components*" (Rasch 2000, 58; emphasis mine). Therefore, for communication to be effective, noise as empirical variation must be excluded or used toward one's ends. In other words, uncertainty can be undesirable or desirable; "uncertainty which arises by virtue of freedom of choice on the part of the sender is desirable uncertainty. Uncertainty which arises because of errors or because of the influence of noise is undesirable uncertainty" (Shannon and Weaver 1949, 109). In this respect, "it is interesting to note how traditional—*one might even say classically rhetorical*—this model of desirable and undesirable uncertainty is. . . . In the end, one must remain certain even about uncertainty" (Rasch 2000, 60; emphasis mine), cf. examples of puns.

So, according to a linear view, communication is effective upon the condition of noise ideally eliminated. Only then can a message be effectively transferred from the subject to its destination. Effective communication, as stated earlier, can be equated with the delivery of a message across space. In this sense, to deliver a message means to take it to a recipient or, more metaphorically, assist in giving birth or putting something into effect. Whether a delivery of a baby or a delivery of a message, the process is a procedure carried out step by step, point by point. However, communication is much more than just delivery: it is also a process of conceiving, e.g., forming or imagining ideas in the mind, and also "being pregnant with," e.g., carrying ideas inside oneself—not carrying them *out*. Such "creative pains" are not yet the focus of communication at this staging.

At this staging of communication, the attention is focused on how a message is transferred rather than sent. The verb "to send" can be traced back to Latin "sentīre" meaning "to feel" (Morris 1982, 1538), while the process of transfer is clearly mechanical with no place for feelings (such as love, as mentioned earlier). It is interesting how the English word "message" has been borrowed into some languages and now exists in its transliterated form alongside the original word for "message," cf. the two Russian words "soobshchenie" ("сообщение") and "messedzh" ("мессэдж"). Such a distinction seems to reflect a difference in meaning between a message transferred ("soobshchenie") and a message sent ("messedzh").

Thus, in communication, understood as message transfer, there is something that cannot be felt by the subject. One can metaphorically speak about a "blind spot" that is outside the subject's awareness. Like the driver who cannot see certain areas by looking through the rearview or side mirrors, the subject can see "what is actually going on" only by turning back. However, "turning back" means having something in the past, cf. living memories; also, it includes the realization that "what is going on now" could have happened otherwise. At this staging of communication, the subject is still blind to all this because objects respond to the subject in predictable and stable ways, provided noise is eliminated or under control. The more noise is viewed as inherently ambiguous and the more communication is seen as an inherently contingent process, the more this blindness will be overcome. What is not realized ("felt") at this staging is that communication "is characterized by extreme contingency, since any selection of information or means of delivery is marked by the interplay of ego and alter, who must always take into account the possibility of selections being selected otherwise" (Rasch 2000, 62). Furthermore, "the concept of contingency is a paradox, involving contact and thus dependency . . . *but also risk, since this contact depends on a context that cannot be determined in advance*" (Grant 2003a, 96; emphasis mine). It is impossible, therefore, to view communication as "the interplay of ego and alter" (to be discussed in detail in the next chapter) by treating this process as a mechanical transfer of message that takes place in the world devoid of time (cf. Prigogine and Stengers 1984). And yet, this is exactly what takes place at this staging of communication; here time is implicitly present as a backdrop to the subject and, *mutatis mutandis*, message transfer (Vyvyan 2003, 236). Thus, communication appears as a timeless (atemporal) process; here time does not count because it does not exist, so to speak. What is not realized ("felt") at this staging of communication is time. Just as the fish does not feel that it swims in the water, the subject does not "see" that every message is not only carried across space, but also unfolds in time.

In communication one cannot simply take an arrow (meaning) and move it from point A to point B, sticking it to the center of the target. One can only shoot an arrow, which is then subject to noise and so can be swayed in any direction on its way to the destination. It is always a somewhat different arrow hitting (even the center of) the target, having experienced "noise"—not so much overcoming it as "coming with," i.e., bringing that noise to the target. So noise is always the "noise of time," to use Osip Mandel'shtam's phrase. "This noise is not analytically decomposable, as communication theory would have it, into a multiplicity of signals, information-bits, that are irrelevant" (Lingis 1994, 47). In Russian, for instance, noise—"shum" ("шум") can mean practically any sound—from the roar of the ocean to the murmur of the heart to the buzzing in the ears to the rustle of leaves to the drumming of rain. One cannot eliminate noise just as one cannot not live one's life, which is another way of saying that one cannot not communicate.

Thus, what takes place not only between the subject and objects, but also between the subject and himself/herself, is time. The subject can receive a message as his/her "Note to Self" only by living or coming to terms with one's life, i.e., dealing with all its "noise." Only this way can communication become successful—not simply effective—and thus truly meaningful.

Time is also what creates communication apprehension, mentioned earlier. It was noted that the term "apprehension" is usually applied to the sender (the subject) rather than the receiver (the object) of communication. Now it is clear why the subject is apprehensive about one's communication with the object; time may sway, like an arrow, the meaning of a message and so there is always a possibility—a contingency—of the message not reaching its destination. However, just as one cannot be taught how to love, one cannot really be taught how to overcome one's communication apprehension; numerous practical recommendations usually given in communication apprehension manuals (cf. Horwitz 2002) are likely to fail precisely because of their being so practical; it may be useful to take deep breaths before making an important speech, but one can really overcome apprehension only by understanding the nature of communication, which can be accomplished by one's going through all its stagings, i.e., becoming a part of communication. Fear of communication will then become fear for communication; henceforth, one will come to view communication as a universe—something not to be afraid of, but to care for. Similarly, by the way, our understanding of communication theorizing undergoes transformations, and we come to conceptualize communication not only as "models of," but also "models for." As reminded by J. Carey, "models of communication are . . . not merely representations of communication but representations for communication: templates that guide, unavailing or not, concrete processes of human interaction, mass and interpersonal. Therefore, to study communication involves examining the construction, apprehension and use of models of communication themselves" (Carey 1992, 32). If we fail to remember that, we fail to understand how communication models "create what we disingenuously pretend they merely describe" (Carey 1992, 32).

So, communication as a contingent process is something liable to occur, something fortuitous. "Contingent" is derived from Latin "contingēns," present participle of "contingere"—"to touch on all sides," "happen" (Morris 1982, 288). Communication thus is not just something invoked, but always a happening that touches us on all sides; as will be shown later in the book, nothing is as deep as a seemingly superficial touch. For communication to reveal its contingent nature and become such a "touching" phenomenon, though, it must be filled up with time as well as space.

Thus, communication is not just a mechanical process of invocation of the object. At the same time, communication cannot be fully understood without seeing it as a process because one cannot step away from it. Hence the nature of technology is more complex than may appear at first glance. For example, M. Heidegger saw the essence of technology in *Gestell* from which one cannot step away, either. *Gestell* in ordinary usage means a piece of apparatus, but for M. Heidegger, it is not something technological. For him, *Gestell*, which literally means "enframing," is not an instrument as gear or an instrumental means to an end, but rather a mode of overall human existence. According to M. Heidegger, one is claimed by technologies, which is how Being shows itself; this way of one being "gathered" by the challenge of technologies into an attitude of ordering things as standing reserve is what M. Heidegger calls *Gestell*. It can be noted that *convenientia*, one of four similitudes discussed by M. Foucault earlier, can be seen as one of the ways "of ordering things as standing reserve"; it is no accident that M. Foucault's book where these similitudes are presented is entitled *The Order of Things*. M. Heidegger writes: "Enframing means the gathering together of that setting-upon which sets upon man, i.e., challenges him forth, to reveal the real, in the mode of ordering, as standing-reserve" (Heidegger 1977, 32). Although one can use technology in the form of various instruments, one cannot control the way in which Being comes into unconcealment (cf. *aletheia*). In this respect, "so long as we represent technology as an instrument, we remain held fast in the will to master it. We press on past the essence of technology" (Heidegger 1977, 32). Only by attending to the truth of Being as its shepherd, according to M. Heidegger, can we answer the challenge of technology. Thus, *Gestell* can be viewed as a call of Being challenging us to rise to the occasion and reach our destination, i.e., Destiny. Communication, therefore, is a challenge for us to bring ourselves into accord with this calling by coming to terms with everything that is (unfolding as) Being, including ourselves. As will be shown later in the book, we can respond to that challenge successfully—responsibly, one might say—not through force, trying to master communication, but passively, as it were, attending to Being like shepherds and thus tending its sacred ground. Right now it must be emphasized that the way to that destiny starts with *Gestell* at this staging of communication as invocation.

At this staging, however, communication is but a faint call. Communication here is still viewed predominantly in spatial terms, with meanings positioned up in the air as immutable stars that cannot change their course; it can be noted that "air" is derived from Old French "aire", originally "place of origin," from Latin "ager"—"place," and Latin "ārea"—"open space" (Morris 1982, 27). It can be recalled that, for Aristotle, stars are incorruptible because they cannot be destroyed, always moving along the same path (Dale 2004, 82). In other words, one knows where exactly to find a star at a particular point and so (spatially) capture its meaning, as it were. So, what else can be manifest in communication is still up in the air, so to speak. Meanings are invoked, called out of chaos by the subject in the form of various objects ("stars"); a star is any object perceived to be a heavenly body, a higher power. This way, we try to "escape uncertainty by trusting a star, chosen for its reassuring brightness, to guide us" (Bauman 2008, 54). However, it is not so much objects as stars that are invoked by the subject; rather, the subject is called out by communication, challenged forth by objects to let Being reveal itself. As a result, "we find out that our choice of guiding star was in the last account our choice, pregnant with risks as all our choices have been and are bound to be" (Bauman 2008, 54). Communication is a constant process of finding that out. In the end, as will become clear later in the book, "uncertainty is the home ground of the moral person and the only soil in which morality can sprout and flourish" (Bauman 2008, 107). Perhaps communication theorizing should also be viewed as a process inherently grounded in uncertainty. Perhaps it is better to constantly question the identity of one's discipline or area of study rather than find the answer to every question and speak to everyone (else) from the position of high moral ground.

It might be tempting to view this staging of communication as the manifestation of the so-called Laplace's Demon, when every state of every object of the universe can be seen as predetermined, given an intellect vast enough to know all the forces affecting them. However, it is impossible to bracket out the "noise of time" from communication; as mentioned earlier, communication is inherently contingent, so meanings constantly change. To use N. Bohr's famous words, "Prediction is very difficult, especially about the future." But, prediction is difficult about the past, as well, for "when a man dies his portraits change" (Anna Akhmatova). One's destiny is to hear a call(ing) of communication (Being) and respond to its challenge. However, understood as response-ability, one's destiny cannot be pre-dicted, i.e., revealed prior to diction. One's destiny cannot simply be outered, it must also be uttered, reaching not only out, but also in—and beyond.

Thus, one (omnipresent Demon) cannot know every state of communication affairs because affairs are always current affairs; everything can always be (seen) happening otherwise. Communication reaches the limit of this staging when objects fail to respond to the call of the subject in a predictable way, when they start moving in other ways and so communication is about to appear as "topology, that is, a relativization of space" (Greimas 1987, 23). It becomes clear that the Other has been standing in the wings of communication, as it were, and is now ready to appear on the stage. In real life, of course, this realization can take various forms, including some tragic ones.

Take, for example, the case of Captain James Cook's fate (the description below is based on: Wexler 2006, 204–206). Cook arrived in Hawaii at the start of the annual two-week-long celebration of the return of the deity Lono. Cook arrived at the town of Kealakekua, which according to legend had been the home of Lono when he had been a man and where he was expected to return. Thousands of natives came to greet Cook—without any weapons, but with lots of pigs, fruit, and sugar cane. Wherever Cook went he was escorted by priests who called him Lono and took him to special temples and offered special foods. All food offerings and religious visits were highly scripted procedures of adoration. After the holiday ended, Cook's ship sailed off, and no one on the ship apparently knew the cause of such a warm welcome. Soon, however, the mast on Cook's ship was damaged, and he had to return to Hawaii for repairs. The natives were clearly confused and even frightened by such a quick return; they were no longer friendly and were unable to understand the reason for the return. When some natives took one of Cook's launches, he decided to take the Hawaiian king hostage so that it could be given back. The king's supporters then killed Cook; his body is said to have been carried off and burnt in sacrifice. It is easy to see that Cook who was perceived by the natives as the object—albeit a deity—met his tragic end when he failed to respond to their call in a predictable way. It is noted that "more recent accounts of first contacts between Euro-Americans and isolated island communities all reveal similar efforts to perceive the Euro-Americans, not as different human beings, but rather as components of the existing indigenous belief systems. A New Guinea culture that included a sky world in its cosmology thought Europeans were powerful spirits from the sky world" (Wexler 2006, 206–207).

To summarize, this staging of communication can be viewed as invocation—an attempt to capture or apprehend the essence of the object and put it in a name. Invocation is expected to generate (ideally) the same response from the object. Communication here can be seen as spatial extension of meaning whereby it reaches the destination step by step. This process seems to be devoid of time—"timeless." However, the subject does not hear the true voice of objects; the call of communication falls on deaf ears, so to speak. Meanwhile, the subject, by attempting to connect to objects, begins one's way of coming into existence oneself. The call of communication, therefore, is a challenge to the subject to reach accord with (everything that comes into) being/Being. The closer one comes to objects, the more likely they are to disobey the subject's call, moving in other (Other) ways. This staging of communication reaches its limit when the challenge of dealing with objects must be met in a way other (Other) than invocation.

~

CHAPTER FOUR

Down the Stream:
Communication as Conversation

Communication, Actually

Let us now see how the nature of communication changes when its participants engage in more interactive symbolic actions. As we remember, the subject's invocation of objects fails to reveal their true meaning; if anything, objects are provoked, as it were, and, as a result of the subject's provocation, start moving in other directions. The harder the subject tries to reach the essence of objects, the more likely they are to move away; a gap between the subject and objects grows wider (and deeper) and still remains to be bridged. It is never revealed what actually happens at that staging of communication; objects there are simply taken for granted as they are invoked. Actually, nothing actually happens at that staging of communication; what does take place between the subject and the object, i.e., time is not actually recognized or rather felt. But, objects are obedient up to a certain point; once provoked, they grow more distant from the subject and so more unfamiliar; as a result, communication is transformed by dividing into two parts, which are now perceived as clearly present. Such division, cf. the so-called actual division of a sentence, cf. topic-comment only reflects the actual world where participants engage in communication *hic et nunc*. Thus, through the fragmentation of space (Foucault 1970, 369), the Other emerges and, along with it, time.

At this staging of communication, objects are experienced in actual situations. The means used by the subject take on a symbolic character, and communication reveals its nature as symbolic action. In K. Burke's terms, communication is transformed from motion to action as willed movement. It must be noted that the roots for that transformation can be found, albeit in an enfolded form, at the staging of communication as invocation where objects are—if only unconsciously—apprehended. As was mentioned in the previous chapter, "the universe cannot be distinguished from how we act upon it. A universe comes into being when a space is severed or taken apart. . . . The act is itself already remembered, *even if unconsciously*" (Spencer-Brown 1979, xxix, emphasis mine). Once the two parts of the universe are perceived more consciously, communication reveals its nature as a symbolic act. To quote G. H. Mead, "*a perception has in it* . . . all the elements of an act—the stimulation, the response represented by an attitude, the ultimate experience which flows upon the reaction, represented by the imagery arising out of past reactions" (Mead 1938, 1; emphasis mine).

The process of communication as symbolic action can no longer be viewed as transmission of a message across space (read: "extension of Man"). Rather, instead of trying to reach the object through various signal means, the subject holds back his/her impulses, i.e. holds a pause, trying to take time and understand what is going on here and now. In other words, instead of further attempts to reach the object for the purpose of its appropriation or calling it his/her own, the subject chooses to increase the gap between oneself and the object in question. Objects need to be questioned because they appear unfamiliar. "The principle of 'distanciation' accounts for our ability to confront something as alien, unfamiliar. This principle is, as Ricoeur points out, . . . the counterpoint to the concept of appropriation" (Gallagher 1992, 125)—the concept characteristic of the staging of communication as invocation. This increased distance creates a space called in German "a *Spielraum*, literally, 'room to play,' or figuratively, 'freeplay.' . . . Gadamer refers to this clearance as *Zeitenabstand*, 'temporal distance'" (Gallagher 1992, 124). Therefore, what is now created between the subject and the object is not simply a spatial distance, but also a temporal one.

A temporal step in the form of a pause (in essence—the subject stepping back to oneself) is one small step for the subject, but one giant leap for communication. By taking this step and pausing, the subject allows for the object to start revealing its meaning. This step into time (cf. Bakhtin 1986), then, is an important act and so, from now on, every symbolic act of communication must be viewed as a decisive act. Here the subject begins to learn how to let the object go; this will become a most decisive moment at another staging of communication, as will be discussed in detail later in the book.

So, turning to the Other and at the same time letting (the Other) reveal its meanings, the subject starts to understand what actually goes on in communication. The eyes of the subject and the object (the Other) meet across space—and communication comes to life. It turns out that communication actually is not transfer of messages between points, but a (spatio)-temporal clearance characterized by tension and drama where (and when) meanings are always in "freeplay." Again, the condition for such "freeplay" was enfolded in communication; however, communication could not be actualized because there was not enough room, so to speak, for the drama of communication to play out. It can be recalled that space was reduced to carrying the same meaning from the subject to the object and thus bridging the gap between words and reality. The existence of objects was thus repressed, and their essence not revealed; for communication to come to life, space must start actively interacting with time, as it is at this staging of communication that their dynamic begins to play out. At this point, it becomes clear that communication is alive—a live process.

This staging of communication is another attempt by the subject to make one's experience meaningful. However, now the subject does not attempt to induce a response; rather, the action taken by the subject is one of inquiring, requesting information or investigating something in order to understand it. With inquiring, instead of presuming a response as a given, one looks into the object; in this respect, the nature of communication can be represented by the concept of the "looking-glass self" (Cooley 1968). According to this view, associated most commonly with G. H. Mead's conception of the Self/mind, meaning is not bound as an entity to a message transferred from person to person (from point to point), but arises in the process of symbolic communication. As the subject unfolds, his/her attitudes reflect those of others and are generalized; the subject thus comes to see himself/herself from the perspective of the Other as if in a mirror. Therefore, we all live in the minds of others.

In this respect, one can recall *aemulatio* as one of M. Foucault's four similitudes "that has been *freed from the law of place*. . . . There is something in emulation of the reflection and the mirror: it is the means whereby things scattered through the universe can answer one another. . . . The relation of emulation enables things to imitate one another from one end of the universe to the other without connection or proximity: by duplicating itself in a mirror the world abolishes the distance proper to it" (Foucault 1970, 18; emphasis mine). It is interesting to note that, according to M. Foucault, *aemulatio* as emulation "traverses the spaces of the universe in silence" (Foucault 1970, 20). A parallel can be drawn between *aemulatio* and the reflective pause, i.e., silence on the part of the subject, discussed earlier, that clears the stage, so to speak, for the "freeplay" of symbolic communication. It is also interesting to note that the gap between the subject and the object "is not annulled by the subtle metaphor of emulation; it remains open to the eye. And in this duel, the two confronting figures seize upon one another" (Foucault 1970, 20). In some translations of M. Foucault's book, too much emphasis is placed on this duel; for example, in Russian, *aemulatio* is rendered as "sopernichestvo" ("соперничество"), literally—"rivalry." However, it should not be forgotten that emulation suggests efforts to equal or surpass someone through imitation; hence the meaning of comparison implied in the process. Emulation is similar in meaning to emulsion: once a thin light-sensitive coating is put on glass, in becomes a mirror. When we look into the Other as if in a mirror, we do not simply compete with the image; rather, we want to be just like that image. This staging of communication could be conceptualized as an attempt by the subject of smoothing out a symbolic glass and "getting even" with the Other (pun intended), i.e., becoming one with the Other.

So, the subject tries to understand the object by inquiring into the situation at hand. By doing this, the subject admits, as it were, his/her earlier inability to apprehend the object; while invocation presupposed an instantaneous and predictable response, now the subject is willing to pause and see how the situation unfolds. Thus, a non-verbal action, manifested in a pause, becomes a catalyst of communication.

To pause and turn to the object as if looking into the eyes of the Other is a hard decision. It is not an easy decision because it amounts, in effect, to the subject admitting his/her guilt for attempting to call the object his/her own and failing to do so. From here it is but one step to the concept of the negative as understood by K. Burke. It turns out that objects are *not* what they appear to be in nature and so can *not* be invoked at will. This way, a connection between the negative and the ethical is established; it is now clear that, to be capable of morality, the subject must have the capacity of choice; to act is always to be moralized by the negative (Burke 1965). The ethical underpinnings of communication will become more prominent as it continues to unfold.

When the subject looks into the eyes of the Other, the latter can be seen as the subject's double. One can view this double as the "negative number" to the "positive number" which is the subject; besides, the notion of the negative number leads to imaginary numbers. In communication, the imagery arises out of past reactions (cf. Mead 1938). Imagination may not be considered very important at the staging of communication which is empirically grounded; however, later, imagination will prove to be an indispensable part of communication. It must be remembered that "the imaginary values . . .

have a deep penetration into the fabric of our description of space and time" (Kauffman 2001, 78). Just as negative and imaginary numbers gradually came to be accepted by the mathematical community and the world at large, it will be shown later in the book how imagination also plays a crucial role in communication and so must be accepted as its indispensible, critical part. In short, at this point, we begin to understand that communication is not only what is, but also what is not.

The Presentation of the Other

By focusing on the Other, the subject begins to come into existence as Self without, however, being fully aware of this process. Every symbolic act of communication produces a certain meaning and so can be viewed in terms of *techné*. It is noted that "an approach to communication as techné demands that we examine what people *actually* do when they are communicating" (Sterne 2006, 93; emphasis mine). A distinction must be kept in mind between making something (*poiêton*) and action (*praktikon*), since the disposition (*hexis*) with respect to making is different from the disposition with respect to acting. Unlike action whose end is in itself, the end of making is a product separate from the activity of making. In other words, the value of *techné* as craft is in what is produced. As Aristotle writes, "all art is concerned with coming into being, i.e., with contriving and considering how something may come into being which is capable of either being or not being, and whose origin is in the maker and not in the thing made" (Aristotle 1947, 1140a10). At this staging of communication, the focus is on the Other, as the maker; it is through the eyes of the Other that meanings come into being in the form of one's verbal and non-verbal behaviors, i.e., certain techniques, based on the Other's responses. At this staging, thus, one's technical skills of communication are produced. These skills may seem simple, but they represent meaningful ways of how one conducts everyday communication, cf.: "The subtle gestures of casual conversation, the split-second decision of whether to meet a stranger's eye on the street, the inflections of the voice— hundreds of different techniques of empathy and avoidance, closeness and distance—are in use at every moment of every day" (Sterne 2006, 93). In all these technical ways, "*participants constitute themselves in conversational practices*" (Krippendorff 2009, 123). One can also note a connection between *techné* and *nous*, cf.: "*Techné*, as a branch of knowledge, was invested with the skill and understanding to create things through enabling them to come into being and *by making manifest articles and objects from nature*" (Bouchard 2005, 24; emphasis mine).

In a way, communication as a technical procedure is based on forgetting rather than the living memory of everything involved in this process. The door-closer in B. Latour's famous example is used "to demarcate space symbolically" (Sterne 2006, 94) and so can be viewed as a case of punctuation of symbolic interactions. In this sense, "when the door-closer works, it disappears from consciousness. . . . When the door-closer does not work the way it is supposed to, it has all sorts of new social significance, simply by virtue of closing the door a little *too quickly* (and batting passersby on the behind) or *too slowly*" (Sterne 2006, 95; emphasis mine). It must be emphasized that communication breaks down when symbolic interactions are not punctuated (synchronized) properly.

Communication as a process of symbolic interactions when one's meaningful behavior is focused on the Other and formed by his/her/its responses, can be successful only insofar as their interactions are synchronized; hence the importance of time as *chronos* at this staging of communication. Following Aristotle who defined *chronos* as the "number of motion with respect to the before and the after" (Aristotle 1961, IV, 219b1–2), *chronos* is associated with change, measure and viewed as quantitative time. It is important to remember that time is simply the metric of motion; any instrument providing such measure, e.g., a clock really measures motion, not time, as such. In this sense, any mechanism at the basis of (un)successful communication is the result of a symbolic act of interaction; for example, skillful (or not) actions by participants themselves lead to smooth (or not) turn-taking. By the same token, defining the success of a communication encounter as a process of "temporalizing" (Heidegger 1992, 368) is a matter of *chronos*. Thus, it must be remembered that participants in every act of symbolic interaction "participate in the creation and formation of one another as they interact *over time*" (Cronen 2001, 18; emphasis mine). In other words, "the idea of timescales should never be thought of as a simple matter of 'objective' calendar time or expectancy" because they are "constructed by the participants in the action under consideration" (Scollon and Scollon 2004, 169). It is interesting to note the dark side of *chronos*, which can start running (and ruining) people's lives; after all, originally *Chronos* (*Krónos*) was a mythological deity who protected his powers by eating his children; hence our mortal bodies are thought of as devoured by Father Time. Not surprisingly, people fight back, so to speak, for instance, by trying to beat the clock. One psychotherapist reports "a significant number of patients, colleagues, relatives and friends who refuse to wear a watch. They thus avoid being bound by the real world of the tyranny of passing time!" (Roberts 2003, 203–204). This subterfuge, however, is only a part of the illusionary nature of communication; by closing one's eyes, it only seems as if reality ceases to exist and time stops.

So, at this staging, the actual nature of communication is revealed: every symbolic act becomes important, every meaning significant. A meaningful message comes to be viewed less an extension of the subject to a class of objects and more in terms of their abstract, conceptual properties. Thus, the narrow referential understanding of the object as an entity that exists only in space is partly overcome, and objects become more meaningful. As signification plays a more prominent role, objects come to be recognized as more significant by those who take the time to try and understand their meaning. The concept of the generalized Other cannot be formed unless general conceptual properties of objects are taken into consideration. What matters more at this staging of communication is whether experiences, interactively constituted and symbolically mediated, begin to make sense. Also, signification goes hand-in-hand with imagination. To make sense of the object, to understand it in terms of some abstract, significant properties, is always, to a degree, to imagine that object in other situations of use. As stated earlier, here the imaginary nature of communication is more fully revealed. Also, it must be remembered that "signification . . . is not exactly, or not simply, 'meaning.' . . . For signification is located meaning, while meaning resides perhaps only in the coming of a possible signification" (Nancy 1997, 10, 22). In other words, meaning reaches out beyond the spatial confines of a concrete situation and must therefore be partly imagined. Thus, in trying to understand the Other, "we do not, so to speak, throw a 'signification' over some naked thing which is present-at-hand" (Heidegger 1962, 190)—exactly what happens at the staging of communication as invocation (or so it seems).

Once the subject starts paying attention to objects, trying to understand them, they turn to the subject as well, opening up their faces, so to speak. While earlier communication was a "faceless" process, now the face of the object as its significance comes to the forefront; it should be mentioned that E. Goffman's concept of face is related to the subject's significance viewed through the eyes of the Other (Goffman 1959, 213). In this light, "signification . . . is not exactly, or not simply, 'meaning'; it is the presentation of meaning" (Nancy 1997, 22). At this staging of communication, then, its "actual being cannot be detached from its presentation" (Gadamer 1989, 122). Meanings, therefore, are not transferred, but presented or played out by those who participate in the process of communication. The performative nature of communication will be manifest more fully as it unfolds; here the presentation of meaning takes, first of all, the form of participants introducing themselves or picturing one another. It is as if each participant says, "Let me introduce myself" all the while trying to picture how he/she is viewed by the Other. In this exchange, each participant is formed, as the subject, by the significant conceptual properties of the Other.

Communication at this staging occurs as a symbolic interaction because objects constantly change as if calling out to the subject, "Pay attention!" For this reason, as mentioned earlier, the focus is on the Other as the source of all meaningful experiences. Any shock one experiences here is, first of all, the shock of the Other, and any wonder one experiences comes from the Other. At this staging, "as in other forms of culture shock, the discovery of difference is the first step to enlightenment" (Farriss 1986, x). In the same vein, "perceptions of change are equally illuminating; change ceases to be a shift from one steady state to another. . . . And *once change over time is accepted* . . . , diachronic analysis based on chronology and causation has to be incorporated into the model-building scheme" (Farriss 1986, x; emphasis mine). Later, one will also experience "self-shock" (Zaharna 1989), finding communication overall as something divine and deeply kindred to oneself. Then, and then only, will one finally become aware of the role that one is destined to play in communication. At this staging, though, it is still impossible to understand all the significance of communication just as it is impossible for one to see all of oneself in the mirror of the Other. Here the subject looks into the mirror (of the Other) rather than looks at oneself into the mirror. By looking at the Other, only a part of the nature of communication can be seen; it will take a steady look fixed at oneself (a gaze) for one to become aware of the deeper significance of (oneself in/as) communication. Such a gaze is more internal than external; also, it is indicative of awe, fascination, or admiration (Morris 1982, 547). It will take time for the subject to develop such a gaze and look into the mirror at oneself *as* the Other.

Meanwhile, at this staging, the subject sees every symbolic action by the Other as potentially face-threatening; communication thus should be carried out as a polite process, cf. the ideas of the politeness theory. To protect one's face, all actions taken by the subject must be politely oriented toward the face of the Other (Brown and Levinson 1987). To look at the Other means to pay polite attention to, or study very carefully, the Other's face or—conceptualized broadly—the Other's bodily presence in the world. While the subject's earlier attitude with respect to objects was "disrespectful," now the subject's actions are full of respect and consideration. In fact, the word "consideration" sums up the nature of polite communication very well: a polite subject is a considerate subject, one who considers the face of the Other.

In the same vein, the subject starts paying more attention to the symbolic means used in communication; now the very instruments of communication are taken into consideration because they make interaction possible. The materiality of symbols becomes thus more significant, cf. language and also non-verbal elements such as kinesics and facial expressions. This way, communication reveals another part of its nature in the form of the Other and various symbolic instruments. It becomes clear that to communicate does not simply mean transferring a message to the object; rather, it means letting the object make something meaningful known to the subject.

By politely orienting actions toward the face of the Other, the subject anticipates a response. Communication, then, appears as a process of anticipation. To anticipate (in) communication means not only to foresee and perhaps prevent in advance, but also to look forward, with eagerness, to certain actions. So, the drama of communication includes decisive actions, guilt, consideration, and anticipation, among other things. Most importantly, as a result of such symbolic (inter)action, objects are observed, i.e., (attempted to be) recognized for, or rather understood as, what they are. In other words, an actual observer appears in communication; in this sense, it is possible to argue that "human action stands apart from the rest of the physical and biological world because of the reflective capacity of human beings" (Baxter and Babbie 2004, 59). The nature of observation here is not as passive as one might think it is. The origins of observation lie in paying attention in order to keep or preserve something, cf. "ser-" in Latin "observāre" meaning "protector" (Morris 1982, 906, 1538). Thus, by observing the Other, the subject's goal, albeit not still completely conscious, is still self-preservation. It can be said that one still experiences some fear of communication (in the form of the Other) although less than before. At this staging of communication, of all objects questioned fear is one questioned least of all; however, steps toward that end are being taken in the form of symbolic acts—if only not completely conscious. Taking a fearless step beyond the immediate empirical situation into communication is still out of the question at this point; such a self-transcendental step will become possible only when one's attention is focused on oneself. How and why this fearless step is taken will be discussed later in the book.

There is always a tension in communication between familiarity and strangeness, and, as W. Dilthey writes, "the art of understanding" always "lies between these two extreme opposites" (quoted by: Gallagher 1992, 124). This interplay between the familiar and the unfamiliar is found in symbolic interaction between the subject—not quite yet Self—and the Other. However, the real drama that unfolds at this staging of communication is the "freeplay" of space and time; we can get a true understanding of what our ends really are in every situation only by reconciling space and time. Bridging the gap between the two extremes—the familiar and the unfamiliar, Self and the Other, space and time—is always an act of interpretation.

Communication in Situ

The ontological view of communication as a process of symbolic interaction, focused primarily on the Other, is best reflected in theories that examine how participants deal with uncertainty as well as their contextualized perspectives and interpretations of meaning, cf. dramaturgically and hermeneutically orientated theories. It might seem that they have little in common: however, they all "search for those moments in which interlocutors create, use, and negotiate meanings and thus constitute a shared life" (Stewart and Philipsen 1984, 193; cf. Sonesson 2000, 543). The need to search for such moments arises each time something or someone unfamiliar comes into the focus of one's attention; in this sense, anything and anyone can become the object of interpretation that requires studying and understanding. There is no difference between the so-called animate or inanimate objects because any object is animated in the process of symbolic interaction. For example, we can read a person like a book, while a book can take on a human image to become our friend or enemy. Overall, the more mundane or bound to the empirical world the object is, the more it has to say about the world. "All" it takes to understand the object is to look thoughtfully into it as if in a mirror. The main goal of communication at this staging is to understand objects in their own terms and, *mutatis mutandis*, the world as well as oneself as its part. Thus, the subject and the object (the Other) become interlocutors in a conversation constituting a shared life.

Communication as "interaction is mediated by the use of symbols, by interpretation, or by ascertaining the meaning of one another's actions. This mediation is equivalent to inserting a process of interpretation between stimulus and response in the case of human behavior" (Blumer 1969, 180). At the staging of communication as invocation, the distance between the subject and the object—"stimulus" and "response"—was not present (or so it seemed). "The medium is the message" effectively makes one forget or not notice "is" as a component of communication. With the insertion of the process of interpretation into communication, while the phrase may sound somewhat behavioristic, it becomes important to understand what the meaning of "is" is, or what actually happens between the subject and the object. In other words, it becomes clear that time is inserted into space, as it were, and so "action may be more than a response to stimuli" (Malhotra 1987, 364).

Thus, the conceptualization of communication moves from the ontological domain to the praxeological domain. For the empirically certain, a claim of what is can have an exact solution—a relationship established between the independent object and our claim about it. The interpretive turn rejects this empirical foundationalism and starts its interpretive activity upon an empirical text (Anderson 1996). All the theoretical approaches mentioned above view communication as the interpretative procedures used by its participants in situ. The process of interpretation unfolds in a gap that now clearly exists between the subject and the object—a clearance or a "room to play," mentioned earlier. It is in this "room" that roles are exchanged and meanings enacted. In a way, interpretation can be seen as an attempt to understand by one what it is like to be the Other.

It is important to remember that such a gap should not be viewed only in spatial terms; "there is always a *temporal* distanciation involved in interpretation" (Gallagher 1992, 131). Only by treating distanciation as a spatio-temporal phenomenon is it possible to see any object as a living being with its own history and significance. It is no accident that, for E. Goffman, the subject "is a product of a scene that comes off, and is not a cause of it. The self, then, as *a performed character, is not an organic thing that has a specific location* . . . ; it is a dramatic effect arising diffusely from a scene" (Goffman 1959, 252–253; emphasis mine). This way, communication reveals even more its ephemeral character—an effect rather than the object causing it.

To understand the object only in spatial terms, cf. G. Frege's extension, convenient as it may be, is to reduce it to something static and atemporal (Uemov 1975, 459). For instance, if a glass falls and breaks, one can continue calling it, for convenience, "a glass" although, in this new empirical situation, a new significant property appears and so it would be more appropriate to call the object "pieces of glass" (Arutyunova and Levotina 2000, 45). Repeatedly stepped upon, such pieces can become smaller and smaller, finally disappearing altogether. In other words, viewed in temporal terms, any object has a life and is therefore important, receiving historical significance in various situations of symbolic interaction. Interpretation and signification, therefore, go hand-in-hand. However, objects are not picked up based upon some pre-given (historically significant) distance between them and the subject; "interpretation does not involve distanciation because of the overtly historical nature of the object of interpretation; rather, objects are able to gain overtly historical significance because of the distanciation involved in interpretation" (Gallagher 1992, 132). So, it is only in the process of symbolic interaction that the significance of objects comes into being; those properties considered more relevant are salvaged and kept, and then the glass is fixed and lives on, albeit with cracks, while those considered unimportant vanish, and then the glass may turn to dust, its meaning vanishing from our memory, and so the object dies.

So, understanding the Other occurs as a symbolic process of conversation wherein meanings grow (or die). It is worth noting that G. H. Mead drew a parallel between symbolic interactionism and Darwinism because "it requires the idea that the forms of things are created inside the process of living. Thus, the elements of a system do not merely affect one another, they participate in the creation and formation of one another as they interact over time" (Cronen 2001, 18). From this perspective, communication is clearly treated as an evolutionary process—a continuous natural process of meaning formation. It is possible to say that communication begins to reveal its ecological roots.

That Which Befalls One

So, every symbolic action presupposes an interpretative effort and is characterized by the "gravity of thought" (J.-L. Nancy). This transition from recognition (apprehension) to understanding, from invocation to interpretation can be viewed as a shift to "dialogic participation" (Anderson 1996, 91). According to M. Bakhtin, one cannot simply contemplate, analyze or define the Other as the object; rather, one can only communicate with them dialogically (Bakhtin 1972, 116). M. Bakhtin's dialogic philosophy was developed vis-à-vis the view of communication as information transfer between a sender and a receiver. In M. Bakhtin's view, meaning in communication constantly emerges at the boundaries of consciousness between people, every utterance performed within a concrete context and infused with multiple voices (Bakhtin 1993, 22–28).

When we communicate with the Other dialogically, we engage in a conversation as a symbolic exchange. It must be noted that "in earlier times, conversation had a more general meaning . . . the action of having dealings with others" (Binding and Tapp 2008, 123). In this sense, conversation can clearly be seen as a part of pragmatics, derived from the Greek "pragmata," meaning "acts," "affairs," or "business" (Hanke 1990). In a manner of speaking, every conversation is a perfect example of current affairs. Not surprisingly, symbolic interactionism and ethnomethodology, which conceptualize conversation as a naturally unfolding phenomenon, are said to have been influenced by the philosophy of pragmatism (Gallant and Kleinman 1983).

It is important to note that conversation as a symbolic exchange should not be understood as simply taking turns to send and receive whatever messages we want. As J. Peters reminds us, "we are bound together in existential and lived ways before we even open our mouths to speak" (Peters 1999, 16). The meaning of Germanic "wurth-"—"fate," "destiny"—is related to "wer-"—the base of the root of the word "conversation" (Morris 1982, 291, 1549); conversation can thus be seen as "that which befalls one." In other words, communication as conversation is not what is chosen, but what is experienced. We are thrown into communication (cf. M. Heidegger), which becomes our destiny. In this sense, we do not engage, but rather are engaged in communication. As H.-G. Gadamer writes, "it is generally more correct to say that we fall into conversation, or even that we become involved in it. The way one word follows another, with the conversation taking its own twists and reaching its own conclusions, may well be conducted in some way, but the partners conversing are far less the leaders of it than the led" (Gadamer 1989, 383). This way, one begins to feel that one's active role in communication cannot be too exaggerated. One begins to appreciate "the virtues of passivity" as "an ethic of receptivity, listening, respect for the material, for plants, animals, and minerals—and for the person" (Peters 2005, 289). From this point of view, "communication here does not involve transmitting information about one's intentionality; rather, it entails bearing oneself in such a way that one is open to hearing the other's otherness" (Peters 1999, 16). One thus begins to open up more to the call made at the staging of communication as invocation; while, at that staging of communication, one hears a faint call of Being, now one takes the time to—actually—start listening to this call.

Communication as (being engaged in a) conversation is not simply the activity of sharing symbolic messages in order to create common meanings, which perhaps is the most common understanding of communication. The Greek root "koino" in the word "communication," as noted by J. Peters (Peters 1999), adds to our understanding of communication the meanings of pollution, contamination or making something unclean. More importantly, "it implies opening the door to the Other, to the unforeseen and the unforeseeable" (Pinchevski 2005, 248). One can never tell ahead of time (and space) how communication, as a conversation, will turn out to be because a conversation is something that twists and turns while "befalling one." "Being engaged" can mean anything—from a pledge to marry to a battle encounter. In Russian, the word similar in meaning is "vstupat'" ("вступать")—"to enter," "to step into." One can thus "enter a new era," "enter (i.e., join) the party," "enter (i.e., step into) cow dung," "enter marriage" (i.e., to marry), etc. It should also be pointed out that what can be discerned in the root of the word "вступать" is "postupok" ("поступок")—"an act." So, communication at this staging begins to reveal its dual nature—good and bad, so to speak. In every situation, one is caught, as it were, between these two extremes. The dual nature of communication is reflected in action itself; it, too, can be conceptualized as a conversation, for example, as G. H. Mead's inner conversation between the "I" and the "Me" (Mead 1967).

Thus, as soon as anything or anyone becomes the focus of one's attention, one is engaged in communication as conversation with those objects (the Other). And, as long as one is open to hearing the other's otherness, communication continues to unfold. When one relates to the Other, one tries to act toward the Other and, eventually, become—indifferent from, or one with—the Other. With every symbolic action, the subject tries—and fails—to close the gap between himself/herself and the objects of interpretation, stepping into the mirror and striving toward the "fusion of horizons" (H.-G. Gadamer). However, one can have "doubts about the way in which H.-G. Gadamer speaks of the 'fusion of horizons.' For 'fusion' does not do adequate justice to those ruptures that dis-turb our attempts to reconcile different [ethical-political] horizons" (Bernstein 1992, 11). Communication as conversation "is not a mere instrument for evidencing one's own viewpoint . . . , but a tragico-comical attempt at closure and indifference, . . . the impossibility of indifference toward the other" (Ponzio 2004, 168). In this light, for example, A. Chekhov's genius—among other things—can be seen in how ordinary conversations carried out by his characters reveal this human condition so well, with all its tenderness and angst.

According to H.-G. Gadamer, the fusion of horizons "does not allow the interpreter to speak of an original meaning of the text without acknowledging that, in understanding it, the interpreter's own meaning enters in as well" (Gadamer 1989, 576). This concept developed by H.-G. Gadamer as part of his hermeneutics of text, can be viewed in broad terms—as a search for the original meaning of any object, including the object of communication overall. The concept of the fusion of horizons raises the following questions: "What is the origin of this or that meaning?" and "Who is the Author of the meaning?" Of course, the answers to these questions are contained within the concept itself: meaning is always a fusion, a blend; it is never entirely original, always coauthored, as will be made clearer later in the book.

The term "fusion of horizons" suggests an act of melting together by heat; meaning, therefore, can be viewed as the "liquid" resulting from fusing. ("Heat" here is to be taken figuratively and can be understood, for example, as emotions, passions, desires, etc.). Thus, communication appears as a process of merging different elements into a union—one (and only) meaning.

However, this process never stops because meaning keeps melting and flowing just like a conversation, always calling for another procedure of fusion. It is important to note that the "liquefied" meaning can still be conceptualized as a tangible empirical phenomenon, existing here and now. In a metaphorical sense, communication at this staging is hot enough to only melt meaning while preserving it in a liquid form. As will be shown later in the book, communication will reach the point of combustion, so to speak, when meaning comes to be "burnt by the fire." It is interesting to mention that the word "combust" denotes "not visible because of proximity to the sun" (Morris 1982, 265). Similarly, meanings that go through the fire will not be visible, unlike those in a liquid form, but will exist nonetheless as the essential and most sacred part of communication.

As mentioned above, the subject conducts a conversation with the object (the Other). The process of communication, then, can be conceptualized in such a way that, "in a conversation, when we have discovered the other person's standpoint and horizon, his ideas become intelligible" (Gadamer 1975, 312). However, all such attempts at understanding as closure toward the Other are never completely successful, always leaving a meaningful trace—still a gap between the subject and the object. Such meaningful traces, accumulated over time, can be viewed as the living memory, which will grow more significant at each consecutive staging of communication. In general, in the words of N. Berdyaev, memory can be seen as the eternal ontological beginning (Berdyaev 1990, 35).

So, communication at this staging can be best conceptualized as an ongoing conversation into which all participants are thrown and so have no choice but to join it. It is important to emphasize the fact that "conversations are the ontological 'stuff' of the human world, *not just a place* where this stuff happens" (Pearce 1994, 39; emphasis mine). In this respect, one can recall the following metaphoric description of communication by K. Burke:

> You come late. When you arrive, others have long preceded you and they are engaged in a heated discussion, a discussion too heated for them to pause and tell you exactly what it is about. . . . You listen for a while until you decide that you have caught the tenor of the argument; then you put in your oar. Someone answers; you answer him; another comes to your defense; another aligns himself against you. . . . The hour grows late, you must depart. And you do depart, with the discussion still vigorously in progress. (Burke 1941, 110–111)

As can be seen, this metaphoric description highlights the ontological and temporal nature of communication as conversation very well. In this view, the most animated (but not heated, cf. combustion, as mentioned above) aspects of communication as conversation are manifest when one's attention is focused on the Other. At this staging, every point of the conversation seems to be important, relevant and significant; in a word, it is communication in all its actuality. Although the word is never used by K. Burke, the essence of communication here clearly lies in "the question" (cf. "Someone answers; you answer him"). It must be noted that communication, understood as conversation and brought into being "through *techné*, is resonant with theatrical questions of illusion and . . . animation. Animation involves the giving of life to something or making it appear vital and spirited . . . where objects, texts and bodies are revitalized in order to create an illusion of reality" (Bouchard 2005, 32). The illusionary nature of communication will become more prominent as it unfolds and will be discussed later. It must also be noted that the most heated, one might say "burning" questions will be raised—and responded to—when communication is between Self and Self, discussed in detail in chapter 6.

It is important to emphasize the role of questioning at this staging of communication. Earlier, no questions were really raised and so the scope of communication was quite limited. If anything, acts of communication characterized by rhetorical questions could really be viewed as assertions while also showing resemblance with exclamative acts (Schrott 1999, 345–347). Although technically questions, they clearly represent communicative forms of invocation. Once questions start being posed in/by every situation of symbolic interaction, communication becomes much more complex, albeit messier and at times more vague. However, it is only by looking into every situation, embodied in the Other, that (shared) experience can be made meaningful. One can recall that Hermes as the messenger of the gods was required always to tell the truth and only the truth, but not required to volunteer it. The truth was available only to those who could ask the right questions. In this light, it is clear why at the staging of communication as conversation the emphasis is on the praxeological domain (cf. Anderson 1996, 118–119).

It does not simply take time to understand the Other, it also takes a certain effort. Meanings clearly do not exist in the form of pre-given answers to be invoked at will. Rather, communication takes one to task in each and every situation of symbolic interaction. Because communication is an ongoing and unfinished conversation, the tasks are always posed somewhat differently, Other-wise. The so-called hermeneutic competence emphasizes interpretive procedures as always reflexive and situated in accordance with symbolically mediated and temporal nature of communication (Kögler 2007, 364). Communication taking one to task can be seen as the further manifestation of *Gestell*, i.e., a challenge for one to come to terms with everything that comes into being. Here, too, the same challenge is posed, i.e., "Is one up to the task?"

The need to understand the object as the Other frees up the subject; as a result, one starts overcoming the fear of communication. It should be remembered that "engagement with a historical text can be modeled on a conversation with another person" (Haney 1999, 39). With that in mind, invocation can be seen turning into conversation and so communication apprehension starts diminishing in spite of the highly emotional nature of symbolic interaction. It can be recalled that the sources of hermeneutics are found in the interpretation of Biblical texts. This way, by overcoming the trepidation before the texts considered sacred or the apprehension before approaching strangers at a party and joining the conversation, one is more and more engaged in communication and so fears it less and less.

At the same time, communication remains an intense process "since immediate human experience is tensional" (Stewart 1997, 166). The tensions in communication are created by the interaction between the subject and the object when one wants to be like the Other; one's conversation with the Other can be viewed as ideally one's conversion into the Other. However, one cannot become the Other; that is why *aemulatio*, as discussed earlier, is conceptualized as "rivalry." The contradictory nature of communication clearly reveals its dialectical underpinnings. It is more appropriate to view such underpinnings in terms of dialectics as understood by Aristotle. "Dialectic, with Aristotle, is the system resulting from the attempt to reduce to rule or generalize modes of argument which rest upon current received doctrines as principles, which move within the region of interests about which *current opinions* pro and con are to be found, and which terminate not in the decisive resolution of a problem, but in *clearing the way for a more profound research*" (*The Encyclopædia Britannica* 1890, 786; emphasis mine). This is exactly how communication as conversation can be conceptualized: it is always an "attempt to reduce to rule or generalize modes of argument," or find a shared meaning; also, such an attempt is based on "*current opinions* pro and con," or views expressed here and now; also, it results "in clearing the way for a more profound research," or more serious discourse (to be discussed in the next chapter). So, the dialogic nature of communication can be viewed as a preliminary search for truth, leading to "the decisive resolution of a problem" that Aristotle saw in apodeictic as a demonstration of knowledge (here one can sense a shift to the epistemological domain). In other words, "phenomenologically speaking, truth happens, first and foremost, as an act of disclosure, a 'showing-forth' (*epi-deixis*) or epideictic display of something that presents itself to us. The assertion and validity of any 'truth claims' pre-supposes the occurrence of such an act" (Hyde 2007, 23).

In this connection, it can be noted that the word "dialogue" is derived from the second part of the Greek word "legein," meaning "to gather" (Morris 1982, 1525), which captures well the essence of communication at this staging: it is a process of gathering opinions coming from different experiences that will later be analytically put in the form of more reliable knowledge that can be demonstrated. To be more precise, at this staging, one pays attention only to those meanings worth gathering (and eventu-ally—saving). Such a process of gathering can be seen as the development of *Gestell* or enframing—the original "gathering together of Man." It is also interesting to note that, in addition to the Greek "legein," the Latin "leg-no" in "lignum" means "wood, firewood" ("that which is gathered") (Morris 1982, 1525). In this sense, communication can be metaphorically viewed as a process of gathering wood for the fire that will be lighted up later when the most burning questions are raised and the most critical steps are taken.

It must be emphasized, though, that such characteristics as its tension-ality in the form of contradictions and a search for their resolution are revealed (actualized) at this staging of communication as conversation. Here communication flows like a stream which carries the boat with the subject and the Other trying to navigate their way to a safe shore. s was stated above, communication is a dialogue in which the subject and the object are engaged. But, it is really space and time that are engaged in "freeplay"; it is space and time that carry on a conversation trying to reach the "fusion of horizons" and become one indivisible whole, which is denied by our every symbolic act.

Through the Looking-Glass, Darkly

So, communication as symbolic interaction can be compared to a conver-sation between the subject and the object. This conversation begins the moment the object moves in a way other than predicted by the subject; the object then comes to life as the Other, and the subject starts the process of its understanding. The subject pauses, taking the time to understand the object. Therefore, understanding for the subject is always an achievement—not in the sense of "accomplishment," but rather as a symbolic movement towards the Other. Communication as a symbolic movement is a process of finding meaning. Being thrown into communication, we must navigate through various situations in order not to be lost, or in order to find meaning in/from our experiences.

To continue with the metaphor of a stream or current, discordant communication whereby interlocuters attempt to mediate tensions can be visualized as a process when its participants are "immersed together in whitewater rapids, engaging and pushing beyond dangers and obstacles improvisationally without upsetting the boat" (Smith 2003, 92). In a way, here, "water is a shifting mirror" (Illich 1985, 25). To be engaged in communication, therefore, is to be constantly performing skillful actions in order to avoid dangers lurking on all sides of the boat. Even when communication is less turbulent, not like whitewater rapids but more like a simple stream, the need for engagement and action is still there, inherent in the very flow of communication manifest in different dialogic rhythms, tensions, collisions, etc. Let us recall that every symbolic act is a skillful response to the circumstances at hand. It is interesting to note that the root "sreu," from which "stream" is derived, is suffixed from the Greek "sru-dhmo-," which means "measure," "recurring motion," and "rhythm" (Morris 1982, 1274, 1542). Thus, communication appears as a live process that is constantly moving in a more or less rhythmic manner. At this staging of communication, however, its participants must deal with its dangers and obstacles.

As mentioned earlier, at this staging of communication, the role of the Other is highlighted. The subject begins to understand oneself from the position of the Other and so one's attention is focused on the Other. Following H.-G. Gadamer, it can be emphasized that "genuine conversation is characterized by a stance of openness to the meanings *offered by the other*, by the awareness that *the other may assist* participants in the dialogue to revise their own partial understandings, and by a willingness to be transformed through the revised understanding of the topic that emerges from the encounter" (Binding and Tapp 2008, 123; emphasis mine). In this respect, the dialogic nature of communication can be equated with the consideration of/for the Other. However, while considering the Other, deep down—not in a completely conscious way—one still strives to protect, first of all, himself/herself. In this light, interpretation, although a process of negotiation of meaning, is still after a certain gain for Self. For example, it is not surprising why "for Nietzsche and Derrida, interpretation is not mediation, as it is for Gadamer, but appropriation" (Rasch 2000, 57). It is also interesting to note that in Greek, the word "interpretation" is derived from "per-n-ē" as in "pernēmi," meaning "I sell," whence "pornē" is "prostitute" (Morris 1982, 685, 1534).

By focusing on the Other, the subject can see only a part of communication. The subject questions the Other by looking into it, and for that process of interpretation to be successful, a significant gap must exist between them because only in this gap meaning as signification appears. Dialogue may be viewed as our corporeal involvement with the world (Ponzio 2004, 168), but here it is only partly so; the gap here is bridged predominantly by symbolic means. Looking at/into, and carrying a conversation with, the Other still leaves a significant distance between the subject and the object, and so a significant part of communication unrevealed. Only later can one almost overcome this gap and come closer to its nature when communication is a corporeal as well as semiotic contact with the world. Once communication is "seen" with the entire body, the gap between the subject and the object (almost) disappears, and the contingent nature of communication is more fully revealed. As mentioned in the previous chapter, "contingent" is derived from Latin "contingēns," present participle of "contingere" and means "to touch on all sides." It will be shown later in the book how one touches, and is touched by, communication "on all sides."

It can be argued that participants in communication as conversation operate on the presumption of a unity as if the gap between them has already been bridged. Thus, the subject in his/her effort to understand the object (the Other) is guided by what H.-G. Gadamer calls *der Vorgriff der Vollkommenheit* or anticipation or preconception of completeness. "This ideal suggests . . . a set of practical guidelines that guide the pursuit of truth" (Wachterhauser 1986, 234). However, with such guidelines, some attention is inevitably taken away from the current moment and placed on a moment, considered "truthful," ahead of time ("preconceived"), from which anticipation is activated. This comes to light in the translation of *Vorgriff der Vollkommenheit* into other languages. For example, it is translated into Russian as "predvoskhishchenie" ("предвосхищение"), meaning both "expectation" and "dealing with something in advance." In other words, meanings are always dealt with somewhat "in advance," hence a more significant delay in experience becoming meaningful. It is also worth mentioning that the Russian word "predvoskhishchenie" ("предвосхищение") literally means "fore-enchantment," "fore-admiration," and "fore-wonder." However, the real experience of wonder leaves as little an interval for expectation as possible; ideally, it seems to arise *with* the experience. The most wonderful experiences are those when but very little, if anything, is anticipated and when communication seems to be but a magical touch. In erotic terms, the staging of communication as conversation is just foreplay, i.e., actions that precede "the event of communication"—a very complex, very passionate act, and the most wonderful experience in which meaning undergoes combustion.

Communication as conversation has a dual and, therefore, contradictory character. At this staging, meanings are seen as naturally arising in the process of symbolic interaction; at the same time, they are also anticipated in the form of practical guidelines. One might say that participants in communication here try to have it both ways—to experience interactions as they are at this particular moment and also to play it safe, if possible, by relying on some elements of a more determinate nature. After all, the main goal here is for the subject to understand objects with which one comes to interact, and so the cognitive underpinnings—still active, still practical—are here unmistakable.

The dual character of this staging of communication is reflected in its theoretical conceptualizations. For example, it is noted that symbolic interactionism is marked by internal tensions manifested in its striving to focus on the interpretation of subjective communicative experiences, on the one hand, and to develop an objective view of communication based on rigorous methods, on the other hand (Makarov 2003, 51). In other words, symbolic interactionism can be seen as trying "to unify intelligent thought and logical method with practical action and appeals to experience" (Plummer 2000, 227).

Similarly, a phenomenological approach strives to present communication as authentic interaction in which true meanings unfold, as if by themselves, through language or—better yet—silence. To that end, however, complex and clearly scientific and analytic in their origin, cf. for example, E. Husserl's background procedures are developed to conceptualize a process of such "natural" growth of meanings, cf. the steps of intuiting, analyzing, and describing; the procedure of bracketing, of course, can be viewed as an impossible task if not *contradictio in adjecto*. It is noted, for example, that "Husserl's primary focus on ideal meanings, rather than the actual situations (such as conversations) in which those meanings are communicated, contrasts with Gadamer's focus on actual communicative activity" (Langsdorf 2007, 58).

One can see a deep problem in the conception of symbolic communication because this "notion of meaning as arising in the social act insists that meaning must be in life and cannot 'occur' other than in activities among people" (Smith 1999, 111). It is possible to state that symbolic interactionism "does not account for how language already has a determinate capacity to mean before it is activated in actual situations of action" and that it "lacks a theorizing of language and discourse (as does this ontological tradition, in general), or a means of making forays into social organization and relations beyond the matrix of the social act in which the self arises" (Smith 1999, 111). However, it can be noted that the seeds for addressing these problems are contained within the conception of symbolic interactionism itself; as was just outlined above, it attempts to present communication as a free flowing conversation and also impose upon it certain structures from outside of a symbolic act. In such attempts one can almost feel the breath of constructivism—broadly conceptualized—standing by in the wings of communication theorizing.

It must be emphasized again that the internal contradictions of the theories with a symbolic interactional, hermeneutical, or phenomenological orientation reflect the tensional nature of communication as conversation. While, at the beginning of this staging of communication, time can be seen as a liberating force, with objects freely moving in new meaningful ways, toward the end of the staging the situation becomes different: one can never completely understand the Other because of its constantly changing character. Objects change time and time again so the culprit for the impossibility to capture the right meaning—once and for all—must be time and time only. While taking the time is deemed crucial for understanding, the patience of participants in communication starts wearing thin, and they are tempted to blame for that each other (read: blame the mirror), looking for something more reliable as a base for their meaningful experiences. The grass may be greener on the other (Other's) side, but it must be greener still—if not the greenest—elsewhere. Thus, one can feel space standing by in the wings of communication, bidding its time (pun intended). Space never disappeared from the process of communication, of course; it simply existed in an enfolded form and is now ready to take another shot at communication.

However, this transformation of communication does not occur as peacefully as passing the baton during relay race. Communication as conversation is an emotional process wherein tensions have been building up, and so reaching a limit of understanding can be agonizing. It must be remembered that communication as a "dialogue is a principle both of connection and of responsibility: it can satisfy a need for belonging and offer a check on unreflective power," but it is still not "exempt from abuse and power"; as a result, we find "agony at the heart of the private sphere" (Peters 1999, 127). In this light, "*dialogue* can be a wonderful method for enforcing imagination of the other's position . . . , but it *is not in itself an adequate communicative vehicle for bearing the full varieties of moral experience*" (Peters 1999, 160; emphasis mine). For example, it is noted that the analysis of local conversations is inadequate to demonstrate the existence of a collective mind (McPhee 2006).

The process of understanding the Other can be presented in terms of the so-called positive and negative face, which are used, for example, in politeness theory (Brown and Levinson 1987) and which are parallel to the concepts of positive and negative freedom (Berlin 1958). When a symbolic action is oriented toward the Other's negative face, communication can discontinue with the distance between its participants going beyond a certain critical point; past that point understanding the Other is not attempted. A similar case is the interlocutors simply talking past each other (cf. Goodman 2007). However, there is a danger in case of symbolic actions oriented toward the Other's positive face, which may be recognized less often, but leads to the same outcome—the end of communication. The subject's actions are driven by the desire of reaching consubstantiation or overlapping of essence (K. Burke). However, the distance between the subject and the Other gets smaller and smaller, but never disappears; hence the potential for blaming the Other for not being able to reach identification, as well as the desire for attempting to look for consubstantiation elsewhere, get bigger and bigger. Engagement in communication, it must be reminded, can turn into a happy marriage or a deadly battle. Familiarity breeds contempt, and from love to hatred there is but one step, one symbolic act. If one understands the Other very well (too well), that knowledge, laid bare in all its vulnerability, can potentially be abused, or used against the Other and thus communication overall. What but a minute ago was a marriage of true hearts the next moment can be ruined forever. Here we find "the *aporia* of conversation itself, which is caught between trust and suspicion" (Gallagher 1992, 23). If suspicion wins over trust, "the dream of consubstantiality in spirit directly leads both to the nightmare of communication breakdowns and to disdain for those who opt out of the game of interpersonal mimesis" (Peters 1999, 66). The saving grace here lies in the fact that, by pulling oneself out of the nightmare of communication, one saves the-not-yet-completely-unfolded-at-this-point Self and, by the same token, communication overall, including the Other as its part.

Thus, communication, similar to one's face, is threatened from both sides—negative as well as positive. The danger lurks at both extremes of communication. It is important to note

> the tendency to reify notions of dialogue and relate them to intersubjectivity. . . . The use of the concept of intersubjectivity . . . renders it blind to deeper implications of communication as an unstable process. . . . As a result, where the monological approach is rightly criticized for the gross simplifications, the dialogical model proposed in its place is over-simplified on a series of cognitive and communicative grounds, and its core concepts—dialogism, intersubjectivity, reciprocity—are easily reified. (Grant 2003a, 98)

So, once one is assigned the status of interpretive authority, communication, similar to a (looking-)glass with its fragile nature, can break if not handled with care.

When communication breaks, it is not so much a break-down as a break-up. It is as if the subject and the Other—or time and space—break up and try to go their separate ways because one challenges, or does not trust, the authority of the other. Paradoxically, communication is ready to break at the moment when it seems so successful, almost reaching the "fusion of horizons" between the subject and the Other (or between time and space). Disagreement ("a break-up") arises when they almost see eye-to-eye on something, almost with the same eyes, as it were. The whitewater rapids cannot be calmed down with skills to the point of being so smooth that the currents stop. In other words, one cannot be completely conversed/converted into the Other, and so communication as conversation cannot stop; it can only turn into something else.

The reason a complete shared experience cannot be achieved by the participants in a conversation is because each side is biased, so to speak, being after a certain gain for itself, cf. the nature of interpretation. Reciprocity or mutuality, the same relationship one has to the other can both connect and cut, and cut lethally; as stated earlier, it is a double-edged weapon. It is not surprising that the root "mei-" that we find in Latin "mūtuus" from which "mutual" is derived, carries the meanings of "going wrong" and "missing" as well as "gift" and "duty" (Morris 1982, 866, 1528). At this staging of communication, the jury on what constitutes its essence is still out; here the verdict cannot be passed because it calls for judging and deciding, not simply producing skillful actions. At the staging of communication as conversation, its participants cannot judge their own actions or make decisions themselves. For that, new meaningful characteristics of communication must become manifest.

Thus, by the end of this staging of communication, "neither the presumption—historical, linguistic, social—nor the proposed situated individuation can account for the generality and its specification without assuming that all rules are understood universally as situated. *As such, nothing is resolved and the issue of communication is merely postponed*" (Mickunas 2007, 142; emphasis mine). In other words, communication must be approached not as a mutual process, but rather as a process of constructing some common ground, something that can be applied to what is shared by each of the participants in communication without (seemingly) implying any further mutual relationship between them. This way, by surviving the agony of the private sphere, the subject and the Other must find out something new about themselves and communication, in general, something that they were unable to see by looking into the looking-glass of each other.

And so, exhausted by trying to navigate the whitewater rapids of communication, its participants, like weary adventures, seek solid land.

To summarize, at this staging of communication, its actual nature is revealed; here participants engage in communication *hic et nunc*. Such engagement takes the form of a symbolic action, with objects questioned by the subject. In other words, one tries to understand objects in their own terms; this process of interpretation can be viewed as a conversation between the subject (still not Self) and the Other. Therefore, more attention is paid to the Other as well as the symbolic means used in this process in the form of different technical skills.

The gap between the subject and the Other is viewed not only in spatial terms, but also in terms of temporality. This gap, though, can never be completely bridged, and communication, conceptualized as conversation, reveals its dark side. Communication reaches the limit when its success in the form of consubstantiation seems to be so near, within reach. As a result, it becomes necessary to focus not on the mutuality, but rather commonality of this process; for communication to continue, another transformation must occur.

~

CHAPTER FIVE

Of This Earth:
Communication as Construction

Terra Firma

As conversation, communication seems to be on the verge of falling through under its own weight—under the gravity of thought of its participants, one might say. The closer it gets to the ultimate identification (which seems so near), the bigger the potential for their ultimate break-up, which takes but one symbolic action. This problem can be addressed only by finding something that "enables participants to move out of burdensome if not oppressive relational practices" (Krippendorff 2009, 125). Communication thus comes to be problematized as the search for something that prevents the agony of the private sphere ending in ending communication altogether. As mentioned in the previous chapter, this lethal danger can be avoided by viewing communication as a process based on commonality rather than mutuality. This view brings up a number of new concepts such as rights, obligations, responsibilities, rules, etc.

At this staging, the unique substances of the subject and the object (the Other) move to the background; now both sides are just communication bureaucrats, as it were, working for the common cause. It is at this point that the subject as (supposedly) the author of messages gets a premonition that, perhaps, one as the author is not as important, or maybe one is not the author of one's messages at all. Indeed, later, "the death of the author" will be proclaimed. However, here such a premonition is fleeting; there is a new hope, and the focus of communication is on some common ground shared by its participants—something solid upon which they feel safe(r).

It turns out that, in a way, the distinction between the subject and the object is quite arbitrary; here one becomes subject to, or the object of, the process of verification of the meaningful experience, formed earlier. Such procedures of verification—affirming meaning or pronouncing it true—provide that firm ground upon which communication continues to unfold. Also, it turns out that the subject can trust the object (the Other), as a source of meaning, up to a point; conversation may be an important and exciting process, but sooner or later, at a certain point in time one wants to find out the accuracy or truthfulness of the image formed in that looking-glass process. The Russian saying "Doveryai, no proveryai!" ("Доверяй, но проверяй!")—"Trust but verify!"—sums up the essence of this staging of communication quite nicely.

Where does one turn for verification in the process of communication, i.e., where can the terra firma of communication be found? It is only natural to look for that solid ground in what participants have in common and that is language as a symbolic means used in/for communication. Participants now shift their attention from the looking-glass of each other, and start paying even more attention to language. Now communication appears to be not so much a process of lived empirical experiences, but rather analytically presented assertions about such experiences. Thus, the actuality of interaction is no longer as significant; now a more important question is what *really* constitutes the nature of communication. A symbolic act viewed predominantly as an assertion, or a claim about a certain state of affairs provides communication with solid ground. It is interesting to note that in the Russian word for "assertion"—"utverzhdenie" ("утверждение")—one can hear the meanings of something hard, solid, and firm, cf. "tverdyi" ("твердый")—"firm." The English word "assertion," in its turn, is also very significant with its root "ser-" carrying the meanings of "arranging," "joining (in speech)," and "discussing" (Morris 1982, 1538). In this light, communication appears as a process wherein affairs are arranged, and participants join (in) this process by speaking about or discussing these affairs.

Thus, communication starts on a positive note, so to speak, with a new hope of capturing the true meaning of experiences. For example, "in the *Tractatus* Wittgenstein laid out a conception of the relationship between propositions and the world, a conception that is nothing if not spatial" (Curry 2000, 93) and so is supposed to provide a clear picture of communication. However, just as positivism by bringing empiricism to extreme logical consequences saw its own propositions turn out unverifiable by experience and thus turn against themselves, i.e., metaphysical, communication also will once again reveal its internal contradictions and undergo another transformation; as a result, communication will appear in a most humanistic—one might say, metaphysical—light. In this connection, it can be noted that "the fundamental break that *Philosophical Investigations* represents with the *Tractatus* is in its denial that it is the business of language to picture the world. *Philosophical Investigations* sets forth a powerfully non-representational view of language" (Flesch 2002, 122; cf. Gay 2010, 144).

Meanwhile, at the beginning of this staging of communication, language is put under the analytic microscope; it is believed that only a careful and rigorous analysis of language can reveal ("unconceal") the true meaning muddied by the turbulent waters at the previous staging. This way, for example, analytic philosophy attempts to clarify the meaningfulness of symbolic expressions; in a manner of speaking, it is an attempt to explain to language what it means.

It is no wonder that such an approach to communication is built upon argumentation and evidence, avoidance of ambiguity, and attention to detail. By the same token, all expressions which cannot be easily broken down into clear(ly verifiable) statements of fact are deemed metaphysical; at best, such affirmations are considered a kind of poetry—curious and inconsequential. The main goal of communication here, to quote L. Wittgenstein, is "to bring words back from their metaphysical to their everyday use" (*Philosophical Investigations*, § 116). This goal can be accomplished, to use L. Wittgenstein's ideas again, through language games, i.e., various rule-governed activities integrated into human social transactions. It is interesting to note that the examples, used to draw a parallel between games and language, consist in "*readily surveyable objects* of comparison to illuminate actual language-games" (Honderich 1995, 461, emphasis mine). Thus the world is beginning to take a more solid and tangible shape, so to speak; its limits, of course, are found in the limits of one's language.

Curiously, communication as conversation is a most serious process of the subject trying to understand the Other; however, that process turns out to be very emotional and dramatic. Communication that exists in the form of language games might seem to be a trivial and playful process; however, here communication turns out to be serious business and so much more than a game. The process of communication here must be viewed as complex discourse, cf. "Discourse can be described as a Wittgensteinian language game" (Krippendorff 2009, 219). What participants do in/through discourse is debating, reasoning, arguing, discussing, etc.; this way, concepts and rules are developed and followed henceforth.

It might still be possible to view communication at this staging as conversation; for example, J. Carey placed conversation at the center of democratic society (Carey 1995). However, "what distinguishes democratic conversation . . . is not equality but publicness. Democratic talk is not necessarily egalitarian but it is essentially *public*, and if this means that democratic talk is talk among people of different values and different backgrounds, it is also profoundly *uncomfortable*" (Schudson 1997, 299). Thus, when participants overcome the agony of the private sphere and lift the relational burden of dialogue, they find themselves in public, facing the common task of creating a certain communication order. In this light, "democratic talk is not essentially spontaneous but essentially rule-governed, essentially civil, and unlike the kinds of conversation often held in highest esteem for their freedom and wit (cf. communication as conversation—I.K.), it is essentially oriented to problem-solving" (Schudson 1997, 298). Communication at this staging, therefore, can be conceptualized as discourse—a process in which participants try to be reasonable and settle a dispute, closing the gap between themselves that they were unable to do through conversation when one stopped on the very brink of the abyss and communication was left as "unfinished business." It can be recalled that, at the staging of communication as conversation, nothing is resolved and "the issue of communication is merely postponed" (Mickunas 2007, 142).

Discourse thus can be seen as the judge that will determine what is meaningful and what is not, putting in order the somewhat messy affairs left by the previous staging. In other words, communication is successful when every participant accepts that order when everyone knows what its concepts mean and so plays by its rules. It must be noted that "recognition of the other is not a simple matter of perception but involves the founding of the human order" (Peters 1999, 230).

At this staging, one must speak about successful rather than effective communication; for communication to be successful, certain conditions must be met, cf. "felicity conditions" in speech act theory (Austin 1962). It is also interesting to note that, while such conditions simply mean those appropriate or fitting for an occasion, one can feel their spatial side emphasized; for example, in the Russian variant of "felicity conditions"—"umestnye usloviya" ("уместные условия")—the root of the word has a clear meaning of "place," cf. "mesto" ("место")—"place," i.e., felicity conditions are those relevant for a certain place. Also, for a speech act to be successful it must occur in a conventionally recognized context; unless participants hold certain beliefs *before* a particular speech act can successfully take place, it is said to "misfire." Only later will communication be performed without, as much as possible, the safety net of preconditions; as will be shown, all true meanings must stand the test of time.

At the staging of communication as conversation, all interactions between the subject and the Other can be viewed as a play (interplay); however, here "play merely reaches presentation through the players" (Gadamer 1989, 106). Now a clear distinction between play and non-play can be drawn, cf. the concept of metacommunication as described, for instance, by G. Bateson using the example of the playful puppies who can tell a playful nip from a real bite. In this sense, "the evolution of play may have been an important step in the evolution of communication" (Bateson 1972, 181). Metacommunication is another attempt, albeit at a different staging, to find the true meaning of experiences. Here, both play and non-play are parts of discourse as language games, and attention is focused on what constitutes this or that game. In other words, the constitutive character of communication here becomes more pronounced. Also, its reflective character (cf. the looking-glass nature of the previous staging) becomes more reflexive (Kasavin 2008, 357).

Thus, "discourse . . . means resorting to a meta-level to inquire into the presuppositions of knowledge" (Johansen 2002, 88). Participants resort to discourse—or rather communication reveals its nature as discourse—because they cannot completely understand each other through conversation and close the gap between themselves. One can say that discourse "necessarily emerges when I and Thou thrive on discovering possibilities that neither could imagine by themselves" (Krippendorff 2009, 125); it is discourse that "enables participants to move out of burdensome if not oppressive relational practices" (Krippendorff 2009, 125). In this process, participants in communication can be seen as "social actors . . . supervising their own and others' action in order to bring into being some larger, collective line of activity" (Anderson 1996, 91); in other words, something large and important was still enfolded under the burden of relational practices. It might be said that participants could not cope with communication as conversation—or rather could cope with it only up to a certain point; now they make another attempt. This time, participants try to join (in) communication, playing by its rules.

With this change in focus, the danger of "a cult of personality" is drastically reduced in the process of communication. Communication appears as an objective and, one might say, impersonal process; it is no longer perceived as a potentially dangerous double-edged weapon. Now communication means business. In fact, now communication is seen as cultivating its participants' attitudes and beliefs, putting their affairs in a certain order. It is tempting to blame communication for the image it cultivates, cf. the concept of "the mean world syndrome" in cultivation theory (Gerbner et al. 2002);

however, any image is cultivated by its participants themselves playing various language games, and so it makes no sense to blame the mirror for the image that it shows.

The focus of discourse is thus on what governs or constitutes communication. It is the inability of the participants in a dialogue to find such a constitutive order that made the staging of communication as conversation limited. On the one hand, "the social-theoretical model of intersubjectivity presupposes the (normative) recognition of rules. . . . In this connection, the influence of Mead becomes especially clear" (Grant 2003b, 8). On the other hand, however, one can note "Mead's failure to take into account self-reflexivity and normativity in the relationship with the other. In other words, Mead never took the process of the internalization of the Other's position seriously. Habermas's language-theoretical correction resides in embedding 'attitude-taking' in the binding force of rules and not in empirical repetitions. This means that the identity of rules does not rest on observable facts, but on the intersubjective acknowledgment of their validity" (Grant 2003b, 8). Thus, a shift can be identified from treating the rules of communication in terms of observable facts in concrete empirical situations of interaction to conceptualizing communication more in terms of norms developed and acknowledged in/by discourse.

At the same time, similar to the influence of G. H. Mead's ideas felt in the more normative theories, which were developed later, one can note that an order, revealed at this staging, is already present in communication, albeit in an enfolded form. As M. Bakhtin writes, "each dialogue takes place against the background of the responsive understanding of an invisibly present third party who stands above all the participants in the dialogue" (Bakhtin 1986, 126). This third party can be conceptualized in terms of any construct; M. Bakhtin himself noted that it can be found in "various ideological expressions (God, absolute truth, the court of dispassionate human conscience, the people, the court of history, science, and so forth)" (Bakhtin 1986, 126). However, this construct is, "strictly speaking, not an ideological but a metalinguistic fact constitutive of all utterances"; its "necessary 'invisible presence' . . . follows from the very nature of discourse" (Morson and Emerson 1990, 136). Thus, the parasitic third party called "noise"—what is considered a common enemy by the participants of a dialogue, something to be excluded—now reveals its constitutive powers. It may be "invisibly present," but it is omnipresent, finding its way into every participant's every utterance. It seems as if this "background of the responsive understanding of an invisibly present third party" can provide a universal backdrop for communication.

Nyack College Library

What takes place at this staging of communication is captured in the concept of *analogy* as another form of similitude. In analogy, *convenientia* and *aemulatio* are superimposed; as a result, *analogy* refers to adjacencies, i.e., bonds and joints, and also the fitting of resemblances across space. Although *analogy* is endowed with a universal field of application, there exists "in this *space* . . . one particularly privileged point. . . . This point is man . . . he stands in relation to the *firmament*. . . ." (Foucault 1970, 21; emphasis mine). In a way, one particularly privileged point—according to M. Foucault, "the man"—can be seen as a metacommunicative fact constitutive of all relationships in the universe.

Thus, communication at this staging is a process constituted and governed by a certain order wherein various resemblances are all (attempted to be) fit together. In the previous chapter, communication was viewed as *techné*; also, the dialogic nature of communication was discussed as a preliminary search for truth, leading to the resolution of a problem that Aristotle saw in apodeictic as a demonstration of knowledge. This shift to the epistemological domain can be conceptualized in terms of *epistêmê*, i.e., scientific knowledge of the order of things in the universe. It is important to note that "*epistêmê* is usually translated as 'science,' but should not in general be identified with modern science. *Epistêmê* is the virtue of theoretical knowledge after competence in some field or activity has been established and analyzed, has received a defined and more or less 'finished form,' and can be articulated adequately in language. It concerns those aspects of its field of study that remain more or less stable independently of our actions or interventions" (Eikeland 2006, 22). It is epistêmê that can be seen as providing a comprehensive account of a stable order derived from indisputable principles; "that what we know through epistêmê cannot be otherwise than it is" (Aristotle 1947, 1139b20). Also, as apodeictic knowledge, epistêmê is demonstrable (Aristotle 1947, 1139b30), i.e., it can be taught by demonstration, which is different from persuasion because demonstration produces knowledge, while persuasion merely opinion (Corcoran 2009). For Aristotle, of course, demonstration means showing by argumentation and reasoning rather than literal (visual) demonstration. From a more performative point of view, one can view any demonstration as a form of argumentation, cf. a political demonstration. Thus, at this staging, the performative nature of communication is also present, albeit in the sense of taking actions in accordance with certain requirements, which places less emphasis on the enactment of meaning and the effects of one's actions, to be discussed in the next two chapters. It is important to note that "the conclusions of demonstration, and all scientific knowledge, follow from first principles" (Aristotle 1140b, 30), hence its relation back to *nous*.

From the scientific (epistemic) point of view, many theoretical views can deductively demonstrate how a communication order can be constructed. For instance, H. P. Grice's cooperative principle looks deeply into the fabric of communication by presenting certain axioms that can guarantee a successful(ly constructed) communication order. However, all approaches similar to H. P. Grice's framework fail to bring to light the complexity of the nature of communication because their depth does not embrace the entire surface of communication. In other words, one might say that such conceptualizations are deep yet not superficial enough. Later, we will see how communication combines both depth and breadth and, respectively, which theories provide a more adequate view of communication.

So, at this staging, communication functions as an order constructed in the process of discourse. Here, everything in communication is supposed to be in order, fit together. One's role as an observer is here different than before. At this staging, the relationships between objects must be stated (ideally—in propositional form) because they cannot be directly observed (cf. Cronen 2001, 16). Consequently, the subject as an observer does not simply watch out for the actions of the Other so that to protect one's face, but constructs something out of what one experiences. This task becomes more important as the experiences observed grow more complex. In other words, meanings are not so much assigned to experiences as constructed from them. Communication thus appears to be less a process of reflection and representation and more a process of construction and organization.

In this respect, (inter)personal aspects of communication are given less attention, replaced with more general and socially sanctioned concepts and procedures. At the same time, there is a lot of value in approaching communication from constructivist positions: "constructivist approaches share the view of the world as a phenomenon constituted through individuals (and communication of) socio-cultural potential of meaning and experiences" (Langer 1999, 77). All such approaches, whether grounded in linguistics, anthropology, cognitive science or sociology, view communication as a process of establishing the most stable order of things in the form of constructs accepted (ideally) by everyone taking part in this process. The old Russian word "struga" ("струга"), meaning "a deep place," captures their essence well: here communication can be conceptualized as an attempt to find the "deepest possible place"—something with which every participant can identify, grounding oneself. Communication as a rational process of discourse wherein meaning is constructed is sometimes linked to the development of the bourgeois society with its compression of living space and appearance of new social institutions. Indeed, when communication becomes institutionalized, it is set up in the form of meanings and places; any place that draws in participants is, in a metaphoric sense, "a deep place," cf. a salon or a coffee-house.

Naturally, as communication increases in complexity with the growing number of participants, the need for its coordination comes to the forefront. As conversation, communication can be conceptualized mostly as a symbolic exchange or sharing of information. As construction, communication can be more adequately viewed in terms of coordination, cf. "Coordination surely is a more appropriate explanation of the use of language than sharing" (Krippendorff 2009, 83). Here communication is not so much a matter of each participant seeing oneself through the eyes of the Other; the focus here is not on participants exchanging looks or voices, but on coordinating them, on agreeing what they mean. Participants thus do not just carry out a conversation, but make arrangements or come to an agreement if only to disagree. It is interesting to note that the Russian word for coordination is "soglasovanie" ("согласование"), which means "coordination of voices" (literally—"co-voicedness"). Also, one finds the meaning of speaking—"govorit'" ("говорить")—in the Russian word for "coming to an agreement"—"dogovarivat'sya" ("договариваться").

Communication as a coordinated process requires that its participants establish rules and follow them. It is impossible to play language games without observing certain rules, and the overriding rule for successful discourse is for participants to bracket all individual motives "save that of a cooperative search for truth," in the words of J. Habermas. (quoted by: Craig and Muller 2007, 448). In other words, rule number one is the agreement to play by the rules for a common cause. Only this way can more specific rules be established in the form of conditions that need to be observed in order for experiences to be recognized by everyone as meaningful (truthful). The English word "rule" emphasizes governing power and authority although the root "reg-" in Latin "rēgula" also carries connotations of something right, just, and correct (Morris 1982, 1536); these meanings are also present in the Russian word for "rule" ("правило"), clearly demonstrating a connection between following rules and searching for truth and making things right. Therefore, it is imperative for successful communication to have everything arranged just right—just and right. It can be recalled that the mood at the beginning of this staging of communication is positive(ly determined).

So, communication at this staging is a process of constructing a certain order that can be viewed as a hierarchically organized system. Every system is a form of social bond, i.e., bonded and bounded because a "system's boundary is a structural manifestation of the system's underlying organization" (Zeleny

1996, 201). Communication here is, to use M. Foucault's metaphor, an attempt to construct a form of similitude by organizing adjacencies and fitting of resemblances across space; everyone is supposed to feel similar to this world and drawn into it. It must be noted, however, that there is something beyond the system's boundary, and the system is like a construction standing on the ground with the edges "out there."

Toward the Common Denominator

It is important to note that "with each communication begins a story" (Langer 1999, 78). A story is what gives our experiences form and shape, thus making them meaningful. This staging of communication highlights the constructed nature of stories, bringing to light "the inextricable connection but irreducible tension between stories lived (interactions) and stories told (narratives)" (Pearce 2004, 206). Every sociocultural order exists as a story, with some stories taking the form of "grand narratives." In one respect, however, all such stories are equal: each story functions—through discourse—as a guide to action. Every order, in essence, tells the story with the same message: "Everything is arranged the way it is because that is how everything must be." It can be pointed out that this conceptualization of communication fits well into its epistemic character; as mentioned earlier, "that what we know through epistêmê cannot be otherwise than it is" (Aristotle 1947, 1139b20).

It is not surprising that communication as constructing a certain order is usually conceptualized as a social process. Neither is surprising the resistance to this conceptualization on the part of traditional rhetorical and interpersonal theories of communication. It is noted, for example, that "rhetoricians opposed the introduction of social science into their field" (Bryant and Miron 2007, 425). However, the new theories of communication should not be seen as a complete ("revolutionary") break with their predecessors; rather, in a more evolutionary way, they build upon their ideas, taking them further into a more complex realm of coordinated action. "In this sense, a constructivist communication theory should not be considered as an entirely new paradigm, but should rather be seen as a widening frame for the analysis of communication, implementing earlier perspectives (e.g., the hermeneutical perspective) into a complex and holistic approach" (Langer 1999, 84). In other words, such "new" approaches to communication should be viewed as deeply rhetorical and psychological in nature. One should talk about such approaches not giving up a human(ist) thrust, but rather taking it further; without that, as we will see later, it will be impossible to recognize communication as a human, humane, and spiritual process. Incidentally, some theorists who focus on the social aspects of meaning construction feel this continuity of ideas very well; cf. the concept of "discursive redemption" in the work of J. Habermas. Such theorists seem to wish—and hope—for their theories to be redeemed. Without a doubt, theorists who view communication as a process of constructing a certain sociocultural order are motivated by noble intentions and have high aspirations. At the same time, it is not enough to treat communication only as a discursive/discoursive process; non-discursive elements play a crucial role in communication, as will be shown later. In this light, the ethical nature of communication cannot be constructed, but must be felt. In other words, one can only be ethical, not simply know what it means to be ethical.

Not all theories where communication is conceptualized as a process of constructing a certain order have an explicit social orientation, but they all have a general character, reflecting a shift from micro- to macro-, from difference to identity, from individuality to totality. The nature of communication at this staging is best captured by such theories as general semantics (Korzybski 1980), general systems theory (von Bertalanffy 1962), universal pragmatics (Habermas 1979), coordinated management of meaning (Cronen and Pearce 1982), symbolic convergence theory (Bormann 1985), cooperative principle (Grice 1989), to name some of the most well-known ones. All these theories share the ontological view of communication, described above; they all strive to show how communication can be brought down to a certain identifiable order as the largest possible class or the common denominator with which all participants identify. In this sense, an individual is viewed as displaying a "class consciousness" if he or she identifies with this class, willing to give one's individuality to the common good; this way, a "person sacrifices his or her will to universal moral laws" (Stoker and Tusinski 2006, 171). The ideological overtones that one hears in such an approach can take on a literal meaning: as mentioned earlier, successful communication means following "the party line." Communication is treated as a conscious process wherein one participates in knowledge (construction) with others.

The essence of bringing communication to the common denominator can be seen in the concept of denomination itself. Denomination as an act of naming makes one recall invocation, discussed earlier, which is also an act of bringing forth the object with the help of a name. In one sense, invocation and denomination are similar due to their active nature: both are clear attempts to act upon the world—more natural in the former case or more constructed in the latter case. In another sense, however, denomination is a more conscious action, which presupposes coordination of meaning with others. In can be said that invocation is a more forceful and unidirectional act, while denomination cannot be successful without an elaborate process of working toward consent. It was mentioned in a previous chapter that modern day political propaganda, which is sometimes traced back to traditional rhetoric, is viewed as "taking the ancient art of 'manufacturing consent' to a new level" (Pinchevski 2005, 30). It must be noted that a process of 'manufacturing consent' is more complex than simply moving from a preexisting situation to a message to an effect on an audience as it presupposes voluntary agreement to an opinion or a course of action. Denomination is still a categorizing name, or a name of a class or a group. In a metaphorical sense, communication strives toward complete equality of a group's members. In mathematics, this takes place if a numerator is equal to a denominator; in real life, such oneness is an ideal never reached, but constantly attempted.

As mentioned earlier, communication at this staging is viewed as a process of constructing a certain hierarchically organized order. Different theories present this hierarchical organization in different terms; cf. the levels from content to cultural archetype in the theory of coordinated management of meaning. Regardless of the number of levels and their labels, communication is treated as an increasingly complex and abstract process. At the same time, ironically, communication appears to be a less and less solidly constructed real world; as a result, its participants seem to turn from real people into incorporeal angels—or demons if they refuse to follow the accepted rules, cf. the maxims of H. P. Grice's cooperative principle. In this respect, to the list of the theories, mentioned above, one can add the theoretical views of St. Augustine—"'a logocentrist,' a devotee of the transcendental signified, an ontotheologian" (Peters 1999, 73).

Thus, what started as an attempt "to bring words back from their metaphysical to their everyday use" (L. Wittgenstein, *Philosophical Investigations*, § 116) now begins to take more and more metaphysical overtones. Language games, it turns out, are not such harmless and rigorous activities supposedly seamlessly integrated into human social transactions; while playing such games, one can get carried away very far—"out there." What started as an attempt to reveal the true meaning, muddied by the turbulent currents flowing at the previous staging of communication, now begins to run the risk of muddying meaning on the other end. It turns out that putting communication on a firm ontological footing is not as easy as it initially seemed.

As mentioned above, a cooperative search for truth is the only constraint effective in discourse; all other individual motives and claims are bracketed. All individual judgment about the world, and consequently all action in the world, is suspended; communication thus is ideal when what is developed in its process forms one general truth—one constructed order accepted by everyone. The paradox of the situation is that the (supposedly) all-inclusive order is still constructed through reduction, and the boundaries ("seams") as a structural manifestation of its underlying organization are showing.

Thus, one's "ego now enters the world . . . within which I abandon my simple and direct awareness of the Other, and suspend my immediate grasp of the Other in all his/her subjective particularity" (Ho 2008, 349). In this process, "the light in which I am looking at him is now a different one: my attention is shifted to those deeper layers that up to now had been unobserved and taken for granted. I no longer experience my fellow man in the sense of sharing his life with him; instead, I 'think about him'" (Schultz 1980, 140–141). As a result, the Other is constituted in one's consciousness as an object of thought. One can recall in this connection E. Levinas's critical attitude toward E. Husserl's method (Levinas 1981). E. Levinas "criticizes that aspect of Husserl's method which presents only phenomenological descriptions of sensations as modalities of consciousness. . . . Husserl's analyses fall short in that they remain essentially epistemological in nature and as such fail to penetrate to the sensible fundamental of subjectivity" (Boothroyd 2009, 341). The fundamental subjectivity of communication cannot be penetrated with conscious thought no matter how deep it may be; to that end, its entire surface must be embraced the way one's sensibility is open to touch. Therefore, "it is sensation . . . which must be subject to further 'reduction' in order to arrive at 'sensibility'" (Boothroyd 2009, 341). In this respect, "the Levinasian 'ethical reduction' is . . . not a reduction by reflection" (Boothroyd 2009, 341). In a later chapter, communication will be discussed as a superficial—and still deep—process, which is ethical through and through. It must now be clear why the attempts to present communication as coordination of action are usually met by phenomenologists with suspicion and resistance—either as too scientific or not scientific enough. Such double standards sometimes find peculiar manifestations in real life, cf. M. Heidegger's case (Peters 1999, 16–17).

So, communication, conceptualized as a cooperative process, is an attempt to ground meaning in a certain state of affairs. The Russian variant of "cooperative"—"sovmestnyi" ("совместный")—has the same root as "umestnye" ("уместные") for "felicity" (conditions) with a clear overtone of "place," cf. "mesto" ("место"), thus highlighting the spatial nature of this process. In a manner of speaking, communication at this staging can be viewed as an attempt to show time its place by spatializing it in a certain constructed order. The goal of communication can be said to consist— although not necessarily explicitly admitted or even realized—"in closing time off—in coercing temporality into spatial icon (the circle)—and hardening this closure into 'tradition'" (Spanos 1976, 462).

It may seem too radical a view to believe that coordinating action toward "tradition" will inevitably bring terror, cf. J.-F. Lyotard's view of J. Habermas's vision of a communicative community leading to conformism and even a terrorist notion of consensus: "There is a desire to return to terror, as a realisation of the fantasy to seize reality" (Lyotard 1984, 82). At the same time, as J. Derrida writes, "the privilege granted to unity, to totality, to organic ensembles, to community as a homogenized whole—this is a danger— . . . for ethics, for politics" (Derrida 1997, 13). In other words, there is a real danger in the assertion of totality by those "who seek to erase difference by invoking the authority of religion, nationalism, and (strategically selected) 'traditional' values" (Rasch 2000, 41). Hence J.-F. Lyotard's call to wage war on totality is quite understandable as is J. Derrida's identification of deconstruction with justice.

Thus, communication at this staging is a process of constructing an order wherein time is (attempted to be) contained. In this light, it is not surprising to read that "social systems . . . are networks characterized by inner coordination of individual action achieved through communication among temporary agents" (Zeleny 1996, 125). Such agents are clearly viewed not simply as transient, but replaceable; not so much as agents of change, but as obedient instruments. In a word, time here is seen as a slave to space. However, all attempts at totality sooner or later fail; "sooner or later" clearly points to the culprit of such failures. Time refuses to be coerced by spatiality; it will be shown later that communication can be seen not only as the coordination of action among temporary agents, but also as an eternal process when every one/every thing becomes its irreplaceable part.

Communication reveals its utopian character because all attempts to construct "the best of all possible worlds" fail as do all attempts at closing time off. A utopia is something that cannot exist in reality because it is a "no-place," cf. Greek "ou" ("not," "no") + "topos" ("place") (Morris 1982, 1411). It turns out that no place can be found where a perfect dwelling—a world order—is constructed. For example, one can notice M. Heidegger's preoccupation with space in his philosophy, cf. the predominance of spatial metaphors in the concept of Dasein (Irigaray 1999; Steelwater 1997). One can recall M. Heidegger's farmhouse in the Black Forest as an attempt to present an ideal being-in-the-world (Heidegger 1962, 300). However, it is noted that this image "seems a little regressive and romantic. Indeed, this image has been connected by some to M. Heidegger's well-known connections with the Nazi Party which often espoused a very similar ideology of rootedness in the deep soils of the Black Forest. The corollary of such a belief was that some kinds of people were unconnected to these deep soils and this manner of dwelling. Jews, gypsies, and urbanites, in general, were all seen as leading rootless or inauthentic existences" (Cresswell 2009, 3). Conceptualizations similar to M. Heidegger's image, then, can be viewed as examples of "how such normative constructions of place exclude 'others' both physically and existentially" (Cresswell 2009, 6).

A utopia is a search for the deepest possible place, cf. "struga" ("струга"), mentioned earlier, something with which all participants can identify. What makes every search for such a place a failed search is time; no meaningful experience can be constructed with space only. For communication to be conceptualized as a truly topological process, it needs time to stretch its spatial properties without tearing or breaking it and thus preserving it as a whole.

Although communication gets more and more complex, its participants continue their search for the perfect world. Communication is driven by the dream of complete identification—a topos that is a true simultaneity. However, "no place in the universe is truly simultaneous with any other; there is no point of shared presence" (Peters 2003, 408). At this staging, participants strive toward a total consensus, but a gap is still there, waiting to be filled in with meaningful experiences. In this respect, it is no accident that the theory developed by J. Habermas is also known as the consensus theory of truth. It might seem that, by going through enough temporary agents, communication can finally be perfectly coordinated and the total order achieved. However, consensus is not simply a general agreement that can be reached as a result of discourse; consensus is not only an expressed general opinion, but also an internal process, a "feeling together," cf. "con" (meaning "with") + "sense." Thus, at the core of the (supposedly) same collective mind, one finds corporeal and non-discursive elements, albeit enfolded.

As communication gets more and more complex, it becomes more and more difficult to coordinate action and manage meaning because of more and more elaborate discourse structures. This staging of communication started, as mentioned earlier, on a positive note in the hopes of capturing the true meaning and constructing the perfect order. Toward the end of this staging, however, doubts seem to creep into such aspirations, and it takes a more forceful effort to construct and manage meaning. It is interesting to note that the Russian word "stroit'" ("строить")—"to construct," "to build"—also means "to order about." In a way, here it still seems possible that reality can be constructed, "ordered about." Only later will communication reveal its nature as "the play of reason on the edge of insanity" (Epstein 2007, 281). It will then become clear that the world does not end, but rather begins at the limits of one's language.

Playing the Devil's Advocate

With discourse constructions getting heavier and heavier, narratives "grander and grander," the process of communication seems to slow down; it seems that one final finishing touch will finish time off, as it were. However, as mentioned earlier, time refuses to be contained. In fact, time does not disappear, but moves into the very flesh of communication. In other words, communication does not slow down let alone stop: it is the same turbulent process, however, now it moves to the nano level, so to speak. All the theories that focus on this staging of communication are too general and too deep, failing to look at what is taking place on its surface.

At this staging, communication begins as a process of clarifying meaning through a rigorous analysis; anything "disagreeable" that muddies meaning is deemed metaphysical and left outside the gates of the constructed order. As always, this process is paved with good intentions, striving toward a total concord and equality of all participants. The goal of communication here is to solve the equation of life, as it were, wishing for oneness when the numerator is equal to the denominator and communication becomes one autopoetic system, cf. the radical constructivist view.

According to H. Maturana and F. Varela, "an autopoietic machine (sic) is a machine organized (defined as a unity) as a network of processes of production (transformation and destruction) of components which: (1) through their interactions and transformations continuously regenerate and realize the network of processes (relations) that produced them; and (2) constitute it (the machine) as a concrete unity in space in which they (the components) exist by specifying the topological domain of its realization as such a network" (Maturana and Varela 1980, 78). This view is driven by noble aspirations of preserving the individuality within a machine that produces the components producing its own organization; in this sense, autopoeic theory can be seen "as a way to reconnect ethics and science" (Hayles 1999, 142). It must be noted that self-producing systems are not closed, they are self-contained. One might say that what they contain within themselves is time, cf. "the communication systems constitute each others' environments in terms of time. To the extent that communication among systems is sustained, the systems also have to communicate frequency distributions in the time dimension" (Leydesdorff 1994, 40). Time here is treated simply as an interval necessary for an interaction to take place; it is a construct determined by the system (observing) itself. The self-reflexive capacity of the system itself (read: time) cannot be observed or felt directly; it can be "only hypothesized as an internal mechanism of the system(s) under study" (Leydesdorff 1994, 40). This construct is taken for reality; in a way, this is the realization of the dream of "the best of all possible worlds"—one self-producing system.

It must be emphasized that "self-organization or *autopoesis* can only be achieved by communication systems which are able to reflexively vary the *organization* of the uncertainty along the time dimension. Self-organizing systems reconstruct their histories so that they can face their future in terms of expectations (Leydesdorff 1994, 40). As mentioned earlier, at this staging of communication, the subject does not completely experience the Other; rather, one constructs something out of one's interactions with the Other. In this respect, "time and causality are not intrinsic to the processes [of communication] themselves but are concepts inferred by an observer" (Hayles 1999, 139). The observer here is nothing but the system itself. It must be noted that, "although the observer's perceptions construct reality . . . , this construction depends on *positionality* rather than *personality*. In autopoeic theory, the opposite of objectivism is not subjectivism but relativism" (Hayles 1999, 143). So, the observer is not really a flesh-and-blood person with psychological depth and uniqueness, but the system itself. From this perspective, any self-contained (and thus time-containing) order can say: "I select and organize structures and observe myself selecting and organizing structures, therefore, I am." Ironically, there is no one/no thing to hear this except the system itself. In this sense, communication can be viewed as functioning like autistic individuals rather than normally responsive people (cf. Hayles 1999, 148). This impression is reinforced by the language used within autopoetic theory, cf. such terms as "coupling," "triggers," or "languaging." For example, language in the process of communication is treated as "languaging," i.e., providing triggers for the observer's self-orientation. This view "seriously understates the transformative effects that language has on human subjects" (Hayles 1999, 147).

Originally presented as a description to explain the nature of living systems, this view of communication appears strangely removed from the real social and psychical world. The search for common meaningful experience no longer is an attempt to bridge the gap between the subject(ive consciousness) and objects; instead, it takes the form of one's agreement with one's own constructs. Now the search for truth is aimed not at real objects, but rather objects as structures selected and organized within one's own system.

Not surprisingly, even the theory developed by J. Habermas can be seen as going around in circles of instrumental questions without any outlet to objects as things (cf. Kasavin 2008, 358). In this connection, it can be argued that "the concept of an ideal communication community, the normative concept of consensus and its political counterpart—discursive democracy—rely heavily on counterfactual ideals that can be intuitively invoked in order to challenge the self-referential logic of systems, abuse of power and 'violations' of language games we witness every day. *Whether the counterfactual ideal is sufficient to repair the reality deficit in such an idealized theory is open to serious doubt*" (Grant 2003a, 114; emphasis mine).

Thus, "according to this view, communications do not establish a connection with external reality, but recursively construct communication networks" (Grant 2003a, 108). Autopoeic theory views communication as a pure and self-contained process, so both the object and the subject (as an individual) seem to disappear in this self-producing machine, reduced to the role of its temporary agents. The only way for communication to keep unfolding is for the subject to keep striving toward freedom, conceptualized as the addition to Being emerging from the structure of Being (cf. Khopfmaister 2006, 268).

In this light, the subject, the object and language must be given the attention they deserve. To that end, however, the subject must still be a part of the system and step outside of it. This act of self-exclusion or benevolent defiance against the system must be viewed as an act of trying to achieve the unity of essence and existence. By taking this step, one does not allow the essence of the system to consume one's entire existence. At the same time, the essence of the self-contained system can be understood only by turning to the subject's existence for the explanation of its meaning. As a result of this radical step, the subject gives up all the earthly possessions found in one's certain world order and now stands alone—face to face with (one)Self. The end result of this staging of communication is not the construction of the total order, but the emergence of the individual Self, willing to lose everything provided by this order, i.e., "the emergence of a new self-conscious subject, the meta-subject, able to *explicitly signify* this loss" (Rotman 1987, 57).

Thus, (self-)excluded from the system, one finds oneself, as it were, beside oneself. This split(ting) personality of the subject was set in motion at the staging of communication as conversation with its mirror-like nature; now, toward the end of the staging of communication as construction, the only way for it to continue is by unfolding. At the staging of communication as conversation, one had to pull oneself from the brink of the abyss or the edge of consubstantiality in order to save oneself and, *mutatis mutandis*, communication overall; similarly, at the staging of communication as construction, one has to split into two, as it were, with one foot still in the system, but the other beyond it—"out there." To that end, the subject must play the devil's advocate, so to speak. It is important to note that the subject does not sell one's soul to the devil, but only *plays* the devil's advocate. It is still a language game only now pushed to its limit—and beyond, as will be discussed later in the book in more detail.

In this connection, it is interesting to draw a parallel between the account, presented above, and J. Peter's view of St. Paul as a normative theorist who sees the problem of universality from the very start "since a world in which only norms were obeyed would lack much of our most precious experiences" (Peters 2005, 60). As a result, St. Paul makes an extraordinary gesture, "sneaking heresy into one's doctrine only to retract it swiftly, and preaching a universal norm that lacks universally binding force" (Peters 2005, 61). In this light, several important points need to be kept in mind. First, it must be emphasized that "the need for the ideal and the limitations of our ability to live up to it is a tragic, not disillusioning, fact" (Peters 2005, 61). In other words, one must come to terms with such a double-consciousness because that is the only way for our communicative experiences to continue. Second, it must be remembered that "this is not to encourage double-dealing or lying" (Peters 2005, 61). As noted above, the subject does not sell one's soul to the devil, but only *plays* the devil's advocate. And, third, one must become aware that such "double-consciousness is a privilege and responsibility, not a curse" (Peters 2005, 61). It will be shown in the next chapter how one becomes aware of communication as one's responsibility.

From the radical point of view of autopoeic theory, the subjectivity of communication receives a peculiar treatment, as shown earlier. For H. Maturana, in the ideal human society one would "see all human beings as equivalent to oneself, . . . without demanding from them a larger surrender of individuality and autonomy than the measure that one is willing to accept for oneself" (quoted by: Hayles 1999, 142). But, communication is not only a process of surrender, i.e., relinquishing possession or control of something to another, in this case—to the system, as such, but also reconciling oneself with, and signifying, that loss; later, we will see what form such signifying takes. The prepositions here are significant—one surrenders *to* and reconciles oneself *with*: the latter clearly expresses the idea of connectedness and continuity. It will be shown in the next chapter how communication can be conceptualized as a process that combines a creative impulse of signification with humility, cf. "loss."

Communication as Poetic Justice

Thus, this staging of communication starts with noble intentions and high aspirations—to construct a perfect order with which every participant can identify. Toward the end of this staging, however, it becomes obvious that such a construction cannot be achieved, with any attempt at a utopia turning into a dictatorship. Communication so forceful and positively determined to reach a total success is now slipping off, the mood of its participants darkening. Conceived as a class act—a conscious process wherein everyone is supposed to participate in coordinated action with others—communication still lacks a perfect class consciousness. Paradoxically, this realization becomes painfully clear when the total success of communication seems to be within reach: one more step—and the perfect order should be constructed. As one tried to understand why this never takes place, "one must keep in mind that a 'we' never speaks. Individual 'Is' do . . . The authoritative assertion of commonalities, while contestable in principle, can silence divergent voices and become oppressive" (Krippendorff 2009, 123).Thus, similar to the agony of the private sphere (cf. Smith 2008), communication experiences the agony of the public sphere.

This agony represents the limit of the staging of communication as construction: the only way for communication to continue is by moving beyond the (almost) perfect world order, seemingly turning against itself. This is exactly the step taken by the subject excluding oneself from the system—the step that appears irrational. In essence, this step goes against the entire thrust of communication as construction, which is an attempt to bring all participants to the common denominator and reach the state of a complete equality. By taking this step, the subject declares, as it were, that he/she does not fit into this project. It is a very painful step: similar to the staging of communication as conversation where one seems to go against consubstantiality, here one seems to go against consensus or construction of meaning. In other words, it seems as if one is no longer *with* communication (let us recall that "con" means "with"). And yet, for the subject to take this step is the only way for communication to continue unfolding.

One cannot overcome the irrationality of this staging by force, though: the more effort is put into discourse, the more agonizing communication becomes. It is only by reconciling oneself with the (seeming) irrationality of communication that one can truly understand (rationalize) its nature and oneself as a part of it. As mentioned earlier, this takes a creative impulse full of imagination combined with humility. Communication that continues beyond the (unsuccessful) attempt to build a totally perfect order can only be partly imagined and thus must be humbly accepted.

This staging of communication brings to mind Plato's well-ordered state where each tribe has its allotment and is denominated after a certain deity (Plato 1804, 139). What did not find any place in that state was poetry as something illusionary and irrational, not fitting into the overall order of things. It is stated that Plato's attitude toward poets stems from his desire to break with the Homeric oral traditions which relied on memory, recital, and a vigilant community. At the same time, it is sometimes noted that Plato's critique of the poets has been misunderstood because the dialectical movement of his rhetorical thought is more nuanced (Wiegmann 1990; cf. Naddaf 2007). Plato's attitude to the poets is considered paradoxical due to his pivotal position in the transition from a predominantly oral culture to a predominantly written one (Lentz 1983). Still, it is commonly argued that, in championing an "abstract intellectualism," "Plato undermined a whole way of life. He asks men that they reexamine experience, instead of merely expressing it" (Russell 2005, 139). "Men reexamining experience, instead of merely expressing it" can be a very good definition of discourse! This is an attempt to exclude from communication everything illusionary and irrational, which, however, will not go away and will be manifest in all its glory later. Interestingly, Plato himself seemed to have a nagging feeling that his rationally constructed world might be vulnerable to something elusive yet ever-present (time?), cf.: "This, however, we ought by all means to consider, that all the particulars which we have just now spoken of will never so opportunely concur as they have happened to do in our discourse. . . . All which particulars have nearly been asserted by us as dreams: and we have fashioned, as it were, from wax a certain city and citizens" (Plato 1804, 140). Plato seems to admit that every solidly constructed world, at its core, has a dreamlike and illusionary nature; the material of wax is a very appropriate and significant metaphor (cf. Epstein 2007, 280).

Thus, for communication to continue, one must reconcile oneself with its poetic nature as something partly illusionary and seemingly irrational. Indeed, one must become a poet, not necessarily as a writer of poems, but in a more general sense as one who is especially gifted in the perception and expression of the beautiful. It takes a poet for communication to overcome its autistic and self-contained character, revealing new sides of its (beautiful) nature. True poetry "is the art of thinking dangerously, the play of reason on the edge of insanity" (Epstein 2007, 281). Each such step is a step toward the beautiful and the dangerous—a step balancing on the edge of insanity. Herein "lies the unique opportunity of poetry to escape the conditions of factual reality and to point out the best possibilities for human life together, possibilities that are concealed by everyday reality" (Wiegmann 1990, 122).

In this light, the nature of communication as *aletheia* can appear only as a poetic process.

A poet is a self-conscious meta-subject who never sees and names things as they are but always differently. In a way, a poet is a master of allegory who always presents both an apparent or superficial sense of something and its deeper sense, as well. An allegory is an art of speaking in other terms; in Russian, for example, "allegory" is "inoskazanie" ("иносказание"), which literally means "other speaking" or "speaking otherwise." It is also significant that the word "allegory" is derived from "allos"—"other" + "agoreuein"—"to speak (in public)," from "agora"—"an assembly" (Morris 1982, 34). In this respect, another staging of communication, discussed in the next chapter, can be viewed not as breaking away from the Homeric oral tradition, as reportedly attempted by Plato, but rather carrying it on, albeit at a new level, when a poet speaks before the entire world as his/her community ("agora").

So, the staging of communication as construction started as an attempt to build a perfect order by taking empiricism to its logical end based upon the clarification of language (discourse) structures; all expressions not easily broken down into clear and clearly verifiable statements of fact were to be deemed metaphysical and left outside of this order. Discourse was supposed to act as the judge, determining what is meaningful and what is not and thus putting everything in order. Taken to its extreme, however, communication turns into a self-producing system and so can be viewed as an observer observing itself observing. It seems as if a full stop could be put here, leaving communication (and its conceptualization) at that. There is just one—most human/istic—question that prevents us from doing so: "Why?" In other words, "Why does communication continue (to exist)?" This question cannot be adequately answered unless the partly metaphysical nature of communication is taken into consideration; the subject's split into a citizen and a poet only parallels the dual nature of communication as a rationally irrational (or vice versa) process. Toward the end of this staging, it becomes clear—at least to those who display a gift and courage for becoming poets—that metacommunication cannot not be metaphysical. By the same token, it becomes clear that a just order cannot be built only through orderly discourse because justice cannot not be poetic.

In this light, the theoretical conceptualization of communication calls for new insights from the disciplines or fields dealing with "such stuff as dreams are made on." Otherwise, "as we work to build a house of communication theory, there is some danger that we will confuse the constitutive character of communication with the powers of the social world and so simply come to exchange the domination of psychology and engineering for the rule of sociology and politics" (Shepherd 1999, 163). With the popularity of social

constructivist theories as well as those of a more normative nature similar to
J. Habermas's ideas, it can be argued that the house of communication theory
needs as always a breath of fresh air, so to speak, a spiritual charge that can
be provided by the humanities, which are better equipped to shed light on
the irrational rationality of human experiences.

The ways of dealing with the irrational rationality of communication
are—more implicitly than explicitly—present in the theories that try to
explain its nature at the staging of communication as construction. While
their focus is "on the reflexive and local production of a social order" (Krippendorff 2009, 6) through the coordination of action, one can find in
them an idea of communication transformation and deconstruction. Even
when directly dealing with language (discourse) structures, they seem to be
looking beyond toward something that drives communication further and
further. For example, general semanticists warn us not to confuse the map
with the territory; in speech act theory the concept of the "direction-of-fit"
reminds us of the complex relationships between words and the world; and
in the theory of coordinated management of meaning the level of a cultural
archetype must be seen not as the limit, but rather as a catalyst of further
communication.

Of course, the theories that focus on a shift from micro- to macro- or from
interpersonal to public communication come very close to the appreciation
of its transformative nature, cf. the view on communication by J. Habermas
and the title of one of his most famous books—*The Structural Transformation
of the Public Sphere* (Habermas 1989). Although grounded in modernity and
criticized for its rigid framework, his theory of communicative action reveals
a number of shifts that can be best understood from a postmodern perspective, e.g., from ethnocentric to global and from logocentric to non-linear.
These shifts take place not *contra* J. Habermas, but in accordance with his
original ideas (see: Sinekopova 2006). Additionally, in the process of such
shifts the role of time is emphasized; in this respect, the "most unsettling
transformation of the public sphere" is "the unstable, *always collapsing transformation from a space to a subject*" (Mah 2000, 182; emphasis mine). However, the unsettling transformation of the public sphere could be viewed in
a positive light: it is in the process of this transformation that Self (finally!)
emerges. As one continuously brackets the world, what is eventually constituted in one's consciousness as the object of one's thought is oneself. Thus,
criticizing J. Habermas for his views, including his possibly terrorist notion of
consensus, is somewhat misplaced; after all, J. Habermas himself noted that
"for every possible communication, the anticipation of the ideal speech situation has the significance of *a constitutive illusion* that is at the same time a
prefiguration [*Vorschein*] of a form of life" (quoted by: Craig and Muller 2007,

455; emphasis mine). One may wonder whether those who criticize J. Habermas are themselves too firmly grounded in the ideas of reason, expecting him to provide the final truth, so to speak, and then blaming him for not doing so. Perhaps such critics are uneasy accepting J. Habermas as partly an illusionist; perhaps they would rather take him for the sage who has all the answers. Could such criticism say more about the critics rather than the criticized?

So, the theories explaining the staging of communication as construction contain the seeds for the theories that will become more suitable for conceptualizing communication as poetic justice. This epistemological continuity reflects the ontological transformation taking place in communication: the point of departure for a total order is the point of arrival (emergence) of Self. In other words, "the agent emerges as a form of retroactivity . . . the moment of the subject's individuation emerges as an effect of the intersubjective" (Bhabha 1994, 185).

To summarize, this staging of communication is conceptualized as a process of constructing a world order common to all its participants. In this light, communication is not as an empirical process of lived experiences, but rather assertions about those experiences, discursively verified. As discourse, communication at this staging exists in the form of language games, and all participants play by their rules. At the same time, communication is a serious and objective process; rather than sharing roles and looking into the eyes of each Other, communication here takes the form (and conceptualized) as coordination of meaning.

At this staging, everyone is supposed to participate in the construction of the same world other; in this sense, the goal of communication is to bring all meanings to the common denominator. This process can be seen as an attempt to close time off by putting temporality into a spatial totality; such attempts, however, have a utopian character and reveal the limitation of this staging of communication. As always, this limitation is realized when the success of communication—"the grandest narrative"—seems to be within reach. Some meaningful characteristics of communication are left beyond the scope of the so-called normative/universal theories. In other words, it becomes necessary to show why communication continues even if (treated) as a supposedly objective process of autopoesis. Toward the end of the staging of communication as construction, it becomes clear that it is impossible to exclude "metaphysical stuff" from communication. The subjectivity of communication calls for a new perspective that would present it as a poetic process of signification combined with a certain loss. And so communication appears as a process where and when experiences are not simply told, but always told differently.

CHAPTER SIX

~

Through the Fire:
Communication as Resignation

The (Un)Bearable Lightness of Being

It is common to equate the main difficulty of communication with misunderstanding or lack of understanding between its participants. This difficulty is mostly a part of the staging of communication as conversation. Without a doubt, misunderstanding or lack of understanding do not contribute to successful communication. A much more serious difficulty, however, is the situation when understanding is (or rather seems to be) achieved; now the subject can no longer wait for the Other (or the system) to clarify meaning or blame the Other (or the system) for not doing enough to clarify it. At this point, the subject must do something himself/herself so that communication can continue. In this light, communication can be conceptualized not so much as a process of understanding or constructing but rather creating meaning; a time comes for the subject to carry out/on the commitment made.

In other words, *the subject situated in a temporal dimension* is aware of the gravity and difficulty of his decisions, but at the same time he is aware that he must decide, that it is he who must decide, and that this process is linked to an indefinite series of necessary decision making that involves all other men. (Eco 1984, 113; emphasis mine)

The process of creating meaning is not the same as representation in the strict referential sense; rather, this process must be viewed the way M. Heidegger viewed representation. For him, "'representation' (*Vorstellung*) means a process of bringing a thing before one's self, and thereby *imagining* it (the

German word is the same) . . . by the word traditionally rendered in English as representation (*Vorstellung*) he means . . . a whole (metaphysical) process of reorganizing the world and producing a new category of being" (Jameson 2002, 46).

It was mentioned earlier that the staging of communication as construction was not complex enough because it was too grounded in reality lacking enough imagination. Now communication reveals its more complex nature; every act of communication can now be viewed as a complex number, combining real and imaginary parts. It becomes clear that the process of communication as creating meaning cannot be successful without a certain degree of imagination. To that end, the subject plays the role of a hyperreflexive observer (cf. Leydesdorff 2000), embracing the entire experience made meaningful up to that point. This way, what is brought before one's self is the entire process of communication: while communication was earlier conceptualized as a process of recognizing objects (cf. the staging of communication as invocation), or understanding the Other (cf. the staging of communication as conversation), or constructing together with the Other a world order (cf. the staging of communication as construction), now communication can be viewed as a process of the subject be(com)ing aware of (one's role in) communication, i.e., be(com)ing self-aware. That is why "properly speaking . . . the Self exists only insofar as one is self-conscious" (Aboulafia 1991, 231). As mentioned in the previous chapter, what is eventually constituted at the end of the staging of communication as construction in one's consciousness as the object of one's thought is oneself.

Communication cannot be successful only as a process of recognizing, understanding and constructing meaning; for communication to be truly successful, one must be(come) aware of one's be(com)ing a part of communication. Hence the subject as Self comes into the spotlight, and communication reveals its new meaningful characteristics. As one looks at the Other in a new light, one's attention is "shifted to those deeper layers that up to now had been unobserved and taken for granted" (Schultz 1980, 140–141). It is in this light that communication can be seen as "the project of reconciling self and other" (Peters 1999, 9). However, communication must also be viewed as a process of reconciling Self and Self. At this staging of communication, one's attention is turned mostly on oneself, and so one becomes aware of one's role in communication as a (co)creator of meaning. In this respect, "we cannot know or understand the Other until we understand ourselves. . . . Any dark corners of ourselves that we leave uninspected will shape our understandings of others without our being aware of it" (Harbeck 2001, 10); at this staging of communication, all such corners are lit up.

When the subject looked into the face of the Other, the goal was to understand oneself; now the subject must look into oneself in order to understand the Other. The difference between these stagings of communication is captured well in the following passage:

> The highest principle of phenomenology, apodictic evidence, is precisely a call for the presentation or bringing forth (*e-videre*) of objects to an immediate and self-present intuition. The notion of transcendental consciousness, as well, is nothing more than the immediate self-presence of this waking life, the realm of what is primordially "my own." By contrast, the concepts of empirical, worldly, corporeal, etc., are precisely what stands opposed to this realm of self-present ownness; they constitute the sphere of otherness, the mediated, what is different from self-present conscious life, etc. (Allison 1973, xxxiii)

The latter realm is clearly related to the staging of communication as conversation, while the former realm—to its staging as a creative process of self-awareness.

So, the key question arising at the staging of creative self-awareness is as follows: "What is to be done in/to communication so it can continue to unfold?" This question must be answered, i.e., something creative must be done, by the subject who, situated in a temporal dimension, is now aware of the gravity and difficulty of this decision.

This decision might appear to be not only difficult, but impossible because the subject seems to have reached the limit of communicability; hence the "unsolvable" task of expressing what cannot be communicated (cf. Chang 1996; Smith 2003), cf. one's helplessness of grasping the unifying nature of language noted by M. Heidegger (1982). Now the subject must come to terms with the necessity and impossibility of observation, or one's defenselessness against communication. Thus, at this limit of communicability, the subject must create (author) new meanings and, at the same time, come to terms with one's death as the author. However, "it is precisely in recognizing the impossibility of communication that the blessing comes" (Peters 1999, 245).

It turns out that the solution to the seemingly unsolvable task is quite simple: the subject's decision as a response to, and response-ability for, communication takes the form of resignation. It is important to emphasize the dual nature of resignation; on the one hand, the subject admits—and submits to—one's inability to embrace the totality of experience, resigning *from* communication, and, on the other hand, the subject creates, at the same time, new possibilities *for* future communication, re-signing communication, as such. In this sense, the act of resignation is similar to the nature of the gaze, which "both acknowledges the desire to own the place of one's look and accepts its impossibility" (Freedman 1991, 64). This dual nature is clearly seen in the Russian equivalent of "resignation"—"ukhod" ("уход"), which means both "leaving" and "taking care of." Through resignation, therefore, the subject gives up any further attempts of grasping the unifying nature of communication (leaves it, so to speak) and also, by the same token, takes care of its continuation. Thus, the decision made by the subject at this staging of communication can be summed up as "I hereby resign/re-sign."

In this act of resignation one finds the most prominent presence and significance of meaning, seen very clearly in the Russian equivalent of "I hereby . . ."—"Nastoyashchim ya . . ." ("Настоящим я . . .") where "hereby"—"nastoyashchim" ("настоящим") means both "the present" and "worthwhile." Thus, at this staging of communication as resignation, the most immediate and meaningful experience is created. As a result of this act, the subject takes another step toward freedom, which, at this point, takes the form of re-signation.

In a similar sense, M. Heidegger finds the unity of the being of language in what he calls "the design." He writes (Heidegger 1971, 121):

> The name demands of us that we see the proper character of the being of language with greater clarity. The "sign" in design (Latin *signum*) is related to *secare*, to cut—as in saw, sector, segment. To design is to cut a trace. Most of us know the word "sign" only in its debased meaning—lines on a surface. But we make a design also when we cut a furrow into the soil to open it to seed and growth. The design is the whole of the traits of that drawing which structures and prevails throughout the open, unlocked freedom of language. The design is the drawing of the being of language, the structure of a show in which are joined the speakers and their speaking: what is spoken and what of it is unspoken in all that is given in the speaking.

It seems that the doubly inscribed creative nature of "resignation" has connotations of an active purposeful action of appointing in "design(nation)." It is possible to view language as a design one works with, metaphorically speaking; the creative work itself, however, is best seen as the act of resignation/re-signation. In this act, one as a "self-conscious subject" (Rotman 1987, 57) seems to lose one's battle to communication, and, at the same time, is "able to *explicitly signify* this loss" (Rotman 1987, 57) thereby, so to speak, "drawing even" with communication.

The Gift That Keeps on Giving

So, at the staging of communication as resignation, the focus shifts from the sender to the receiver of a message who turns out to be its (co)author. It becomes clear that one cannot simply transmit a message, having sent it to someone else once and for all. Any message happens to be a "Note to (one) Self," i.e., a message sent by the subject—through others—to himself/herself. A message is not simply a letter written by one and sent to the Other; rather, it is a constant process of writing or re-signing meaning. In this sense, communication is a process of correspondence between the subject and everything/everyone that the subject (cor)responds to, including oneself. It is interesting to note that the Russian word for "correspondence" is "perepiska" ("переписка") or "perepisyvanie" ("переписывание"), which means both "writing letters or communicating with each other," i.e., correspondence and also "re-writing," i.e., re-signation.

Through re-signation, one's fate is revealed as striving to correspond to/with communication. In this process, one's fate unfolds, and the subject becomes commensurate with communication. One cannot escape one's fate, but one can—and must—come to terms with it through communication as a process of correspondence and resignation. The connection between communication and fate is profound. The word "fate" is derived from Latin "fātum," formed from the neuter past participle of "fāri"—"to speak" (Morris 1982, 478). Thus, one's fate is what is spoken, communicated. In this light, the subject can be viewed as an utterance generated in every creative act of re-signation and so passed from generation to generation.

Communication is a process when the subject, as a message, is sent back to himself/herself and, by the same token, to everything/everyone that he or she corresponds to. In this sense, one cannot carry out a conversation or discuss/debate things with/in communication—just as one cannot communicate with one's fate; rather, one can (cor)respond to it. From this point of view, communication must be treated as "the paradoxical task that can be solved only provisionally, or that can be solved only by creating new problems" (Rasch 2000, 49). In this light, communication appears, in U. Eco's words, as "an indefinite series of necessary decision making that involves all other men" (Eco 1984, 113).

Communication as conversation took the form of inquiry when the subject looked into the object (the Other), trying to understand its meaning. At the staging of communication as resignation, it becomes clear that the subject must respond to one's inquiry himself/herself, corresponding to everything/everyone that he/she comes into contact with. The subject's ability to communicate at this staging takes the form of response-ability. At its core, this "responsibility for the Other is not a conscious choice I made, nor is it an unconscious involvement understood in a psychoanalytic sense. It is, rather, a responsibility expressing itself by interrupting self-consciousness, as if reminding me of a commitment I have never made but which is still incumbent upon me" (Pinchevski 2005, 80). In this sense, "it is possible to view subjectivity as an elemental site of interruption . . . a space-time opening not intended as such but one that nevertheless takes place" (Pinchevski 2005, 11).

Also, at this staging, it becomes clear that communication as a language (discourse) game cannot be "won" by the subject. The subject attempted to "win the game" with communication when the subject tried to step through the looking-glass and unsuccessfully identifies with the Other, or when a total order failed to be constructed. At the staging of communication as resignation, it becomes clear that the best one can do is to (keep trying to) draw even with communication, so to speak, submitting to its rules, on the one hand, and changing them (re-signing), on the other hand. In other words, as will be discussed in detail in the next chapter, the best possible scenario for all participants in communication is a tie.

Communication at this staging takes the form of an attempt at closure when the subject turns into "punctum" as a meta-sign (Rotman 1987, 40–41), trying this time with more passion and creativity to close the gap in one's experiences. The subject, as punctum, is, in essence, one's internal gaze. R. Decartes, for example, in his *La dioptrique* presents a little person, looking from out of the darkness at the images on the screen (one's eyes); thus, within every big person, there is, as it were, a little person observing what the eye can see. M. Merleau-Ponty draws our attention to this little person, asking: "Who will see the image painted in the eyes or in the brain? . . . Descartes already sees that we always put a little man in man, that our objectifying view of our own body always obliges us to seek *still further inside* that *seeing man* we thought we had under our eyes. But what he does not see is that the primordial vision that one must indeed come to cannot be *the thought of seeing*" (Merleau-Ponty 1968, 210). To M. Merleau-Ponty, the "world is not what I think, but what I live through (mais ce que je vis)" (Merleau-Ponty 2004, xviii). Thus he criticizes the idea of a little person, calling on us to face the world and see how its poetry unfolds as if without our involvement. This way, one's fate unfolds, and the subject turns from a little person—an observer-voyeur, as it were—into a big person, who, as a poet, opens up to the world by corresponding to everything/everyone that he/she comes into contact with. To that end, one must let the world reveal its beauty, which can be done not by observing it from within one's self, but only by giving one's entire existence to the world and opening up one's internal gaze to it; it is no accident that we often close our eyes during a love act or a creative act.

Punctum, perceived only by internal gaze, represents one's personal sense that motivates (moves) the subject. The nature of such personal sense is non-discursive because it is beyond denomination. However, in spite of, or rather because of this, it can be so effective; the spatiotemporal fabric of experience can be punctured everywhere and everywhen—by anything that causes the subject to (cor)respond to it. Conscience as a response to the call to take care of other beings and being-in-the-world is compunction; it is what one feels with an act of puncture, cf. "con" meaning "with." If one acts without any conscience, one does not feel anything during contact with the Other, the world and, ultimately, oneself. Any act of communication as response-ability is not only a conscious, but also conscientious act.

The subject's acts can be considered response-able when a certain distance exists between one's gaze and everything/everyone that one corresponds to. In reality, the ideal zone of one's external gaze is determined as a correspondence between one's body and what one comes into contact with, or a point of accommodation (Yampol'ski 2001, 30). It seems possible and even necessary, however, to speak about the ideal zone of one's internal gaze, as well, which cannot be determined only in spatial terms because it is filled with time. For this reason, different subjects' gazes can take the form of very different responses to one and the same experience; overall, the most response-able act is one of resignation by which one attempts to bind space and time as far and as deeply as one possibly is able to, displaying humility at communication and also making sure it continues. A responsible act of communication is a binding act; as a result of such an act, the subject is now committed to communication.

At this staging, the subject feels the need for the most conscientious, most responsible consideration of the entire process of communication, in-cluding one's role in this process; according to Aristotle, people who have practical wisdom "possess a faculty of discerning what things are good for themselves and for mankind" (Aristotle 1947, 1140b5). To that end, "the ability to deliberate well is the most characteristic activity of *phrónêsis*" (Aristotle 1947, 1141b2, 12). For one to deliberate well, "phrónêsis must take into consideration where the others are, emotionally, intellectually, and in their skills and attitudes, in trying to find the right thing to do" (Eikeland 2006, 34). At the staging of communication as resignation, one is aware of the gravity of one's decisions, but is also aware that it is time to decide; hence it becomes critical that one deliberate about what is good and expedient. It is important to note that "there is a difference between inquiry and deliberation" (Aristotle 1947, 1141b30).

Phrónêsis is not simply a crafty procedure toward achieving a certain end (cf. *technê*), it is also the ability to reflect upon and decide that end. Thus, at this staging, communication is conceptualized as *phrónêsis*, and "good action itself is its end" (Aristotle 1947, 1140b5). With *phrónêsis* one must "act with regard to the things that are good and bad for man" (Aristotle 1947, 1140b2, 5). Aristotle says that *phrónêsis* is best represented in politics and war; however, "even rhetoric is not restricted to these arenas, but may operate in private spheres" where we are "concerned with things about which we deliberate" (Eikeland 2006, 32). While *technê* is assigned to activities of making, which produce or bring (changes in external) objects into existence, "*phrónêsis* is assigned to praxis or 'doing,' i.e., to activities having their ends and objectives within themselves, as with acts of justice, or more generally with processes of perfection" (Eikeland 2006, 23). Also, it must be noted that, at the staging of communication as conversation, one takes a step toward appreciating the nature of uncertainty or "the noise of time." This makes sense because "what Aristotle called 'phrónêsis,' i.e., the virtue of making practiced practical judgments, is the power to deal with the ambiguity of the concrete" (Caputo 2005, 29). In this light, any symbolic act could be seen as a matter of *phrónêsis*. *Phrónêsis* is enacted in every symbolic act for "it is only when we are confronted by the demand of action *in context of a particular set of* circumstances that we get a true understanding of what our ends really are. . . . Action in the particular cir-cumstances of life is a continuing dialogue between what we think our life is about, and the particularities of moral and practical exigency" (Beiner 1984, 24). Thus, communication is "a continuing dialogue" and so one can see continuity between the stagings of communication as conversation and resignation: communication is still a dialogue, a conversation, but now its moral and practical exigency is brought out to the foreground. It is common to think of communication problems as social or interpersonal exigencies that can be resolved through the artful use of symbolic means (cf. Bitzer 1968). However, any situation of communication is exigent in-sofar as it requires urgent attention and thus *phrónêsis*, which can be seen as a matter of intrapersonal communication, in the first place. From this perspective, every successful action as praxis is a courageous act.

Communication in terms of *phrónêsis* can be viewed as the *timely* use of appropriate means. It is from similar positions that M. Heidegger, while in-terpreting Aristotle's ideas, presents the unfolding of life as "temporalizing" (Heidegger 1992, 368). Also, M. Heidegger makes the connection between *phrónêsis* and *kairos*, noting "how the being which is *kairos* constitutes itself in *phrónêsis*" (Heidegger 1992, 381; cf. Rämö 1999, 313). This connection is reflected in the Russian word "pora" ("пора"), which can be used as an utterance and literally means "(It is) time." This word/utterance is concrete in meaning and denotes getting down to business and doing something urgent that cannot be put off any longer. It is noted that "pora" ("пора") means a response to time's call, a vocation to the moment (Kostetskii 2005, 111). Thus, a kairotic opportunity is "relative to *all* of its attendant temporal circumstances—its occasion, audience, their aims, the constraints of time and place, relevant events and actions, and so on" (Jost 2003, 318).

It is emphasized that *kairos* has "profound connotations of generation" (Carter 1988, 102). To generate (resign) a new meaning, it is not enough to understand an act of communication in terms of quantitative measure, cf. *chronos*. For example, it is noted that "we know exactly how much input from the media it takes to put a new political topic on the public agenda, even to the point of how many articles and TV reports raise the public awareness by how many percentage points" (Donsbach 2006, 444). However, factually doing it, e.g., creating a new news segment is still a matter of not missing the right opening, a matter of *kairos*. In other words, it must be remembered that "*kairos* presupposes *chronos*, which is thus a necessary condition underlying qualitative times, but that, by itself, the *chronos* aspect does not suffice for understanding either specifically historical interpretations or those processes of . . . human experience where the *chronos* aspect reaches certain *critical points* at which a qualitative character begins to emerge" (Smith 2002, 48). Of course, *chronos* and *kairos* are the two sides of the same coin, which is time. When the emphasis is made on the latter, though, it seems—more so than before—that time is running out, so to speak, and one must not miss the moment to act; every action thus must be viewed as momentous. In a previous chapter, communication was metaphorically presented as a process of gathering wood for the fire to be lighted up later when the most burning questions are raised and the most critical steps are taken. It is at the staging of resignation that the decisive resolution of the problem of communication is (attempted to be) found, when the meaning is consummated.

It can be recalled that originally *kairos* referred to physical openings, e.g., in weaving, and so combines the meanings of temporality and spatiality (Stephenson 2009). It signifies, therefore, not simply the timely use of something, but rather "critical points in time and space" (Carter 1988, 102). Thus, toward the end of the staging of communication as resignation, it becomes especially clear that communication is a joint activity of space and time where/when every "critical point" is made in the spatiotemporal continuum of meaningful experiences.

Aristotle considers practical wisdom (*phrónêsis*) and political wisdom to be of the same frame of mind; in this respect, politicians "'do things' as manual labourers 'do things'" (Aristotle 1947, 1141b25). Here, one sees how *phrónêsis* is compared and contrasted with *techné*. Besides, the performative nature of both is clearly highlighted; whether as a technique, cf. the staging of communication as conversation or a decisive act, cf. the staging of communication as resignation, one "does things" with words (or non-verbals). At the staging of communication as resignation, however, "practical wisdom issues commands, since its end is what ought to be done or not to be done" (Aristotle 1947, 1143a5). In this sense, every act of communication, although it may not be preceded by "I hereby," may be viewed as a performative act (cf. Austin 1962).

By the same token, every act of communication at this staging is truly an event, i.e., not simply any incidental occurrence (cf. Durig 1995), but one of significant coincidence, cf. "cō"—"together." It is interesting to point out that the Russian equivalent of "event"—"sobytie" ("событие")—means both "event" (with the emphasis on the second syllable of "событие") and, with the emphasis shifted to the last vowel of "событие," "co-being." It is also interesting to note that, etymologically, the word "event" can be traced back to the root "gwa," which has such meanings as "to arrive," "to come to be," or "a welcome guest" (Morris 1982, 454, 1519). Hence a communicative event is something that comes as a welcome guest, and one must not miss the opportunity to welcome him/her/it.

At this staging, the subject becomes fully aware of the nature of communication as a gift, cf. the Latin root "munia" in the word "communication," which means, among other things, "service performed for the community" and "gift" (Morris 1982, 1528). It was mentioned earlier that "gift" is etymologically related to the word "mania." At this staging, the maniacal view of communication is overcome, and communication comes to be viewed as a gift. Respectively (and respectfully), the subject accepts communication as a gift and also gives oneself as a gift to the process of communication itself. In other words, communication becomes a process of passing one's meanings (oneself) from generation to generation, thus generating communication. In this light, communication is an existential act through which the subject devotes to communication all meanings that one re-signs, i.e., one devotes to communication one's entire life. The more dedicated to communication one's resignation, the more likely communication is to continue.

For experiences to be re-signed, they must be re-membered. In this sense, the subject's "act of self-definition . . . involves responsibility to memory" (Rasch 2000, 140). Memory, therefore, is not only an eternal ontological beginning (Berdyaev 1990), but also an eternal ontological continuation. (In this respect, the growing popularity of the so-called memory studies is not surprising.) Memory as re-membering here is identified not with storage but rather the power to call things to remembrance, cf. Mnemosyne's powers. There are certain speech genres that, by definition, are infused with memory through and through, cf. autobiography, considered by some to be the highest form of communication (see: Radford 2005, 163–164). In this light, a memoir is treated as "a temporal manifold as well as a linear temporality . . . , a story punctuated by acts of retrospection and projection" (Struever 2004, 428). Here the "focus on timefullness is the devotion that fuels and disseminates the practices of memory" (Struever 2004, 438). It is important to note that such forms of communication describe meaningful experiences which are presented as singular. In other words, "the memoir is not an exemplum. The life is not exemplary, it is not presented for imitation; the isolation topos defines the speaker's relation to the reader as well: the inimitable nature suggests the need for the reader's own apt, revisionary effort" (Struever 2004, 428); in other words, it highlights the nature of communication as re-signation. Such forms of communication are the most intimate genres because, in them, the subject shares one's fate with everyone/everything insofar as it is possible, taking this risk and showing how one corresponds to oneself and thus to communication, in general. In a way, "this risk and commitment essentially means that one lives the future with a willingness to reconfigure the past" (Smith 1993, 239). In this sense, one can say that "communication . . . is sooner a matter of faith and risk that of technique and method" (Peters 1999, 30). How successfully the subject overcomes this risk and how faithfully the subject's autobiography or memoir shows this correspondence to everyone/everything, we can usually tell—or rather re-tell.

The Proteism of Communication

So, at this staging, it becomes clear that the creative nature of communication cannot be revealed without the subject's imagination, conscience, and devotion: only this way can one correspond to/with communication and thus oneself. Anyone can be viewed as a poet, or a (co)creator of meaning, as long as one's actions take the form of re-signation. It should be emphasized that, for experiences to be meaningful, the subject must engage in communication as a creative process; nothing makes sense unless re-signed. The subject's role in that process should not be overrated, though; the subject does not "make sense"; rather, something makes sense, revealing—with the subject's help—its meaning. Any creative act of communication thus is a revelation.

As revelation, communication at this staging is similar to what C. Jung described as a visionary mode. The visionary mode of artistic creation is personal in nature, unlike the psychological mode, which is collective. The experiences expressed through the latter mode are drawn from human consciousness and always within the realm of the understandable, while the former derives its existence from the hinterland of the unconscious—something "out there." The latter mode is closer to the staging of communication as construction while the former taps into the depths of the archetypes of the collective unconscious and is a higher mode of creation, clearly belonging to the staging of communication as resignation. The visionary mode is an experience emerging "from the abyss of the prehuman ages . . . , which surpasses man's understanding and *to which in his weakness he may easily succumb*" (Jung 1993, 90; emphasis mine). In other words, one can reach the visionary mode not by force, but only through a weakness, resigning (to) the experiences that can never be completely understood and therefore constructed at the conscious level.

So, at this staging of communication, the subject is an artist, operating or rather living, to this or that degree, in the visionary mode, trying to look beyond communication and resigning (to) its primordial flow. As a visionary, the subject's look beyond communication must be understood, of course, figuratively: this look can be seen as punctum, mentioned earlier. This internal gaze, however, fills up one's entire existence, bridging the depths and the surface of communication. In this respect, the subject as a poet—a (co) creator of meaning—is one who looks beyond communication by sensing it with one's entire existence, by trying to be(come) communication.

Meaning is created (re-signed) at the very limit of communicability, at the edge of the abyss, as it were. In this sense, a person acts as a poet inspired by the Muses and calling things to remembrance; in Plato's words, "without the madness that is the gift of the Muses, a man will be no more than a poet manqué" (*Phaedrus* 245a) (see: Naddaf 2007, 330). One tries to bridge this abyss with one's entire existence, or all meaningful experiences (to) which one resigned. This transcendental step is extremely dangerous because (re-signed) "meaning is a gamble. It comes belatedly, if at all" (Peters 2005, 178). In other words, in every act of resignation, one blinks one's internal eye, so to speak; during this ("abysmal") interval anything can happen. One, for the time being, lets communication be(come) what it will. At this staging, "the slightest split second can be a potential portal through which the Messiah can come" (Peters 2005, 63), or it may be(come) the last second of one's existence. That is why this staging is so critical in communication; what is at stake here is one's fate—and communication's continuation.

At the staging of communication as resignation, one becomes aware of the nature of communication, not as a transfer of a message through space, but rather as an attempt to carry it on in time; to put it another way, communication can now be conceptualized as initiation. In this respect, an act of communication as re-signation during "the present moment is an open door for any fresh departure" (Peters 2005, 63). Communication as initiation is impossible without imagination (cf. Lanigan 1995), transcending any constraints; here an act of communication is a springboard to new meanings. This staging of communication is one where/when meanings are created, or conceived. At this staging, "we are sites of transcendence, concernful openings of space and time, articulate clearings of care over that world" (Anton 2002, 202). Earlier, while discussing the staging of communication as conversation, H.-G. Gadamer's *Spielraum* was mentioned as a figurative room to play or a clearance in the form of temporal distance. At the staging of communication as resignation, everyone becomes an articulate clearing—one through whom/what communication itself is expressed.

The initiation of meaning should be viewed in (temporal) terms of "proto" rather than "post," cf. postmodernism. "Proto" expresses the idea of new beginnings and open possibilities. The staging of communication as resignation is that of proteism (cf. Epshtein 2004; Stepanov 2005) where/when the highly dynamic nature of communication borders on the illusionary. This staging of communication, therefore, can be identified with modernism rather than postmodernism because, at this staging, "all that is solid melts into air" (Berman 1983). In this sense, "to be modern is to live a life of paradox and contradiction. It is to be . . . alive to new possibilities for experiences and adventures, frightened by nihilistic depths to which so many modern adventures lead, *longing to create and to hold on to something real even as everything melts*" (Berman 1983, 13–14; emphasis mine). The meanings that are created at this staging oscillate in all directions like waves and are thus perceived as the most immediately present wherever/whenever they reach out. In this sense, for example, Shakespeare's works are modern because they have resonated with any period throughout the centuries and still correspond to today's times. Shakespeare is perceived as (every)one's contemporary because his work bridges the gap with meaning so successfully.

So, the moment of communication is always an interval—a gap to be bridged by one's creative act of re-signation. This gap has a highly dynamic and illusionary nature, appearing as a surface upon which communication is (being) played out. At the staging of communication as conversation, its surface took the form of the looking-glass; yet, the focus was still clearly on the Other. The staging of communication as resignation might be compared to M. Duchamp's *The Large Glass* where "the surface palpitates, signs appear and disappear, yet we cannot tell whether this takes place in fictive depth or on the real surface" (Greenberg 1993, 8). In other words, although it appears transparent, this "Glass" captures meaning if only for a period of time—if only for a moment (Yampolski 2001, 25). M. Duchamp's *Glass*, then, should be understood not as a completely transparent surface, devoid of time, but as an act of prolongation of meaning. This is exactly what takes place at this staging of communication where/when meaning is captured in the creative act of prolongation. Here communication overall can be seen as "The Large Glass," oscillating in such a way that its depth and surface become almost indistinguishable. In the creative act of communication, meaning glimmers, and one can scare it away or wait for its revelation too long; in other words, one can rush where angels fear to tread, or one can delay meaning, which then equals death. Or, one can let meaning glimmer, grow through oneself—and capture it at the right moment. If meaning is captured at the right moment, then prolongation equals life.

While discussing communication as a creative act of resignation, one can recall Proteus—the prophetic god that can see through the depths of the sea as he tends the flocks of Poseidon. Proteus would assume every possible shape to escape the necessity of prophesying; however, once someone could get hold of him and Proteus saw that his endeavors were of no avail, he would foretell the future. A parallel can be drawn between the figures of Proteus and Hermes; both used their prophetic powers only if pushed to the limit—if caught (Proteus) or asked the right question (Hermes). Then, they would tell the truth, and the way to the future would be marked. Proteus can be viewed as the counterpart of Hermes, only his domain is more fluid and illusionary.

Thus, at some point in time, Proteus tells the truth, or becomes sincere. Communication at this staging is successful on the condition of its sincerity. The sincerity condition (cf. one of the felicity conditions in speech act theory) might appear vague. However, its nature is quite simple: an act of communication is sincere if it re-signs, or generates new meanings by inspiring others to carry them on. In a word, sincere communication is inspiring communication. There can be no new (re-signed) meaning without a spark of inspiration; this point becomes very clear by turning to the Russian word for "sincerity"—"iskrennost'" ("искренность")—where "iskra" ("искра") means "a spark." Every act of communication is aimed at meeting the condition of sincerity as it generates, to various degrees, a spark of inspiration. It can be noted that the word "sincerity" is derived from the Latin *sincērus*, meaning "clean," "pure," "genuine"; its root "*ker*" means "to cause to grow" (Morris 1982, 1208, 1522). So, a sincere act of communication is supposed to be characterized by purity; the purer one's intentions, the more likely the meanings so conceived are to grow and continue.

Thus, communication cannot be considered successful unless the sincerity condition is met. In the theory of the universal pragmatics, developed by J. Habermas, one of the claims is redeemed not discursively, but through action. In this light, the sincerity condition can be met only through one's resignation, or corresponding at every point of one's life to communication, as such. To put it simply, one must perform all actions, i.e., live one's life oneself. This way, one's vocation is revealed as a response to the call that manifested itself at the staging of communication as invocation. Everyone's vocation is different, of course: one responds to communication by be(com)ing a doctor, another one—a carpenter, etc. However, it is everyone's common fate to (cor) respond to communication by be(com)ing what one cannot help be(com)ing.

So, communication at this staging takes the form of response-ability. In this sense, communication is something that never leaves one; similar to Ch. S. Peirce's dynamic object, "it is something that urges us to speak or at least turns our attention to it" (Farronato 2003, 194). The nature of communication at this staging, therefore, consists in one's response-ability to something that allows and calls for one's correspondence; every response to it is an act of resignation. Thus, at this staging, a time comes for one to respond to the call of communication, re-signing (to) it. What was but a faint (enfolded) call at the staging of communication as invocation is now heard more loudly—if only by the internal punctum. In other words, it is now unfolded and must be answered in the creative act of resignation.

The Author Is Dead—
Long Live the Author!

At the staging of communication as resignation, its creative potential becomes especially clear, including, first of all, the nature of language. One fails to become aware of the creative potential of language if one views it as a seemingly external and immutable system; it is here that the roots of communication apprehension can be found. However, once one becomes aware of the highly dynamic nature of language, which reveals its profound meanings, it becomes clear that language is not one's enemy, but rather an ally—a benevolent means of communication. From this perspective, language is perceived as a living entity, generating communication. In this sense, it is important not to treat language as an instrument, using up its resources; rather, we are all indebted to language and must constantly repay our debt to it in every act of resignation of meaning, including the creation of new signs, cf. the ideas of semiurgy (Epstein 2008). That is why "Thrice blessed is he, who introduces a name into a song" (Osip Mandel'shtam). For example, Shakespeare and Pushkin are thrice blessed because, to a large degree, it is their languages that are spoken by the Engligh-speaking and Russian-speaking cultures, respectively. At the same time, everyone is at least once blessed for, through one's very life, one re-signs communication. One's life, whatever it may be, is meaningful insofar as it makes a difference. Overall, one's entire life can be viewed as one whole utterance, one prolongated act of creativity by which one participates in communication, be(com)ing its part.

The creative character of communication is revealed best of all in the so-called language of art. However, language in general, in any of its manifestations, can be viewed as the "language of art" (Heidegger 1971); every act of communication, to a degree, is an aesthetic act when one feels the beauty of the creation of meaning. In this sense, writing a beautiful poem, giving a beautiful lecture, and making a beautiful chair are all examples of aesthetic communication.

Similar to language of art and aesthetic communication, the concept of the subject should be treated in the broadest possible—bordering on metaphysical—sense, i.e., as anything taking in itself, and resigning (to), communication experiences. In this sense, the role of a person, as the subject, should not be overrated because meanings are created not so much by people, but by time into which one is thrown and which one cannot help expressing. From this point of view, the essence of language is made up by/of time, and any fight for the purity of language is a losing battle; it is in the nature of language, as subject to time, to change in every act of re-signation. It is impossible to make language pure, transparent; one must look at/into language as a glass where meanings glimmer, revealing themselves only in the creative act of prolongation. Not surprisingly, poets understand the temporal nature of language best of all. Thrice blessed for introducing a name into a song, they are aware of the illusionary character of their copyright. They understand that the author dies in every act of creation; in other words, it is not so much the individual author that creates meanings, but rather language on the whole, infused with time, cf. "What I am saying now is being said not by me" (Osip Mandel'shtam). In this light, "language is not a tool used by an individual to deliver messages; rather, language is a universe in which individuals (addresses) emerge when called" (Rasch 2000, 70).

Thus, people become free only thanks to/through language. One can say that people are spoken, sentenced (uttered) to creative freedom. That is why one should treat language, not as an instrument, but as the author. The other side of the so-called death of (the individual subject as) the author is the "birth of (language as) the author." The author is dead—long live the author! In this respect, one should speak about language ability as the creative aspect of language, as such. Language ability is a constant search for new ways of resignation of meaning, for what (else) language is able to say. In this light, "words often understand themselves better than do those who use them" (Schlegel 1971, 260). The so-called feeling of language, therefore, is not so much how well one uses language, but rather how well language can reveal one's meaningful experiences. It is interesting to note that the names of certain fields of study can be understood in two ways; for example, "communication studies" and "memory studies" can mean not only the areas of study with their own object of investigation, but also the study of people themselves by communication or memory.

Thus, one's experiences become meaningful through language. Of course, one always deals with specific texts as one resigns meaning because every text harbors "a contradiction between what it says but does not know and what it knows but cannot say" (Chang 1996, xiv). It is out of this contradiction or gap that re-signed meanings emerge.

So, language, as a whole, can be viewed as a measure of one's correspondence to everything/everyone that one comes into contact with. Here this measure is pushed to the outer edges of communication and often can be found in its nano elements, as it were. In this respect, it becomes clear why "modernity is marked by an interest in small units of time. . . . We no longer live in the continuous, analog, infinitesimal universe dreamed of by nineteenth-century luminaries. . . . Ours is one of quanta, bits, and digits, a world jagged and fractally stepwise at the lowest—at all—levels of analysis" (Peters 2006, 149). It is interesting to note that, according to Aristotle, "practical wisdom . . . is concerned with a man himself—with the individual" (Aristotle 1947, 1141b25). Elsewhere, he says that "practical wisdom is . . . concerned with the ultimate particular" (Aristotle 1947, 1142a20). One can view such "ultimate particulars" (including "a man himself") as the smallest units that make up the focus of attention in modernity. In this sense, *phrónêsis* and Self clearly belong to the staging of communication as resignation.

Applied to communication, this interest can be found in the smallest, most seemingly insignificant signs. For example, the Hebrew of the Torah privileges the oral form of communication, and it is the responsibility of the reader to add vowels to roots; otherwise, no meaning can be formed. As the reader, in effect, creates meaning, "*small variation* in vowels can produce very disparate meanings from the same root" (Russell 2005, 133; emphasis mine). Thus, vowels as the "souls of the letters" (Russell 2005, 133) are literally breathed into communication, creating meaning. In Russian, the word for "consonants" is "soglasnye" ("согласные")—literally "agreeable or agreeing with," while the word for "vowels" is "glasnye" ("гласные")—literally "voiced/full of voice." In this light, communication cannot be reduced only to "consonants," or the complete identity of meaning; communication calls for "vowels," or one's voice—a breathing life that manifests itself in re-signation. One is creative, resigning (to) communication, if one can supply one's voice (read: life) to an otherwise lifeless order made up of "agreeable consonants." Again, it is at the lowest level that one finds language capable of generating the most significant meanings; it is no accident that such auxiliary, seemingly unimportant words are found at the top of the lists in frequency dictionaries, cf. prepositions, articles, or link verbs.

Communication as a process of creative activity is characterized, at the same time, by a certain degree of passivity; the subject of communication is subject to meaning, cf. the concept of passibilité proposed by J.-L. Nancy (1997). In this sense, one is "passible" to communication, suffering or undergoing the event of meaning, cf.: "Passibilité, not unlike the Kantian notion of receptivity, which, as such, includes a certain 'creativity,' is then defined as the capacity of being affected" (Raffoul 1997, xviii). Passibilité as creative, expressive receptivity is a crucial part of communication, revealed most fully at its staging as resignation. Actively fighting passibilité does not do anyone—and thus communication overall—any good.

Of course, it is not easy to admit that one's active role in communication should not be overrated, cf. the following critical comment on H.-G. Gadamer's work: "this formidable contemporary thinker has a disconcerting habit of presenting what theorists of social cognition regard as active attribution processes in the passive voice. So, we 'are led,' meaning 'speaks itself through us,' and so forth" (Farrell 1987, 128). In the same vein, S. Freud, despite being Viennese, is said to have been incapable of enjoying music, cf.: "Some rationalistic, or perhaps analytic, turn of my mind in me rebels against being moved by a thing without knowing why I am thus affected and what it is that affects me" (Gottlieb 2007, 16).

Still, one cannot be in complete control of meaning, affecting it any way one chooses; one is also affected by meaning, suffering or undergoing its event. The more actively one tries to become conscious of meaning, the less "passible" to communication one becomes. Communication is impossible (and "impassible") without the so-called tacit knowledge, which has many roots, including empathy and indwelling (Polanyi 1966). It can be said that "communication works . . . only because there is this tacit dimension. *We can only know what we know by not knowing why we know what we know*" (Thayer 1997, 13). Also, parallels can be drawn between M. Polanyi's "tacit knowledge" and A. Giddens's "practical consciousness" as well as M. Johnson's "non-propositional meanings" (see: Krippendorff 2009, 83). In this light, communication calls for one's creative humility, i.e., re-signation. According to Ch. S. Peirce, "the self-centered self is an analytical force. Such a self rests upon the most vulgar delusion of vanity" (Colapietro 1989, 96). The "true self can emerge only when the futile ego dissolves . . ." through "the most complete surrender of egoism" (Colapietro 1989, 96). The true self that emerges at this staging strives toward be(com)ing one with communication, though feeling and imagination.

To Be and Not to Be

Communication as re-signation is an act of one's be(com)ing in contact with the entire world of one's experiences. This contact or being-with-the-world is nothing but the manifestation of one's creative humility; for example, the Russian word for "humility"—"smirenie" ("смирение")—literally means "with-the-world." Thus, this staging of communication is "rather like the contact I have with the universe" (Peters 1999, 152).

Being in touch should be understood, first of all, in the literal sense—as one being in physical contact with another one or others. Such tactility presupposes one's tactful concern for anyone/anything that one comes into contact with, i.e., those that one touches/is touched by; not surprisingly, tactility and tactfulness have the same root. Touch as contact is an act of communication performed with (cf. "con") tact, hence "con-tact." Communication as a tactile act is one's be(com)ing in physical contact—in touch—with someone/something. For such an act to be successful, one must rely on—literally rest upon—or trust those one comes into contact with; a love act is a good example of tactile communication where/when bodies literally touch each other, i.e., rely/rest upon each other. In such an act, the intimate nature of communication is revealed most fully. One wishes for the meaningful experience of this act to never end, to continue on and on, to be prolongated as far as possible. It is noted that a woman's breasts can be viewed as the most erogenous and resilient part of the body: one wants the breasts to never lose their elasticity, feeling and caressing them (Epstein 2006, 50). By the same token, a creative act is the most erogenous and resilient act of communication.

Any creative act of communication is a love act because in it meaning is conceived. One can speak about tactility not only in the literal (corporeal) sense, but also in the figurative sense—as any creative touch leading to the generation of meaning. One is in touch with reality if this act—corporeal or not—sparks a flame, which one craves and fears, at the same time; in every creative act of communication, Eros and Tanatos are inseparable, touching each other, as it were.

So, any meaningful experience that touches us can be viewed in terms of tactility; we not only touch each other physically, we touch each other semiotically. In this respect, communication can continue long after the disappearance of the physical bodies of those who had created its meanings. For example, it is said that Shakespeare created the modern person (Bloom 1999); as a result, each of us is, in a very small part, Shakespeare. At the same time, Shakespeare, as a sign, lives in each of us; this way, meanings are carried on, constantly re-signed. It is this never ending process of communication as contact of signs that Ch. S. Peirce called "unlimited semiosis" (see: Merrell 1997).

Thus, communication at this staging can also be conceptualized as contact or touch. In this light, the creation of meaning occurs at the outer edges of communication, so to speak, cf. the skin of one's body or the sign vehicle (representamen). It is commonly believed that the true meaning can be found only in the depths of communication; consequently, the surface of communication is usually viewed with disdain or disregarded (Epstein 2006, 133–134). However, all deep meanings must come up to the surface so that communication as contact can take place. Communication is a superficial process in that it takes place on the surface; yet, its superficialness is profound. Every act of communication as touch can be seen as a message "To Whom It May Concern." In Russian, this expression literally says "To All It Touches"—"Vsem, kogo eto kasaetsya" ("Всем, кого это касается"). Thus, by definition, communication is a process that touches everyone/everything.

As mentioned earlier, at the staging of communication as resignation, the oscillations of meaning are highly dynamic; to make the right decision and act, one must span large distances between Self and everyone/everything else very quickly. Small variation in expressive means can create significant, and significantly disparate, meanings. Overall, communication here appears as a large glass where/when the difference between the depth and the surface almost disappears; communication thus reveals even more its illusionary character. The creation of meaning, therefore, always appears, to a degree, as an act of the illusionist/illusionary. Similar to R. Magritte's paintings, which are seen as "an exercise in suggesting what reality lacks in order to become itself" (Roudaut 2003, 37), communication is but a playful initiation for reality to become meaningful. The root of the word "illusion" is "ludus" ("play"), and, indeed, at this staging of communication, its playful nature can be seen best of all. One can say that, at this stage, *Homo Homini Ludus Est*: a man is not a wolf to his fellow men but rather a playful creature.

Thus, the nature of communication at this staging predominantly consists in the play of imagination. Imagination is inherent to communication because "I never feel how you feel; I can only feel how *I imagine* I would feel if I were you" (Peters 2005, 117; emphasis mine). Here meaning is partly real, cf. real numbers, and partly imagined, cf. imaginary numbers, associated with time (Marks-Tarlow 2005, 53). It is through imagination that experiences are (playfully) made or rather created meaningful. Earlier, it was mentioned that communication was still not complex enough because it was too empirically grounded or too constrained by in the reality of a world order. At this staging, an act of communication can be viewed as a complex number (cf. Mamardashvili 1997, 32).

At the staging of communication as resignation, meaning reveals its fractal nature, cf. fractals' quality of being between the real and the imaginary (Marks-Tarlow 2005, 53). This way, every participant tries to maintain one's self-identity, while (cor)responding to the entire process of communication. The most stable form of such correspondence is represented by the Golden ratio—the fraction that never repeats itself and never ends. The closer one's act, as the event or the moment of communication, comes to the Golden ratio, the more momentous it is; such an act makes it possible for communication to continue longer. At this staging, it becomes clear that any attempted closure in one's contact with the world is impossible; what is supposed to be a period turns out to be but another comma.

Everyone—through one's actions—turns out to be closer or further away from the Golden ratio. Any act is a break (a fracture) in the living fabric of communication, a distinction drawn by one within oneself (cf. Spencer-Brown 1979; Rasch 2005, 15). This "originary" distinction, conceptualized in this book as an opening between space and time, can be viewed as an open wound, as it were, where/when communication "passes." It can only be hoped that one feels this fraction while undergoing meaning.

That the fractal (character of the) subject at this staging of communication must not be equated with J. Baudrilliard's fractal subject, "which—instead of transcending into a finality beyond itself—is diffracted into a multitude of identical minaturized egos, multiplying in an embryonic mode as in a biological culture, and completely saturating its environment through an infinite process of scissiparity" (Baudrilliard 1988, 40). Unlike this subject who dreams of reproducing oneself into infinity, the subject at this staging is concerned with communication overall. It should be noted that "fractals point the way to the invisible, interconnected ground of all being" (Marks-Tarlow 2005, 61). The nature of communication as such ground is discussed in detail in the next chapter.

Although communication at this staging is conceptualized as the play of imagination, it should not be viewed as an easy and trivial process. In fact, here one undergoes the most serious trial when every moment of communication represents a momentous decision. An act of resignation is the most intense moment of communication, and all subjects can tolerate this tension to various degrees. It is as if one holds a meaningful pause; it is called "meaningful" because, as a result of it, meaning is generated. Communication overall can be seen as nothing but one unending pause, "waiting for Godot" (S. Beckett). Sooner or later, however, everyone resigns (to) communication; in a manner of speaking, everyone interrupts the Golden ratio (read: Self) and steps into the flame of communication. The range of oscillations of meaning depends on how far (out there) one's response-ability to/for communication reaches. Indeed, the key question at this point—"a question at once philosophical, moral, and political—is how wide and deep our empathy for otherness can reach" (Peters 1999, 230).

The horizon of meaning, therefore, is formed by the Golden ratio with its never repeating itself and never-ending line of points or moments of communication. At this staging of communication, it becomes clear that one can only keep moving toward this horizon; the fusion of horizons can be reached only in the transcendental and partly irrational creative act of re-signation.

The staging of communication as resignation can be viewed as facticity with its real and imagined character. "Despite the emergence and dominance of empiricism and positivism, and thus the model of empirical factuality, the words *fact* and *facticity* have retained a wealth of meaning that should be kept in mind in interpreting their significance" (Raffoul and Nelson 2008, 2). Facts are commonly treated as something objective, having real and demonstrable existence; in this sense, facts cannot be empirical and are associated with the data gathered in various concrete situations. The staging of communication as conversation, described in the present book earlier, deals with facts. "Facticity," meanwhile, retains the original meaning of "the Roman *factum*, which is not an assertion about nature, but primarily associated with human activity and production. . . . Giambattista Vico continued to use the word in this sense in the principle of *verum factum* ('the true is made')" (Raffoul and Nelson 2008, 2). Communication, while its roots are certainly empirically grounded, is partly (poetically) created in the act of resignation. It must also be remembered that the Latin *factum* is derived from *factus*, which is the past participle of *facere*, "to do," and means "a deed" (Morris 1982, 469). The act of resignation, indeed, is a deed, i.e., not only something that exists objectively, but also—more importantly—something created, i.e., a step taken, a truth partly made, a meaning re-signed.

Thus, communication at the staging of communication as resignation reveals its nature as a highly creative and intense process when the gap between one and everyone/everything that one (cor)responds to seems to be bridged. However, it only seems so, i.e., it is partly an illusion. Communication as a process of sending and receiving messages is nothing but "the illusion that no time elapsed between sending and receiving" (Peters 2008, 150). Earlier, communication was discussed as a process that concerns/touches everyone; but, even the physical (let alone semiotic) "touch is an illusion stemming from one's organs' insensitivity to the microscopic but infinite distances between bodies and the even greater chasms between souls" (Peters 1999, 178). Communication, therefore, appears at this staging as a virtual process when every meaningful experience seems to be the most immediate and the most real one. At this staging, "the experience of our body reveals to us an ambiguous mode of existence" (Merleau-Ponty 2004, 230). Here one learns what it means to live with "as if," what it means to be and not to be, at the same time. In a similar sense, it seems, T. Adorno writes about the necessity of coming to terms with the fact that "the transcendent is, and it is not" (Adorno 1973, 375).

The roots of communication as a virtual process can be found at the staging of communication as conversation with its mirrorlike nature, e.g., in the ideas of the early symbolic interactionsists who refereed "to the 'as if' behavior of social actors in an attempt to define the future reference of conduct. The potential virtuality of social behaviors thus comes to the fore" (Grant 2003a, 116). Similarly, it is possible to state that "Cooley's social reality is already virtual reality. With the looking-glass self comes the looking-glass other" (Peters 1999, 187). Of course, the phenomenon of virtual communication is first of all identified with electronic technologies. However, "one can question whether the phenomenon of virtuality is itself electronic, whether computation or communication networks are intrinsic to the virtual" (Rotman 2008, 111). In fact, "virtuality is ancient. Far from being tied to contemporary electronic technologies, its lineage long antedates its current technological matrix" (Rotman 2008, 112). Virtuality should be viewed as an inherent part of communication, most prominently coming to the forefront at this staging. Every intense moment of the creation of meaning (re-signation) is an example of virtual communication. In such moments, one's consciousness is altered, as it were, cf. the so-called altered states of consciousness, often induced by certain drugs and characteristic of creative personalities. It seems as if, in such extreme situations of communication, one's creative thought overcomes space and catches up with time, reaching the singular point of the fusion of horizons. This way, a subject becomes everyone else's contemporary, cf. "con" meaning "with"; for example, Shakespeare is the most virtual author considered a contemporary by numerous generations of readers over the centuries because he was able to capture and express the ideas (read: time itself, or so it seems) that have touched millions and millions of people.

As a virtual process, communication is addictive: one feels drawn to its generative power, trying to reach that singular meaning the way one tries to reach the horizon, resigning (to) communication in every creative act. At this staging of communication, one cannot help the gravity of one's thought. The gravity of one's creative mind is more powerful that the gravity of this Earth for the former can overcome the latter, and one can leave this Earth for the outer space and boldly go to places once only imagined. In this sense, virtuality turns out to be more important than reality itself.

Thus, communication reveals its virtual nature as the play of imagination. It can be recalled that earlier communication was presented in terms of language games. Unlike the word "game," used as a countable noun and presupposing a set of rules to be followed, the word "play," which carries such extra meanings as "risking" and "pledging" (Morris 1982, 1005), is a collective noun, denoting something continuous and never-ending—like the Golden ratio or the horizon. Virtual communication should be understood in this very meaning of continuously unfolding play.

So, virtual communication can be viewed as a process when reality constantly turns as a gem playing with all its facets. In this play new meanings are constantly created (re-signed). The real virtual—if such an oxymoron is allowed—communication is such play in which one (the player) both knows and does not know who he/she is and what exactly might happen in the next moment; one acts as if drawn by the gravity of one's creative mind, resigning (to) communication. A good example of such communication is found in the phenomenon of the so-called flow (cf. Csikszentmihalyi 1990). In such moments, it seems as if everything happens by itself, and one is but a fluid facet of communication, playing with, and played by, its flow. It is interesting to note that the staging of conversation was earlier presented as a process of navigating the currents of communication; at the staging of resignation, practical decisions (cf. *phrónêsis*) are crucial, and here one needs a spark of imagination with a touch of (creative) irrationality. Only this way can one go with the flow. One cannot "go with the current"—only with the flow. Also, successful communication at this staging means acting at the right moment; in other words, "trust in virtual communication somehow contains a sense of phrónêsis, and of kairos" (Rämö 1999, 321).

The Present of the World

Thus, communication at this staging reveals its most decisive, extreme, one might say, critical moments. Not surprisingly, this staging can be conceptualized in terms of the so-called critical theories of communication. Such theories by definition are critical of, and call for, changing the existing order of things. In this sense, they are quite revolutionary, seeing communication as "the theatre of struggle" (Hall 1989). With their active thrust, such theories seem to be more appropriate for the explanation of the staging of communication as construction; their authors seem to know how to build the perfect world and so provide a guide for action to that end. That is why, perhaps, such theories are aimed at exposing the pathologies of communication, for example, in the form of dominant ideologies.

The so-called postmodern theories of communication are developed in the same vein, taking the deconstructive view to its extreme. According to such views, communication is equated with the erasure of meanings. In J. Derrida's "différance," which has a reference to both spatiality (being apart) and temporality (action put off) (Derrida 1973, 82), one can see an attempt to get rid of (the difference between) space and time.

Strange as it may seem, in order to explain the creative nature of communication more adequately, critical theories must become even more critical, while postmodern theories must become even more radical. In other words, "the norms should not be abandoned, but instead be radicalized and redeemed" (Peters 2005, 179). In this light, communication can be best conceptualized by performative theories. The performative roots of communication can be found at the staging of conversation where participants present themselves to each other. One can say that, at the staging of communication as conversation, participants are warming up to their parts; at the staging of communication as resignation, one must play one's part to the fullest, in earnest, with dedication, (cor)responding in each performance to those with whom/what one has come into contact and so resigning (to) those experiences. This understanding of communication as performance is expressed well by the verb "to render." It should be noted that its etymology includes such semantic components as "to (re)turn" and "to give back" (Morris 1982, 1101). This is exactly what happens when one performs (re-signs) communication; one attempts to express oneself, giving oneself back to those who/what made one's act of communication (read: one's life) possible, i.e., to communication, as such. It is no accident that virtuality is said to exist as performance (Openkov 1997, 32).

Communication as performance—in the sense of rendition—is always a creative act; rendition is identified with distinctiveness. In other words, one performs communication the way a musician performs music—in one's own way. In the act of performance, one is all by oneself and also, at the same time, together ("in touch"), or a contemporary, with the entire process of communication. In such moments, one performs communication as if its very continuation depended upon how one renders (resigns to) it. In this respect, it is essential that the well-known Golden Rule, emphasizing sameness, be supplemented with the "gem component," emphasizing difference, i.e., one's uniqueness and distinctiveness. The Golden-Gem Rule thus takes the following form: "Do that which anyone including yourself could wish and no one else but you could do" (Epshtein 2004, 759). In other words, in communication one must do everything oneself. Indeed (in-every-deed), "we should act as if our choices shape the universe" (Peters 1999, 156), as if the fate of the entire communication universe depended upon our performance.

In this respect, it can be noted that, according to M. Heidegger, "to be a self is to be the temporal openness of truth in which beings can be revealed. To be a self in the most suitable way is to be wholly open to those possibilities which are uniquely one's own" (quoted in Zimmerman 1981, 31). It can also be mentioned that "this sense of the uniqueness of the existential moment is not thematized by Mead" (Malhotra 1987, 377), which points to another difference between the stagings of ommunication as resignation and conversation.

Thus, everyone renders or re-signs (to) communication as creatively as one possibly—and "passibly"—can. While everyone tries to perform it as best as possible, no one can predict, or tell ahead of time when or if one's wishes will come true. All one can—and must—do at this staging is to perform communication as creatively and lovingly as possible—with devotion bordering on the irrational. The staging of communication as resignation is when wishes are rendered; whether and how they will be carried out/on depends upon how faithfully they are performed.

Every act of communication at this staging, then, is an act of rendition when meanings are created (re-signed). For example, conceptual artists create works of art into which a singular thing is inserted as a metaphysical sign with its signifier becoming its signified (Epshtein 2001, 225). However, everyone can be viewed as a conceptual artist because everyone, like a singular thing into an installation, installs oneself, one's entire life, into the very process of communication. In this light, communication is an act "of guiding one's body into discourse . . . the insertion of agency—wound and bow, death and life—into discourse" (Bhabha 1994, 184). Here one finally becomes aware of the nature of communication as a process of bricolage when everything is at hand, so to speak, and the last missing part is oneself. In this (cont)act, one resigns (to) communication; such a self-transcendental act is an essential part of communication as resignation.

Communication at this staging reveals its nature as creative inscription. This "is a doubly inscribed designation . . . it is the . . . 'split' subject that articulates, with the greatest intensity, the disjunction of time and being" (Bhabha 1994, 214). Thus, the main gap one has to bridge now is one between Self and Self. This way, one takes the most radical transcendental step one can—the step beyond oneself and into the fire of communication. In taking this step into the fire of communication "one is not supposed to anticipate the response, only to act" (Peters 1999, 61). Only this way can the universe of communication be (trans)formed. Otheriwse, "how is it that we become available to a transformation of who we are . . . if we demand, in advance, to know that, as subjects, we are intact, uneroded, uncontested, presupposed, and necessary?" (Butler 1995, 131). This self-transcendental step toward the metaphysical "out there" is crucial because "what is 'outside' is not simply the Other—the 'not me'—but a notion of futurity—the 'not yet'—and these constitute the defining limit of the subject itself" (Butler 1995, 142–143).

It is often noted that with postmodernity the very process of becoming seems to come to an end (Merrell 1995, 267). It is also noted that time does not seem to have any relation to one's active experience, which turns into an ever-present spatiality (Jameson 1998). Thus, it is common to view postmodernism as "the historical moment that is paradigmatically 'about' spatiality (as opposed to a rigidly linear temporality), as a host of theorists (Innis, Jameson, Giddens, Harvey, Lefebre, Baudrillard, Soja, Foucault, Gregory, and others) have argued" (Cavell 2002, 7). In this light, virtual communication is often called cyberspace. However, it only seems that space pushed time out of communication, as it were; communication moves (takes place) so quickly that time is barely felt, i.e., one factually fails to feel it. As mentioned earlier, communication at this staging reveals its most dynamic character; here any distance can be overcome given enough time, and often it takes but a split second. Significantly, it is noted that "the notions of virtual communication . . . could . . . be characterized as . . . based on human right moments to act judiciously in an abstract 'virtual' space . . . that no longer 'take place'—only time" (Rämö 1999, 321). Thus, cyberspace can be viewed as one more unsuccessful attempt made by space to conquer time; virtual communication, therefore, should be treated as cybertime rather than cyberspace.

By the same token, it might appear as if time (finally!) conquers space, what with the new communication technologies that seem to instantaneously create an effect of presence. It is noted that

> contemporary communication technologies have doubtlessly come close to fulfilling the dream of omnipresence, which is *the dream* of making lived experience independent of the locations that our bodies occupy in space . . . the more we approach the fulfillment of our dreams of omnipresence and the more definite the subsequent loss of our bodies and of the spatial dimension in our existence *seems to be*, the greater the possibility becomes of reigniting the desire that attracts us to the things of the world. (Gumbrecht 2004, 139; emphasis mine)

In other words, the meaningful gap between space and time at the staging of communication as resignation—as all the other stagings—only seems to be bridged; if there were no gaps, no meaning would be generated. The difference between them is simply barely noticeable or rather it is factually unnoticeable as long as communication is resigned in loving and creative acts, which border on the illusionary and transcendental. At this staging, communication must be conceptualized, not as "différance," but "deference," or actions full of respect and concern for communication. In the etymology of "deference," one finds such meanings as "enduring" and "bearing children" (Morris 1982, 346, 1509), and, indeed, communication at this staging gives birth to new meanings and so endures. The factual character of this process is reflected in the Russian equivalent of "deference"—"pochtitel'nost'" ("почтительность"), which literally means "almost-in-the-flesh," i.e., "almost wholeness," ("pochtitsel'nost'"—"почтицельность"). This is exactly how the virtual character of communication must be viewed, cf. "the virtual has meanings of . . . being 'almost-so' or 'almost-there'" (Shields 2003, 4). Communication at this staging can be conceptualized in terms of "barely," "almost," "as if," "factually." Here one *barely* feels the difference between space and time; one *almost* bridges the gap between them; one feels *as if* one becomes one whole with communication; and, *factually*, this is, indeed, the case. Communication, therefore, is presented to one only insofar as one resigns (to) it. In this light, communication can be viewed as "the present of the world that appears through the breakdown of temporality" (Bhabha 1994, 219). Overall, communication is a constant search for that present— the most immediate and important, the "almost-whole," "almost-in-the-flesh" experience. As mentioned earlier, the Russian word for "present"— "nastoyashchee" ("настоящее")—means not only "present tense," but also "real" and "worthwhile."

Overall, the nature of communication at this staging can be interpreted as *sympathy*, which is another form of similitude discussed by M. Foucault. The following passage captures the essence of this staging of communication very well:

> Lastly, the fourth form of resemblance is provided by *the play* of sympathies. And here, no path has been determined in advance, no distance laid down, no links prescribed. Sympathy plays through the depths of the universe in a free state. It *can traverse the vastest spaces* in an instant: it falls like a thunderbolt from the distant planet upon the man ruled by that planet; on the other hand, it can be *brought into being by a simple contact*. . . . But such is its power that sympathy is not content to spring from a single contact and speed through space; *it excites the things of the world* to movement and can draw even the most distant of them together. . . . Moreover, by drawing things towards one another in an exterior and visible movement, it also gives rise to a hidden interior movement—a displacement of qualities that take over from one another in a series of relays: *fire*, because it is warm and light, rises up into the air, towards which its flames untiringly strive; . . . it disappears . . . into light vapour, into blue smoke, into clouds: it has become air. (Foucault 1970, 22; emphasis mine)

Also, "*sympathy transforms*. It alters, but in the direction of identity" (Foucalut 1970, 23; emphasis mine), in other words, in the direction of the invisible, interconnected ground of all being, mentioned earlier, and discussed in detail in the next chapter.

To summarize, at this staging, one becomes aware of one's role in communication, which can be formulated as resignation, or one's response to, and responsibility for, communication overall. Through resignation, one's fate is revealed as an attempt to measure up against communication, as such. Also, at this staging, communication reveals its nature as a creative process; here one is a visionary, resigning (to) the flow of communication. Thus, one becomes aware of the temporal nature of communication seen as a process of the initiation of meaning.

One comes in touch with communication not only corporeally, but semi-otically. As a result, communication in its tactility, while appearing a super-ficial process, reveals its depth. At the same time, communication reveals its illusionary nature; at this staging, communication exists as a virtual process, which is impossible without the play of imagination. Virtual communication exists as performance when every act is an act of resignation or rendition of meaning. Whether—and how—communication will continue depends on how creatively one plays one's role. Finally, at this staging, communication happens so quickly that the meaningful gap between time and space is factu-ally unnoticeable.

At this staging, communication can be viewed as the "present of the world"; it is presented to one whenever one brings something into being by a simple contact. For example, I touch the paper by writing this sentence and put a period. And . . .

PART III

COMMUNICATION BEING: THE PAST IN FRONT OF US

~

CHAPTER SEVEN

Airy Nothing:
Communication as Transformation

Return: Back to the Things Themselves

And . . . communication continues, coming back to where/when it started; however, now we look at everything in the light of all our experiences. As T. S. Eliot noted in *Little Gidding*, we return to the beginning and come to understand the place as if for the first time. Communication is now revealed in all its wholeness, i.e., the entire universe of communication opens up. This staging coincides with the staging of communication as invocation and is also qualitatively different from it. Between/in these stagings is the entire universe of communication.

For communication to reveal its nature as constant return, one must pay (return) one's duty to everyone/everything that made it possible for one to become a part of communication. Any act of self-definition by way of exclusion involves a "responsibility to memory" (Cornell 1992, 149). One's duty in communication must be constantly returned because, otherwise, communication will discontinue. At the staging of communication as invocation, no respect was paid to objects because it seemed that their (spatial) essence can be invoked at (one's) will. Now it becomes clear that objects are living beings that exist in time as well as space. For example, as discussed in a previous chapter, if a glass falls and breaks, it can still be called "a glass," cf. "a broken glass." However, the empirical situation now is a bit different, a new semantic feature is identified in the meaning of the word, calling for a somewhat different expression, cf. "pieces of a glass." If the life of this glass continues to be more and more dynamic (fractured), this object may die, i.e., disappear as a meaningful experience from the universe of communication, cf. "pieces of glass." Thus, all objects—animate as well as the so-called (by people) inanimate—live and may die. To prevent all objectified meaningful experiences from dying, communication must be constantly re-turned.

This way, one constantly returns to oneself, transformed in every act of communication. In other words, at this staging, all meaningful experiences are revived. It becomes clear that one cannot escape the reality of communication—one can only constantly return (to) it. This staging of communication is what B. Latour calls "the second empiricism," or "the return to a realist attitude" when "objects become things" and "when matters of fact . . . become matters of concern" (Latour 2004, 41). And so, at this staging, communication returns back to the things themselves where/when "the objective essence of things *in themselves*" (Seifert 1987, 9) finally appears, or the appearance of things finally finds its essence; thus essence and appearance finally meet in things, and the nature of communication is revealed as *aletheia*. This way, all objects, filled with spatiotemporal meaningful experience, are transformed and (re)turned into things, which are now meaningful and make sense. One's attitude toward every thing is transformed, as well; now it is clear that every thing is an indispensable part of the universe of communication and must be prevented from dying, saved in the constant process of its revival. At this staging, communication can be viewed as "a 'repetition' or 'retrieval,' a process of dis-covering and re-membering . . . of being and thus the truth as a-letheia (un-hiddenness)" (Spanos 1976, 462).

Through transformation, communication revealed its nature as invocation, conversation, construction, and resignation. Through the transformation of meaning, at this staging, communication reveals its nature as transformation. In other words, at this point "the identity of experience [is] instaneously present to itself" (Derrida 1973, 60). At this point, every object returns back to itself, its existence returning to its essence.

This way, communication reveals its most ephemeral nature. Here communication can be compared to the air made up of all the meaningful experiences. It can be recalled that communication at the previous stage is compared to the fire, which, "warm and light, rises up into the air, towards which its flames untiringly strive" (Foucault 1970, 23). Now, at this staging, communication is like that air, and all participants in/of communication breathe it as they inhabit or make up the universe of communication. Air here can be viewed as "the condition of possibility, the resource, the groundless ground" (Irigaray 1999, 5). Moreover, as L. Irigaray (1999, 8) so passionately argues,

Is not air the whole of our habitation as mortals? Is there a dwelling more vast, more spacious, or even more generally peaceful than that of air? Can man live elsewhere that in air? . . .

No other element is as light, as free, and as much in the "fundamental" mode of a permanent, available, "there is"? . . .

Doubtless, no other element is as originally constitutive of the whole of the world, without this generativity ever coming to completion. . . .

In this sense, the staging of communication as the airy transformation is the most ecological staging of communication, cf. the Greek "oikos"—"house," and its derivative "oikia"—"dwelling" (Morris 1982, 413, 1548; cf. Peshkov 1998, 9–10). Thus, the "Note to Self," sent at the staging of communication as invocation, finally reaches its destination (its "home"), the Self himself/ herself/itself, and the message of that note turns out to be both simple (on the surface) and profound (deep): "Communication has no beginning or end, and wherever/whenever one(Self) is/goes, he/she/it is at home."

At this staging, the (trans)cultural character of communication is re-vealed because culture is the "invisible, interconnected ground of all being" (Marks-Tarlow 2005, 61). Culture is everything that needs to be cultivated, tended, constantly revived. Culture is our home, cf. the Latin root "kwel" in the word "cultivate," meaning "to inhabit" (Morris 1982, 321, 1524). This staging is where/when communication is (trans)cultural and (trans)culture is communicated. In other words, at this point, communication and culture are one.

So, the nature of communication at the staging of transformation can be conceptualized as constant return; a return of Self back to (one)self; a return by Self of one's duty to everyone/everything that made it possible for one Self to become a part of communication; and a return of everyone/everything back to communication, i.e., home which, however, they never really left. It finally becomes clear that "we are never not in contact; the world is never not constituted" (Anton 2002, 186). And, that we are never not at home.

The Breath of Pleroma

At the staging of communication as transformation, its nature is manifested in the form of a ritual. One can view a communication ritual as any symbolic act by which a certain ordered state of things is sanctioned and maintained (Cheal 1992; Rothenbuhler 1998). Through a ritual, meanings are revived again and again; it seems as if nothing else matters, and "only the moment of recognition is sweet to us" (Osip Mandel'shtam). Here, the meanings of things are recognized in the sense of being acknowledged and revered.

When a ritual is performed, it "is never invented in the moment of its action, it is always action according to pre-existing conceptions" (Rothenbuhler 1998, 9). It must be noted, however, that communication can be conceptualized as ritual at the staging of communication as conversation, as well (just as any other staging, for that matter), where its focus is more on the empirical moment of symbolic interaction, cf. the concept of the ritual order as developed by E. Goffman. Describing someone who broke the truce with society, E. Goffman writes that, "the main principle of the ritual order is . . . face, . . . *what will sustain for the moment* the line to which he has committed himself and through this line to which he has committed the interaction" (Goffman 2005, 44; emphasis mine). At the staging of transformation, communication overall is sustained as/through ritual; in other words, the performance of communication is driven by a certain force. However, this is not an external, evil force, making one act against one's will; rather, it is an internal force, constituted within the process of communication itself and reflected in the form of culturally sanctioned symbolic actions. This force allows one to remember—or rather never fail—to perform the most significant actions in one's life; thus one's life continues, and so does communication. To put it more accurately, one's life continues in/through communication, and communication continues in/through one's life. This staging of communication is one of ritual services, so to speak, where/when one serves communication, and communication serves one; here, they are one (and the same).

A ritual can be viewed as the ultimate care of/by communication. Communication was earlier presented as a process that concerns (touches) everyone and where one shows one's concern in the act of re-signation. At the staging of transformation, communication is more than a matter of concern—it is a matter of care. It is noted that "'care' contains a suggestion of anxiety and watchful attention" (Scott 2007, 137–138). However, such an anxiety over communication is very different from the fear of communication, cf. communication apprehension, mentioned earlier. At this staging, communication apprehension is overcome, and one is only anxious that communication can continue, its nature (being) constantly (trans)formed.

All re-signed meanings are now revived, and, in this respect, a ritual can be conceptualized as a form of congregation of meanings—an act of their gathering, "flocking" together. The root of the word "congregation"— "ger"—means "agora," "marketplace" (Morris 1982, 281, 1516); thus, the nature of ritual can be traced back to communication in Ancient Greece with its democratic traditions where/when the voice of an individual participant of communication was significant. Overall, communication as congregation is a process of care of everyone/everything of/for everyone/everything else—a process where/when all are one integral whole.

The ecological nature of communication makes it possible to look in a new light at nature, as such, and the so-called protection of the environment. In this light, it must be pointed out that one cannot protect something that surrounds one (Grois 1993, 174). Hence it is more accurate to speak about a culture, which encircles nature, as it were, or takes care of it through watchful attention. In other words, culture protects nature from itself. In this process, nature is cultivated ("culturized") while culture is naturalized. At the staging of communication as transformation, it becomes clear that culture and nature cannot be separated from each other as they form one integral whole. At this point, therefore, the cultural nature of communication is, figuratively, its nature and appears as the most natural process. Here, every (ritual) act of communication is considered sacred because the naturalness of its meanings is not questioned. "In any given cultural community, the sacred is whatever it treated as unquestionable, 'beyond interdiction,' as Durkheim puts it" (Rothenbuhler 1998, 24).

Thus, in every act of communication as ritual one is on the "sacred ground" (Bateson and Bateson, 1987, 81). It must be noted that "ground" here should be understood not only in the literal, but in the figurative— transformed—sense. Of course, certain parts of land can be, and often are, treated as "the sacred ground." However, "ground" at this point has a more ephemeral meaning and should be viewed as the spirit, which is stronger than flesh and more firm than any terra firma.

One can see the transition from the staging of resignation to the staging of transformation in the following lines:

> . . . The poet's eye, in a fine frenzy rolling,
> Doth glance from heaven to earth, from earth to heaven;
> And as imagination bodies forth
> The forms of things unknown, the poet's pen
> Turns them to shapes and gives to airy nothing
> A local habitation and a name
>
> (William Shakespeare, A *Midsummer Night's Dream*)

The staging of communication as transformation is one of "airy nothing" where/ when everyone/everything finds "a local habitation and a name." At this staging, communication can be viewed in terms of *habitus*, to use P. Bourdieu's well-known term. It is important to note that *habitus* is conceptualized as "the mediating link between objective social structures and individual action" (Painter 2000, 242); in other words, *habitus* should be viewed as the ever-present phenomenological force that makes it possible for every one/every thing to be in perfect harmony with every one/every thing else.

So, the staging of communication as transformation is where/when communication exists as—and has the essence of—"the sacred ground." At this staging, one is no longer scared of communication, cf. communication apprehension; rather, one cares about communication, and communication, in return, cares about every one and every thing. There is but a small difference between the words "scared" and "sacred"—only two letters switched, and yet, between these two words lies the entire way of a communication universe. This way leads to the sacred singularity of every one/every thing. This is the way from trying to invoke the essence of a thing by calling it out with a signal to acknowledging every object as a divine thing and calling it by its "sacred" name; at the staging of communication as transformation, every thing and every one has "a local habitation and a name."

In this respect, communication is truly a free process because "freedom, in fact, is . . . exposure to the singular existence of things" (Scott 2000, 83). In other words, one can feel truly free only by be(com)ing exposed to, and taking care of, the existence of every single thing. Of course, no one can really cover this entire way, be(com)ing this path. In other words, no one can really feel/fill the entire communication universe by being exposed to the singular existence of every one/every thing simply because one's spatiotemporal experience is (alas) limited. One can only feel the breath of pleroma as the totality of divine powers. It can be suggested that pleroma—fullness or plenitude—be added as a form of similitude to the classification discussed by M. Foucault. As pleroma, communication unfolds in its fullest form, totally filled with space and time. Here communication is seen most clearly as a universe—one constantly re-turned/ing being.

It is not easy to acknowledge, i.e., to admit into oneself the sacredness of every thing and every one, especially the so-called inanimate objects; one can simply look at what people as animate objects—objects supposedly with a soul—do to their natural environment. Similarly, even people—especially from other cultures—are seldom viewed by others as part of the sacred ground; they are usually found foreign or exotic. But, "it is already a failure of recognition that we think of these creatures rather than ourselves as exotic" (Peters 1999, 260). Communication can never reveal its nature as a whole—and holy—universe unless we recognize that

the foreigner lives within us: he is the hidden face of our identity. . . . By recognizing him within ourselves, we are spared detesting him in himself. . . . The foreigner comes in when the consciousness of my difference arises, and he disappears when we all acknowledge ourselves as foreigners, unamenable to bonds and communities. (Kristeva 1991, 1)

Only this way can we see that we are all one and the same, i.e., see the Other in oneself and oneself in the Other. This way, the Moebius strip is turned (transformed), and the subject becomes the object, while the object becomes the subject; the inside part becomes the outside part, while the outside part becomes the inside part. In other words, it *turns out* that they are—or it is—all the same. And so one comes to one's starting point, having traversed both sides of the Moebius strip, successfully filling all the gaps of communication with meaning and yet without ever breaking it or crossing an edge. Thus communication reveals its topological nature—one (seemingly) without any breaks and edges.

Communion with Eternity

Every thing and every one can be viewed as a part of a communication universe. Once careful attention is paid (re-turned) to a thing, its universal character is revealed. Every ritual act of communication in which the meaning of a thing is revived, is a beautiful act; even those rituals that are sad or heart-rending are full of care and beauty because of their spiritual charge. Their meanings are full of beauty and care because, at the previous stage, they were rendered (re-signed) full-heartedly, with a loving devotion. And now, through these meanings, communication is revived, constantly saved in every ritual act; it is said for a reason that only beauty can save the world.

The beauty of a communication ritual is mesmerizing. At the staging of communication as resignation, one can also be put under the spell, or intoxicated by, its virtual flow; in this respect, the dangers of virtual communication can be quite real, cf. the phenomenon of the so-called Internet addiction (Chou 2005). At this point, a communication universe has not yet been formed and so one has not yet come back (returned) to oneself. In this case, it can be said that those addicted to communication are the experienced users of the Internet, but are not the experienced users of/by communication because they are not yet one with the entire communication universe. It is only by breaking this spell and overcoming this addiction that one can return back to the things themselves and find oneself on the sacred ground of communication, be(com)ing free as a part of the integral whole. In other words, by reaching the staging of communication as transformation, one can be cured. To be cured means to be restored to health or to become whole. It is interesting to note that the Russian word for "to cure"—"istselyat'" ("исцелять")—literally means "to make whole," cf. "to heal," meaning "to become whole and sound" (Morris 1982, 607). So, communication has a therapeutic, healing effect because it restores meanings. Again, it must be emphasized that only those meanings can be cured by/in communication, or made whole, that were re-signed as a result of a corresponding step—the step by which one creatively corresponds to (steps into) communication with love and without fear.

Thus, a ritual can be seen as the fullest, the most spiritual form of communication. In a communication ritual, the highest virtue is found—*sophia* (wisdom). According to Aristotle, "it is absurd to think that Political Science or Prudence is the loftiest kind of knowledge, inasmuch as man is not the highest thing in the world" (Aristotle 1141a, 21–23). It is only through/ in wisdom as "the most perfect of the modes of knowledge" (Aristotle 1141a, 17) that the divine bliss can be reached or rather constantly revived.

Aristotle views wisdom as "intuitive reason combined with scientific knowledge" (Aristotle 1141a, 15). However, wisdom as "the most finished form of the form of knowledge" (Aristotle 1141a, 15), must, by definition, include *all* the forms that knowledge takes on its way of (trans)formation. In other words, *techné* and *phrónêsis* must be viewed as constituting wisdom along with intuitive reason (*nous*) and scientific knowledge (*epistêmê*). Without them, the picture is not complete/d, not "finished"; after all, it is important for meanings to be produced and decisively acted upon. It may be that Aristotle, with his focus on knowledge per se, simply took those other two forms for granted.

Any thing in communication can—and must—reveal its ritual nature. For example, an American saluting the flag or one watching *Melrose Place* are both rituals although the former is more longstanding while the latter—more transient; "notwithstanding these differences, in texture and longevity, none of these actions is intrinsically more basic or central or fundamental than the others" (Curry 2000, 109). Even a simple "jug of wine, to use Heidegger's example, presents itself to a Dasein open to its appearing as made from the earth and filled with its fruits, ripened and nourished by the sky's sun and rain. The wine is made by mortals and is consumed by them most meaningfully in awareness of their mortality and of their relations to the immortal meanings of the occasion" (Malhotra 1987, 368). This way, different things come together into a ritual of drinking wine—one of the oldest rituals across cultures. Here, of course, the reference is to M. Heidegger's view of a fourfold universe made up of earth, sky, mortals, and immortals.

So, a ritual is a form of communication in which meaning is revived, saved through constant transformation of the spatiotemporal continuum of experience; this form exists in the dynamic state of divine bliss. A ritual exists toward no other end than constant transformation of meaning. In this light, ritual communication appears as non-instrumental action, i.e., action "not useful for specifically technical purposes" (Rothenbuhler 1998, 11). A ritual seems to be an irrational, unnecessary form of communication; however, it is in this seeming unusefulness that ritual communication reveals its profound significance.

So, at this staging, the nature of communication consists in the ritual revival of all the significant—worthwhile, sacred—experiences that became meaningful as a result of its previous transformations. The main function of a ritual act of communication, thus, is the constant revival of communication itself. In every ritual act, communication is brought back to life or rather is maintained as "airy nothing" where/when every one/every thing has "a local habitation and a name." (Considering that every one/every thing now is a part of the universe, i.e., something global, a better term, perhaps, would be "glocal," in the sense of "a global dimension of the inhabiting, continually oscillating in the re-creation of that inhabiting itself" [Sedda 2009, 16].) A communication ritual is re-membering or, rather, unforgetting of everything that, it seems, has been forgotten (like the door-closer from B. Latour's example), or broken (like the glass, mentioned earlier), or simply seems to have disappeared in the flame of the horizon. It turns out that, indeed, "manuscripts do not burn," to use the famous phrase from M. Bulgakov's *The Master and Margarita*. In other words, the meaning of every thing endures: every thing is sacred and, therefore, saved, re-turned. In a ritual act of communication, the meaning of every thing is retrieved, revived, unforgotten.

At this staging, every one/every thing has the same part, which is the easiest and the most significant one—to make sure that communication, as such, is unforgotten; in this sense, every one/every thing authors the same meaning, which is constantly returned. One can no longer claim an individual authorship (copyright) of this or that meaning. For example, when a groom during a wedding ceremony says "I do," it is not the groom, but communication itself speaking. In other words, "in a ritual . . . authors are unimportant" (Krippendorff 2009, 61). Here communication is represented by language material, which, manifested in a ritual act, is beyond interdiction; unlike the text that must be interpreted, language material is not questioned—it is simply revived as it is. In this respect, "language material" can be understood somewhat similar to L. Shcherba's definition of language material as "the totality of what is spoken and understood in a specific concrete environment in this or that epoch of the life of a social group" (Shcherba 2004, 26; see also: Lähteenmäki 2008, 188). However, language material as the totality of what is spoken and understood should not be identified with texts, discourse, or language as a system. Rather, language material should be viewed as a vocabulary of winged words. In Russian, such sayings are called "krylatye vyrazheniya" ("крылатые выражения")—literally, "saying with wings"; indeed, such sayings "give wings" to every one who is a part of a communication ritual. Overall, any element of language material can be viewed as winged words or an expression with wings; the simpler the meaning, the more significant it is and the more eternal it appears. Such everyday expressions as "Hello" and "Good-bye" are full of wonder and beauty because, in/through them, communication endures.

Earlier, it was noted that the gap between one and everyone/everything else is filled in a creative act of inscription of meaning (resignation). At this staging, communication is taken beyond inscription-resignation; the nature of communication as ritual is such that nothing (else) can be inscribed or resigned. At this staging, it is all communication wrote.

Language material as a vocabulary of winged words is represented by the sum total of all the cultural names created (resigned) to this point—not simply isolated words, but rather appellations as acts of entreatment or calling by name. It is interesting to note that the process of appellation can be related to—literally—cultivating the soil; appellations are protected names under which a wine may be sold, indicating that the grapes used in making the wine come from a specific area. Thus, language material must be viewed as the vocabulary of the most protected, sacred acts of appellation or naming. It is also interesting to note that one of the meanings of "vocabulary" is "a reserve of expressive techniques, repertoire: *'a dancer's vocabulary of movement'*" (Morris 1982, 1434). In other words, a vocabulary is what acts as a resource or stands in reserve, which, of course, brings to mind *Gestell* as a way of ordering things as standing reserve, discussed earlier in the book. It is possible to say that, at the staging of communication as transformation, the challenge of *Gestell* is constantly answered, the truth of every, as well the overall, being of communication (at)tended—just as the soil is tended to grow grapes for making wine. At this staging, every being of communication is called by name. Thus, through the vocabulary of the most protected appellations, the true voice of (the e/very being) of communication is heard.

Language material should be understood in a broad semiotic sense—not only as the elements of the verbal nature, but as non-verbal elements, as well. In fact, communication rituals often have a predominantly non-verbal character. It is only natural for non-verbal elements to be part of a ritual because a ritual is a form of communication where/when everything takes place naturally, without much speaking. A ritual act of communication goes without saying. That is why, perhaps, silence as a non-verbal element of communication has immense ontological significance (Dauenhauer 1980). If every motion "is relative and can be transformed into a rest by an appropriate change of the frame of reference" (Čapek 1961, 346), then "a rest" can be viewed as a point where communication, usually associated with speaking, rests its case, as it were, and non-verbals take over. At this point, the rest is silence. In such a case, there is no need for one to waste one's—and the Other's—space and time on unnecessary words: communication can be saved, as a whole, if everything takes place as if by itself, going without saying.

So, a ritual is a form of communication where/when all worthwhile meanings are constantly sanctified. A ritual highlights "the transformative, efficacious quality of the liminal" (Crosby 2009, 9) in the process of communication. It is noted that, following E. Levinas (1981), "the skin . . . is a much used and widely deployed figure of liminality" (Boothroyd 2009, 343). However, it can be argued that any of the five senses can be discussed as a figure of liminality as long as a distinction in perception is marked. For instance, it is pointed out that "to ancient Greeks, including Aristotle, luminosity was more important than hue in characterizing color. For example, the Greek words *melas* and *leukos* can be translated not only as 'black' and 'white' but also as 'dark' and 'light'" (Hoeppe 2007, 14). In this sense, "seeing the light" can be literally seen as a transformative, liminal act of communication. If we view luminosity more metaphorically, the overall nature of communication can be conceptualized as *luminality*, combining the ideas of the transformative quality of an act of communication, cf. liminality with its effect as seeing the light, cf. luminosity.

In this light (pun intended), communication must be treated as a passage or (re)generation of (trans)cultural meanings connecting one generation with another. Every ritual can be seen as an act of intergenerational communication (cf. Williams and Nussbaum 2000). In this respect, memory, without which no ritual can be performed, is not only an eternal ontological beginning or continuation, as mentioned earlier, but also an eternal ontological "unending." A good example of the most liminal nature of a ritual in intergenerational communication is the ritual Djugurba practiced by the Australian Walbiri Aborigines (see: TenHouten 2005, 32–34). The word *Djugurba* means the ancestral inhabitants of the country and also the times when they traveled around, creating the world where the present-day Walbiri live. Also, this word means "dream" and "story." This story, as the Dreaming, is told on the sand; it exists in the form of drawings made, erased, and drawn again in the sand. In this sense, *Djugurba*, as the marks on the sand, means "Look, a story." Such stories are usually told/drawn by tribal women who refer to their ancestors as "anonymous persons." "When asked where the story took place, the storyteller would answer "*Djugurba*," in this context, meaning 'no place'" (TenHouten 2005, 33). It is also important to note that "Dreaming does not die and does not get washed away, rather existing forever" (TenHouten 2005, 33). One can notice clear parallels between the new postmodern ideas and the old ritual of *Djugurba*, cf. the concept of erasure and literally drawing and erasing stories on the sand. According to postmodernists, writing must be viewed as the condition of possibility not only of oral speech, but language and signification overall. To the Australian Walbiri Aborigines, it is clear that speech ("a story") has "always been a writing" (Derrida 1998, 56), cf. drawing on the sand. In fact, to them, nothing is deeper than the clean, smooth, "erased" sand viewed as the source of healing energy, which will continue as long as life continues in the form of the Dreaming, and stories are drawn and redrawn, told about the events in "no place." Thus, at the staging of communication as transformation, the two extremes of postmodernists and "traditionalists" meet as oral speech and writing meet; here speech is (equals) writing, and writing is (equals) speech for they are one process of signification—a meaningful dreamlike experience that is constantly (trans)formed.

In a ritual act of communication, no new meanings are created that can be used toward a certain practical end; communication at this staging does not have any instrumental character. However, in the non-instrumental sense, everything and everyone, i.e., transculture, as such, is constantly revived. In this sense, the very possibility of communication is constantly revived; this way, communication reveals its nature as potentiality. It is no accident that the liminal, mentioned above, is viewed as "a realm of pure possibility" (Turner 1967, 97). This staging is one of perfection, not because a certain end has been reached, a certain goal (perfectly) accomplished, but because here communication *is* being carried out/accomplished without any end; here no clear boundary exists between an end and a beginning, the inside and the outside. Communication is perfect because it is without a beginning or an end. This is the staging where/when communication being is revealed most clearly: communication can be perfect only as pure possibility.

Thus, communication as pure possibility is manifested in a ritual. The more frequently an act takes place, the more ritual and the more pure communication is. In other words, the degree to which communication can be considered ritual depends on the number of times an act occurs. In general, communication reveals its ritual character most clearly if the same action takes place time and time again. It is easy to see that many rituals have a predominantly biological basis, the act of communication related to eating, drinking, birth, death, etc. Such actions occur most frequently in the overall process of communication so it is easy to identify them as ritual.

At this staging, communication is pleroma completely filled with time and space where/when "all previous spatio-temporal unfoldings are integrated and made meaningful" (Arneson 2007, 202), hence the motion of communication seems to stop. Here,

> of time it may be said: time times. Of space it may be said: space spaces. The customary notion of time and space takes offense at such talk, and rightly so. For in order to understand it, we need the thinking experience of what is called *identity*. . . .
>
> Time in its timing removes us into its threefold simultaneity. . . . In removing us and bringing towards us, time moves on its way what simultaneity yields and throws open to it: time-space. But time itself, in the wholeness of its nature, does not move; it rests in stillness.
>
> The same is to be said about space: it spaces, throws open locality and places, vacates them and at the same time gives them free for all things and receives what is simultaneous as space-time. But space itself, in the wholeness of its nature, does not move; it rests in stillness. Time's removing and bringing to us, and space's throwing open, admitting and releasing—they all belong together in the Same, the play of stillness, something to which we cannot here give further thought. The Same, which holds space and time gathered up in their nature, might be called the free scope, that is, the time-space that gives free scope to all things." (Heidegger 1982, 106)

At this staging, then, time and space are held "gathered up in their nature," which brings us back to the concept of *Gestell* when one is "gathered" by the challenge of technologies into an attitude of ordering things as standing reserve. Conceptualized as pure possibility, communication can be seen as a process where/when anything and everything seems possible; at this staging, one comes to the impossible as close as possible. Figuratively speaking, every thing seems divine, and one finds oneself in the state of eternal bliss. This (state/moment of) being can be reached or rather constantly maintained only by treating *Gestell*, as mentioned earlier in the book, not as an instrument gear or an instrumental means to an end, but as a mode of overall existence. At this staging, it becomes clear that one cannot control the way in which Being comes into unconcealment. One constantly meets the challenge of communication by bringing oneself into accord with the call of *Gestell*, i.e., by coming to terms with everything that comes into being, including oneself. One can respond to this challenge successfully not through force, willing to master communication, but inactively, through stillness, by attending to communication being like shepherds and tending its sacred, (trans)cultural ground.

This way, "we can bring technology 'into its yet concealed truth' by way of fundamental thinking and through a type of poetry that reaches into the destitution of the age. Heidegger details this restoration in terms of a turning described metaphorically—thinking as craftsmanship, then as the inflashing or lightening flash that brings Being into presence, and finally as the mirroring of the fourfold: earth, sky, mortals, and divinities" (Wyschogrod 1985, 199). It is easy to see how "thinking as craftsmanship" can be viewed as *techné* of the communication-as-conversation staging, "the inflashing or lightening flash that brings Being into presence" can be seen as *phrónêsis* of the communication-as-resignation staging, and "the mirroring of the fourfold" can be conceptualized as wisdom of the communication-as-transformation staging. To this process of "a turning," two more stagings must be added: thinking as intuitively grasping the first principles, cf. *nous* of the communication-as-invocation staging and thinking as scientific knowledge, cf. *epistêmê* of the communication-as-construction staging. Together these stagings make up the process in which meaning is "turned" (transformed) or "restored," and communication Being comes into unconcealment.

It was noted earlier that, at the staging of transformation, communication returns back to the things themselves; as a result of such "second empiricism" (B. Latour), the virtual character of communication goes into the background, and communication becomes a process where/when every thing and every one is the way it is, not "as if." However, at this staging, it—still—only seems, albeit most seamlessly, without breaks or edges, that space and time are one, and anything is possible. It is noted that rituals "are 'not indicative' (many make this mistake) . . . rituals . . . occur in the subjunctive mood. They are . . . not about what is, but what . . . ought to be" (Rothenbuhler 1998, 15). That is why communication rituals teach one humility; it turns out that one can be(come) one with communication only *in potentia*, in one common wish for communication to simply be, i.e., without any instrumental gain for oneself. One gives up everything one has, i.e., one's individual space and time (read: one's life) so that communication, as such, can be possible. This way, one has communion with eternity.

The Democracy of Transspecies

So, at this staging, due to its ritual character, communication appears as perfect, as ideal as possible. Here, as mentioned earlier, the depth of meaning comes all the way up to the outer edges of the surface and becomes "smooth," while the "smooth" surface of meaning reaches to the very core of communication and turns out to be profound (deep). Here everyone's actions are in perfect harmony with everyone else's acts; as a result, the process of communication becomes as rhythmic as can be. It is worth mentioning that the etymology of the word "ritual" includes the meaning of rhythm (Morris 1982, 1121, 1506). In other words, this staging is characterized by a perfect correspondence (one might say, correspon-dance) between every one/every thing and every one/every thing else. In this sense, "communication as dance . . . stresses . . . the harmonious complementarity of movements: ceremonially asking *how are you* and saying *good-bye*, taking turns at talk, the punctuations that mark the progression of legal procedures, and the public ceremonies of political succession. . . . The dance-ritual metaphor entails . . . *continuity* and *repetitiveness*, . . . the sameness of the process" (Krippendorff 2009, 61).

At this staging, communication can be viewed as the manifestation of "Ch. S. Peirce's vision of the communicative universe as a true democracy of transspecies" (Peters 1999, 258). In this democracy of transspecies, the voice of every being is equally significant, i.e., it counts. It is interesting to note that "numbers are the signifying system that bears the burden of the political *dream* of transparency" (Peters 2005, 191; emphasis mine). A good example of this is the ritual of voting as a form of political communication (cf. Peters 2005, 192). In this ritual, everyone's vote is equal to the vote of everyone else; all other characteristics such as one's wealth, status, religion, etc., are deemed insignificant; in other words, they do not count. The only thing that does count is the voice of every singular sacred being; when one casts one's ballot, one, in effect, gives one's life toward the common good. This is how democracy is maintained, and this is how the universe of communication, as a democracy of transspecies, is constantly revived. Through this ritual, the very voice of communication is heard; this is how communication speaks.

Thus, in ritual communication everyone gives one's voice (read: one's authorship of meaning) toward the common good; this way, the soul of every one/every thing is constantly revived, and not simply the soul of humans, but the soul as what gives life (authors) being itself. Of course, it is easier to recognize the soul of human beings that physically move in timespace. However, every inanimate thing that one comes into contact with could be recognized as having a soul, as well, because it generates a meaningful experience. The universe of communication, then, should be viewed as a living being made up of every one/every thing as its significant part, cf. Ch. S. Peirce's approach to signs as every thing/every one with a meaning, including words, people or natural phenomena. In this sense, "determining the range of creatures we will communicate with is a political question, perhaps *the* political question. It may be the key question of politics in our century, when we treat animals as if they were human and humans as if they were animals" (Peters 1999, 230).

The staging where/when the universe of communication is transformed, can be represented with the sign of equality. It is noted that this sign "refers to the world equally. It is really the source out of which mathematics flows" (Sarukkai 2002, 104). In this light, this staging can be seen as the source out of which all communication flows.

In his chapter on the myth of A. Einstein, R. Barthes (1972) "shows how this equation conjures up the old alchemists' dream of knowledge reduced to a kind of magical formula" (MacDonald 2006, 515). Indeed, as argued by R. Barthes, A. Einstein's formula gives us access to the "unity of nature, the ideal possibility of a fundamental reduction of the world, the unfastening power of the word, the age-old struggle between a secret and an utterance, and the idea that total knowledge can only be discovered at once, like a lock which suddenly opens after a thousand unsuccessful attempts" (Barthes 1972, 69). This chapter "raises a serious question: are we now fulfilling [in our age of new information technologies] the old alchemists' desire to dominate man and nature by means of system of secret knowledge?" (MacDonald 2006, 515). More importantly, are we still searching for the magical formula with which to transform water into gold, i.e., which will help us to discover the secret to such a meaningful transformation? At the staging of communication as transformation, it becomes clear that no such secret formula exists. Or, rather, any equation will do because, as mentioned above, the sign of equality "refers to the world equally" (Sarukkai 2002, 104). In other words, any equation is magical because its only "secret" is to treat its parts as the same, i.e., to treat every one and every thing equally significant to every one and every thing else. Water cannot and must not be turned into gold because water is the same as gold, i.e., equally significant.

At this staging, the nature of communication is most fully freed up. It was noted earlier that freedom is an exposure of every thing and everyone, as a singular existence, to the singular existence of every thing and every one else. Here, every one/every thing is free because every one/every thing equally matters; every one/every thing is equal to every one/every thing else, every one/every thing is equally significant. Here it is (all are) all the same, equal, even, smooth, harmonious. It should be noted that the transformational nature of the liminal reveals a bond characterized by "complete equality" with no "distinctions and gradations" (Turner 1967, 99). At this point, we are all the same because "we all share the trait of being selves" (Peters 2005, 51).

They say that everything has its place and time; this is exactly what occurs at this staging: without even the smallest, the most seemingly insignificant thing the universe of communication is incomplete, "not the same." In this sense, although it can be argued that "in a ritual . . . authors are unimportant and *performers replaceable*" (Krippendorff 2009, 61; emphasis mine), it should be remembered that, without them, a ritual does not exist.

At this staging, all one's longings are satisfied, and communication is a process where/when every one/every thing be-longs; "the key concept here is surely not 'sharing,' but rather 'fitting,' or 'belonging'" (Curry 2000, 106). It becomes clear that no language game can be won by any one or any thing; the best possible scenario for all participants in communication is a tie. Communication is a tie because it brings together, binds, unites every one and every thing into a (trans)culture—the invisible, interconnected ground of all being, the sacred ground. In this light, communication can be viewed as *singlarity*, which combines the undivided and uniform nature of "single" with the uniqueness and individuality of "singular." At this point, "we are singular in our universality and universal in our singularity" (Peters 2005, 51).

At this staging, it also becomes clear that space and time are invisibly connected, because they are one (and the same) being. It turns out that they cannot exist without each other because they form one whole. If, for the sake of simplicity, space can be identified with denotation (roughly speaking, the world of objects that exist at certain distances from one another), while time—with signification (roughly speaking, the world of senses that exist at certain intervals from one another), at this staging, every object makes sense, and every sense is objectified, i.e., space and time are unified into one communication universe.

When ritual communication is discussed in terms of space and time, it is sometimes noted that "in ritual there is less of a temporal dimension. The point of ritual is that it is a timeless reflection of the culture and community to which we belong" (Stenning 2006, 7). However, it only seems that ritual communication is timeless, or devoid of time. In fact, every ritual act of communication should be viewed as filled with time, cf. J. Carey's views on ritual communication, mentioned earlier in the book. In this respect, the staging of communication as invocation is timeless in the sense of (yet) lacking time, while the staging of communication as transformation is timeless in the sense of being timefull, or having significance throughout times.

The emphasis on the temporal nature of a ritual means that "a ritual is not a thing but rather a how, a quality" (Rothenbuhler 1998, 5). In this sense, the so-called quality time is identified with the time spent on the most significant and worthwhile activities. In ritual communication, the quantity of time of an act, i.e., the number of times an activity takes place, cannot be separated from its quality; in other words, they form one inseparable whole. As mentioned earlier, *chronos* and *kairos* are the two sides of the same coin.

Thus, a ritual act of communication is infused with time. In this respect, communication rituals can be "viewed as time-outs from the usual constraints of affairs" (Rothenbuhler 1998, 15), i.e., from the instrumental character of communication. It may seem as if time is taken out of communication, while, on the contrary, all communication here is put out, as it were, into a ritual; hence a ritual is an act of communication filled with time. Time permeates ritual communication, and it seems as if a ritual act of communication could exist (be returned) forever. In a way, a ritual act is like a birthday because it generates (gives birth to) the possibility of meanings to continue. Figuratively speaking, a communication ritual is an act meant to have many—ideally, the infinite number of "returns of the day."

At this staging, not only the importance of time should be emphasized, but also—equally—the importance of space. Ritual communication is a process that appears not only timeless, but also borderless, without any bounds. In a ritual act of communication, one can visit the places that do not—yet or already—exist in reality; here the sky is not the limit. Here anything is (or rather seems to be) possible—anywhere, anywhen. In other words, at this staging, the role of time should not be emphasized at the expense of space, and vice versa; they both are equally significant as they form one whole universe of communication in the form of *singularity*.

Thus, it can be said that, at the staging of communication as transformation, time seems to slow down and stop, finally giving in to space. Or, it can be said that here time finally seems to catch up with space, filling its objects with one's spirit. By the same token, it can be said that space seems to no longer keep distances between its objects and so gives in to time. Or, it can be said that space seems to let time into itself, filling time with one's spirit. The point is that there is no point in looking for one "winner" because it is a tie. At this staging, the "winner" is communication itself—the universe as a whole where/when all are one and, first of all, space and time.

Communication as ritual is a process in which meanings are revived over and over again. In this respect, communication as ritual is different from communication as the construction of a certain order, discussed earlier. The latter can be viewed as a prototype for the former. Indeed, a certain form of communication can be constructed, described, explained, or discussed; however, it is only at the staging of transformation that this prototype becomes dynamic, i.e., it becomes possible as a ritual act of communication.

Earlier, the ritual of voting was discussed as a process when the voice of communication, as such, is heard. In this broad and metaphoric sense of the word,

the voice is ultimately linked with the dimension of the sacred and ritual in intricately structured social situations where using the voice makes it possible to perform a certain act . . . words, carefully stored on paper and in memory, can acquire performative strength only if they are relegated to the voice, and it is as if the use of the voice will ultimately endow those words with the character of sacredness and ensure their ritual efficacy. (Dolar 2006, 107)

It must be emphasized, however, that communication as a democracy of transspecies "cannot successfully mandate outcomes. . . . Democratic discussion simply reproduces the conditions for its own possibility, . . . highly fragile condition" (Rasch 2000, 150). It is "this condition—not project" (Rasch 2000, 150), i.e., that most fragile nature of communication at this staging, not its prototype in the form of a project at the staging of communication as construction, that is invested "with an ethical imperative" (Rasch 2000, 150).

Thus, at this staging, the prototype is filled with the dynamic spirit, and communication is truly transformed: it (be)comes alive. The spirit that fills communication can be viewed as Aristotle's *dynamis*, which "maintains the life of an organism, and it is the very same *dynamis* that generates its offsprings; thus the same *dynamis*, which is the cause of both an organism's existence and its offsprings, is passed from one generation to another" (Katayama 1999, 2). Filled with this dynamic spirit, communication can now communicate as a self-sufficient process—timeless and unbounded. As K. Hales writes (with F. Varela's later work in mind), "here the boundaries of the liberal subject are not so much penetrated, stretched, or dissolved as they are *revealed to have been an illusion all along*. . . . No longer Wiener's island of life in a sea of entropy or Maturana's autonomous circularity, awareness realizes itself as a part of a larger whole—unbounded, empty, and serene" (Hayles 1999, 156; emphasis mine). In other words, at this staging the nature of communication is revealed as living the dream, or the living dream.

At this staging, one cannot be separate/d from communication; one is its inherent part, one is communication, i.e., they are one. Here the entire communication universe speaks with one voice of *singlarity*, and the ideal of the public sphere is reached. Of course, this ideal can be reached only *in potentia*, and so the public sphere can never be constructed, it can—or rather must—only be constantly revived.

So, at this staging, it makes no sense for (any)one to measure oneself against anyone else and to claim oneself as the "winner"—most "significant one." It becomes clear that there is really no point in any measurement; in every act of communication "we probe, at best, the limits of our instruments. . . . The history of our knowledge is the history of our media" (Peters 2003, 409). In other words, how can any thing be deemed more—or most—valuable (significant) "if *no sharp values* in nature exist and if the whole concept of infinite divisibility of space and time is an unwarranted extrapolation of our limited microscopic experience?" (Čapek 1961, 322). Here every one/every thing is equally significant and can equally relate to every one/every thing else; as a result, one exists in the state of eternal, divine bliss, which is boundless and immeasurable. The staging of communication as transformation is similar to the staging of communication as invocation as far as its syncretic nature; however, the feeling of fear of a chaotic stream of experiences is no longer present at this staging nor is the desire to control objects.

Love Equals Communication

In the previous chapter, communication was presented as a creative process of resignation, in which one finds—or rather which gives one—pleasure. It is noted that pleasure, as a realm of contact, has no object (Epshtein 2006, 120). Indeed, pleasure is experienced in the act of touch—corporeal as well as semiotic. However, for this very reason pleasure *is* directed at an object—it is just that one can barely feel the difference between oneself and the object or rather one fails to see this gap, cf. the description of communication in terms of "barely" and "almost" in the previous chapter. The expression "to take pleasure" must be in agreement—"in contact"—with a noun in the objective case, cf. "to take pleasure in something/someone." The divine bliss experienced at the staging of communication as transformation is different from pleasure: unlike the latter, the former has no object (or subject because they are one and the same). Here, one (communication overall) simply *is* in a state of bliss. It is interesting to note that the Russian equivalent of "object" is, in this context, "dopolnenie" ("дополнение")—literally, "something additional, supplemental." At this staging, the universe of communication is complete and needs no "supplements"; it is organic, self-sufficient and plentiful *singularity* full of space and time. There is no instrumental need to create more meanings; it is simply necessary to revive everything that is.

It is important to emphasize the non-instrumental nature of ritual communication. A parallel can be drawn between communication as ritual and the sabbatical passivity in Judaism. For example, while discussing Saint Paul as a theorist of communication, J. Peters notes that the verb "katargeō," which combines the meanings of "down" and "work," "catches precisely Paul's conception of hang-time and foreshadows the idea that sabbatical passivity (inertness) can be worthy. In this dialectical knot of language influences, we find Paul anticipating much in modern thought, especially the modes of ethical suspension" (Peters 2005, 55). However, just as pleasure differs from bliss, passivity is different from inertness (inactivity). In "passivity" one can still hear the echoes of suffering; according to the etymology of this word, "passive" means "capable of suffering" (Morris 1982, 958). It is no accident that "passivity" and "passibilité," mentioned earlier, have the same root. In inertness suffering disappears, and a complete lack of artful craft is revealed, leading to divine bliss. In this sense, communication appears as artful lack of art, crafty naturalness. This is the most vulnerable, fragile, dreamlike communication; that is why it must be handled with the utmost care and brought back to life in each ritual act.

Inertness/inactivity can be viewed as the manifestation of the meaningful pause that appeared as part of communication when the subject stepped back from the object to look into its eyes as the Other; that would not be contained in the utopian world order that was attempted to be constructed; that was held in the creative act of prolongation; and that becomes the very essence of communication where/when there is nothing else one can do about it: at this staging, communication is beyond interdiction. This "limit of communication is precisely what gives rise to communication as an ethical event" (Pinchevski 2005, 67). Following E. Levinas, it is usually stated that "one is oneself when and insofar as one is for-the-other, for-the-other-before-oneself" (Cohen 2001, 9). In this light, an ethical event is considered to be different from an ontological event or an aesthetic event (cf. Cohen 2001, 8). The roots of an ethical event can, indeed, be found in communication which consists in one's response-ability to/for something that allows, and calls for, one's correspondence; such response-able action takes the predominantly aesthetic form of resignation. At the staging of communication as transformation, communication does take place (and time) as an ethical event; however, it is not different from an ontological event, but rather is equally an ontological event. In other words, one is oneself when and insofar as one is the other. At this staging, the opposites meet, and every event of communication is equally ontological and ethical.

The fundamental dynamic force that keeps communication in motion is love. To use Dante's famous words from *Divine Comedy* (*Paradise*, 33.145), it is love "that moves the sun and the other stars," or the entire universe of communication. Any event of communication is about love (cf. Scannell 2005); for example, as J. Peters remarks, "in the *Phaedrus* the question is not about media, but about love" (Peters 1999, 37). J. Peters further notes that "Christianity calls for a love based not in comradeship (as in Aristotle's *philia*), the desire for beauty (eros), or the 'natural' ties of the clan or city, but in the recognition of the kinship of all of God's creatures" (Peters 1999,

61). Parallels can be drawn between these well-known kinds of love and the main stagings of communication, discussed in the present book: at the staging of communication as invocation, love is still vague, syncretic, and so has no name (it can be recalled that love is not part of the theories focusing on this staging of communication); *philia* can be said to characterize the staging of communication as conversation—a love based in comradeship; *storge* is found at the staging of communication as construction (a world order as the "natural" ties of the clan or city); *eros* is found at the staging of communication as resignation; while at the staging of communication as transformation, the highest form of love is found—*agapē*, "a love as indiscriminate as rainfall, one that embraces all humanity alike, including one's enemies" (Peters 1999, 55). It is possible to say that this love embraces not simply all humanity, but every being in the entire universe—nature "culturized" as well as culture "naturalized." In this light, J. Peters considers dissemination to be the essence of communication because "open scatter is more fundamental than coupled sharing; it is the stuff from which, on rare, splendid occasions, dialogue may arise. Dissemination is not wreckage; it is our lot" (Peters 1999, 62). However, one can say that coupled sharing is as fundamental as open scatter because it is the stuff from which, on rare, splendid occasions, creative dissemination may arise. Our lot is not only dissemination, but dialogue, as well. As mentioned in a previous chapter, conversation means "that which befalls one," and the meaning of Germanic "wurth-"—"fate," "destiny"—is related to the root of the word "conversation" (Morris 1982, 291, 1549). In other words, at this staging, the opposites meet, and dissemination equals dialogue, or vice versa: they are now one (and the same) fundamental, generative process of communication where/when "love . . . is not only individuated care but also undeviating constancy, 'an ever-fixed mark'" (Peters 1999, 57).

Communication as a process of artful naturalness (or natural art) can be related to the virtue of *sophia*. By this point, it becomes clear that communication cannot be a simple matter of one's intuition, cf. *nous*, or overcome (solved) by various techniques, cf. *techné*, or reduced to a rational order ruled by discourse, cf. *epistêmê*, or resigned in the decisive act of meaning rendition, cf. *phrónêsis*.

The difference between the stagings of communication as conversation and transformation is the difference between *techné* and *sophia*, cf. "Two people can be doing the same things . . . that is, they may be performing virtually the same physical motions and saying virtually the same things but performing different actions. One person may be performing it as a self-contained activity that is intrinsically valuable, the other as a process structured and motivated by external goals" (Rorty 1980, 217). The latter is an example of *techné*, while the former is an example of *sophia*. Wisdom consists in the ability to revive life itself, making it possible. Out of the main variants suggested as translation of *techné*—"art," "craft," "skill,"—the latter seems to be the most appropriate one. Communication as a skill is simply an activity toward a certain end. Wisdom, in its turn, is not just a skill, but an ability; thus, at the staging of transformation, communication is one's ability to simply (seemingly) do nothing in the instrumental sense, yet, in this inactivity, to do everything, making sure that the very possibility of communication is constantly returned. A skill is making a boat in order to cross the river; wisdom is making a boat as a possibility in order to keep making boats. Wisdom consists in knowing that nothing can be done and doing exactly that—nothing; this way, the ethical nature of communication is revealed most fully.

Of course, one can see ethical action in any sphere of communication, called for by the pragmatics of the context-dependent situation. Thus, it is possible to state that "ethical activity brings things into being that are distinct from the activity itself—it introduces some sort of change in the external world" (Nightingale 2006, 213), cf. *techné*. Also, although *phrónêsis* does not have an end beyond itself because here "doing well is itself the end" (Artistole 1140, 5), Aristotle adds that those who have practical wisdom "possess a faculty of discerning what things are good for themselves and for mankind" (Aristotle 1140b, 5). In other words, both forms of activity presuppose active production of meaning—making, cf. *techné*, or doing, cf. *phrónêsis*; in both cases (more so in the latter), as was noted earlier, the communication ethics must "call on our unrelenting creativity" (Krippendorff 2009, 154). The staging of communication as transformation, however, is one of the most pure ethical activities; here nothing is produced but everything reproduced. The nature of communication here can be viewed in terms of the most "minimalist liberalism" (Rasch 2000, 149)—reproducing nothing but possibility.

So, this staging is the staging of constant reunification of every one/every thing with every one/every thing else where/when all are (equal part[icipant]s of) communication. It can be said that here one does not feel any difference, any gap between oneself and everyone else, or one is one with everyone else, or one is everyone else. This is the staging of oneness—*singlarity*. It seems as if the gap between all participants of communication is filled (finally!) with the sign of equality, as it were. Taking this sign out—first, mentally, and then, literally—the most adequate verbal representation of the nature of communication would take the form of its parts (reunited) without any gaps, cf. "spacetime" or "timespace." From this perspective, the radical difference between humans and technology is overcome, as well; it is suggested (Epshtein 2004, 611) that their communication be studied within the so-called humanology, which equally focuses on the ecology of humans and anthropology of machines, the "technozation" of humans and "humaniziation" of technology. Hence all participants of communication take the form of "humanologs" as transformed beings; it is no accident that such beings are often found in science fiction where they are *made* possible.

Becoming Undead

Thus, at this staging, the universe of communication is (trans)formed; communication re-turns to its origins, to the eternal source of all meaning. The healing powers of this source make (every participant of) communication whole, one. The wishes rendered with creativity, love and devotion, are now carried on, like the "happy returns of the day," with the gap between space and time, one and everyone else, oneself and oneself (seemingly) filled.

Communication up to this point has been theorized from various perspectives. The information theory especially, in W. Weaver's words, "has so penetratingly cleared the air that one is now, perhaps for the first time, ready for a real theory of meaning" (Weaver 1964, 27). At this staging, meaning(ful experience) that is constantly (trans)formed can be best understood from the performative perspective. From the performative point of view, communication can be viewed as a process of the rendition of meaning, cf. the staging of communication as resignation, or its constantly return/ing, cf. the staging of communication as transformation. Once communication reveals its nature as performance in the latter sense, it appears as one self-sufficient meaningful whole. Thus, the way from the staging of communication as invocation to the staging of communication as transformation is traversed, the gap between them filled. The "beginning" and the "end" of communication meet, and we walk, as S. Kierkegaard notes, backwards into the future (Peters 2003, 409). And so communication appears again as *nous*—"both beginning and end" (Aristotle 1947, 1143b5).

This way can be viewed as the way from blindly trying to master objects to seeing the light, which, of course, is a metaphor for communication turning spiritual. At this staging, communication reveals its most *liminary* nature: on the one hand, meanings constantly pass or are transformed over the least perceptible threshold, cf. "liminal," and, on the other hand, communication is a constant source of meaningful light, cf. "luminary." For communication to be successful as a *liminary* process, everyone must completely trust everyone else; communication overall is possible only if based on trust. Because it exists in the form of the air that is invisible to the eye, it is trust that holds communication together. Trust is a matter not of physical matter, but faith—"airy nothing." In Russian, the words for "before trust" and "trust" differ in but one space, cf. "do verie" ("до верие") and "doverie" ("доверие"). Once the universe of communication is (trans)formed, this gap is filled with spirit, as it were, and communication becomes a matter of faith, based on trust. Nothing is more firm than trust, and, at the same time, nothing can be more easily broken than trust because communication here is at its most defenseless. One yawn during a religious service, one look at the watch during the singing of the national anthem—and the spirit is gone from communication, the trust broken. Communication is a process where/when every action must be performed in good faith.

As mentioned earlier, at this staging, communication is as a process where/when the motion of spatio-temporal continuum of meaning only seems to stop, the state of complete equality seems to be reached. At some point, the straight (even) lines of the equality sign begin to oscillate, as it were, turning into the waves of the more and more turbulent currents. And so, with the transition from potentiality to actuality, the Dreaming ends.

Just as there was no point in looking for the "winner" during the reunification of space and time, i.e., for the one that made it all possible, there is no point in trying to place the blame on one or the other for breaking their union. It can be said that time can no longer wait, staying at this staging only for the duration of a ritual; after that, it must fill (the objects arranged in) space with new meanings. Or, it can be equally said that space refuses to remain in the form of frozen objects and allows time to fill them with new meanings, letting them in. One way or the other, the Dreaming ends, and empiricism sets in again, as if for the first time.

In more prosaic terms, a quantum mechanics analogy can be used. Then, potentiality

> is like a wave function, a manifold buzz of possibilities, awaiting final determination at each successive moment . . . the particular configuration of particles observed at time t depends, in large part, on when and how the observer makes the observation. The act of making the observation itself serves as the singular or unlikely event that collapses the wave function, elevating one possibility to actuality. (Sheldon and Vansteenkiste 2005, 145)

For that to happen, one must wake up from the Dreaming, as it were, and become once again an observer of what actually takes place.

The staging of communication as transformation lasts (and takes place) only as long as a ritual lasts; once it is over, the messiness of communication, in all its actual manifestation *hic et nunc* comes back into focus. This way, communication moves to the staging of conversation where attention is paid (again) to a certain object as the Other. In other words, a certain object appears to move in a different way, causing one's wonderment; what but a moment ago seemed only natural, eternal and going without saying, now seems new and calls for looking into, i.e., interpretation. True wisdom calls for one to return to the Platonic cave, back to life with all its actual trials and tribulations. One faces again the tests of time; one wonders at objects again, but fears them no more. One is now wise and strong, having been rejuvenated in the healing springs of communication. One has traversed the entire universe of communication, becoming a part of the communication universe; in other words, one has already become undead.

To summarize, following its staging as transformation, communication is turned into one, and thus a communication universe is formed. At this staging, every one and every thing returns to itself, constantly transformed in every act of communication, which reveals its ecological character. Here the nature of communication is manifested in the form of a ritual as care and cure; at this point, every one and every thing is cared for and cured—restored to itself, made whole.

Ritual communication does not have any instrumental purpose; here the very possibility of communication is revived, which can be identified with the virtue of *sophia*. Hence communication here exists as potentiality. At this staging, communication is as close to being perfect and ideal as possible, appearing as *singularity*—a true democracy of transspecies where/when the voice of every singular thing matters. Here every one/every thing, as a singular existence, is exposed to the singular existence of every thing and every one else; at this point, communication can be viewed as pleroma. Communication is completely filled with time and space and so its motion seems to stop. However, "the thing itself always escapes" (Derrida 1973, 104), and so, at some point, the transition from potentiality to actuality takes place. And so the (trans)formation of the communication universe begins again—or rather continues.

~

CHAPTER EIGHT

Communication: Infinite Return

Summing Up

Thus, communication comes back to where/when it started so that it can keep moving forward. So, too, this book comes back to the questions raised in the very first chapter—"What is the nature of communication?" and "How can it be theoretically conceptualized?" To answer these questions, it was necessary to step out of communication, as it were, looking at it from a distance, and also become communication itself, as much as possible. In this sense, our theorizing took the form of inquiry where/when "we are not only always 'on-the-way' traveling the path but we are intrinsically that pathway itself" (Heidegger 2005, 62).

The first step on/of that way of inquiry was making an ontological commitment and defining communication as a process of motion in which experience becomes meaningful. In this process, common experience undergoes a number of transformations, communication being (trans)formed. As a result of each transformation, communication is conceptualized as a point where/ when experience seems to be captured, becoming meaningful. It seems as if, at this point, the motion stops; however, another transformation always takes place and time because the motion of meaningful experience is an everlasting and ever-changing process.

In the present book, four transformations of meaning are identified; respectively, five stagings of communication, caused by these transformations, are discussed. The fourfold framework is commonly associated with stability. It is noted that the triadic frameworks, while widespread in the history of culture, came into being only following the binary, and the fourfold, based upon the binary, conceptualizations (Ivanov 1999, 529). This may be one reason why four, and not three, main views of communication are usually discussed (Rosengren 1983). One of the latest attempts to present communication in terms of a fourfold approach is the work by J. Anderson and G. Baym (2004) where communication is viewed in terms of four quadrants and discussed using the coordinates of ontology, epistemology, praxeology, and axiology.

All the views of communication, based upon the fourfold framework, are similar to the approach developed in the present book. However, in the present book, all such views of communication are taken further: first, the nature of communication is conceptualized as a process of experience becoming meaningful, and, second, a measure for this process, in which meaning is transformed, is identified with the interplay of space and time. As a result, communication is presented as experience becoming meaningful to those involved in it, or as motion of spatiotemporal continuum of meaning.

Thus, communication is conceptualized as a living being, trying to return to itself—to the point where/when there was no gap between space and time and so communication was one whole. This way, communication continues on and on, moving back to its future. In other words, communication is a process of (one) striving to, and distancing from, a constantly dis/appearing point; it is a simultaneous motion to/from meaning. On the one hand, time seems to get ahead of space, drawing it after itself, while, on the other hand, striving to catch up with it. The same can be said about space in its relation to time. This is how space and time try to fill each other with one's spirit, getting close to each other and still keeping apart from each other. As mentioned earlier, a gap between them is unavoidable because it is where/when meaning is (trans)formed; in this respect, one can speak about "the gaps of which communication is made" (Peters 1999, 251). The endpoints of the four transformations are the points (places/moments) where/when this gap is (or rather seems to be) bridged.

Once we made our certain ontological commitment, it became possible to present different theoretical conceptualizations of communication as gravitating toward one of its stagings. It was shown that the linear views, for example, the information theory or traditional rhetorical theory, are more appropriate for the staging of communication as invocation; those of a more interactive nature, for example, dialogical or dramaturgical—for the staging of communication as conversation; more normative views, for example, universal pragmatics or the theory of coordinated management of meaning—for the staging of communication as construction; those with a critical and what is considered postmodern orientation—for the staging of communication as resignation; and, finally, at the staging of communication as transformation, its nature can be best explained/understood in terms of performative theories.

There is an isomorphic relationship between the ontological and epistemological approaches to communication. Ontologically, communication can be viewed as moving from stable and observable structures, which exist in supposedly pure space, to ever-changing semiotic relationships, which exist in supposedly pure time, to the dynamic state where/when they form one whole. Respectively, knowledge claims about communication move from resting as if in space on empirically obtained and verifiable facts, to based on seemingly nothing but an intersubjective agreement reached over time, to the state where/when (it seems) nothing else can be said about the nature of communication.

As was noted at the beginning of the book, theorizing the nature of communication can be viewed as a journey which one, similar to the *theoros* in ancient Greece, undertakes for the purpose of looking at an object in all its cosmic beauty and then publicizing one's findings upon return. In this sense, every theoretical study of communication is a communication itself where/when one attempts to bridge the gap between one's views and those expressed earlier—the gap that exists as a spatiotemporal interval. By resigning one's experiences, one opens up a new gap to be bridged (one hopes) by someone else at a later point in time and space. This way, communication (about communication) continues. Any theoretical attempt to explain/understand an object is "to be continued" because any conceptual framework is incomplete and open to new meanings. We may claim things and ideas as our own all we want, but we do not really own anything; rather, communication itself carries us to new and newer shores. Ironically, it is physicists and mathematicians—the scientists dealing with the supposedly soulless matter and cold numbers—who speak of the indeterminacy and incompleteness of life. In the so-called communication studies or sciences, we tend to search for certainty, craving closure. Fortunately, there are voices such as Ch. S. Peirce's and M. Bakhtin's, reminding us that semiosis is unlimited, communication unfinalizable. Therefore, "we should not hold our breath waiting for methods of documentation that will finally settle what really happened. . . . Description may be inexhaustible not only because language is generative but also because the universe is incomplete" (Peters 2008, 31).

Let us briefly look back at the stagings of communication, described in the previous chapters.

The staging of communication as invocation can be viewed as a (seemingly only spatial) process of calling forth the object. In this respect, communication can be conceptualized as transmission of a message from the subject to the object, which then responds to it in a predictable, seemingly timeless manner. Ideally, this procedure is expected to generate the same response from the object and so can be viewed as spatial extension of meaning. At the staging of communication as conversation, its actual nature is revealed. Here communication is a process of symbolic (inter)action that takes place between the subject and the Other in concrete situations. In such engagement, which is viewed not only in spatial terms but also in terms of temporality, objects are questioned by the subject because one tries to understand objects in their own terms. The staging of communication as construction is an attempt to build a perfect world order common to all its participants. Here communication is a process of conscious coordination of actions, based on the discursive verification rather than the lived experiences of actual interactions. The goal of communication here is to bring all its meanings to the common denominator. At the staging of communication as resignation, it is a creative process when one is consumed by communication, taking a transcendental step into its flow and resigning (to) it. Here the meaningful gap between time and space is factually unnoticeable. Finally, at the staging of communication as transformation, it is a ritual process in which meanings are constantly revived; it is the most ephemeral staging of communication. Communication here is completely filled with time and space and so its motion seems to stop.

The nature of communication at these stagings can be correlated—figuratively and quite loosely—with the natural elements as understood by some thinkers in ancient Greece, for example, Parmenides. From this perspective, the staging of communication as invocationcan can be viewed as the air in the vast spaces of the sky in which meanings are arranged as if immutable (timeless) stars that cannot change their course. The staging of communication as conversation can be viewed as the currents of the water flowing like a stream which carries the boat with the Self and the Other trying to navigate their way to a safe shore. The staging of communication as construction can be viewed as the firm earth upon which a certain world order is constructed by using certain rules. At the staging of communication as resignation, it is enflamed, so to speak, and one steps into this fire, which is always so near and so far, like the horizon. If this step of re-signation turns out to be truly creative, full of loving care, then meanings are revived at the staging of communication as transformation where/when it is conceptualized as the spirit—similar to the air yet beyond any objectification. For this reason, the nature of communication at the staging of transformation cannot be represented visually and can never be expressed adequately (to its nature) in a verbal form. As the "airy nothing," the spirit cannot be framed, by definition; although "airy" it is still "nothing."

The key element is the fifth element, cf. "quintessence" ("quint" meaning "five"), in/which the overall nature of communication is revealed. This quintessential element can be identified with the entire communication universe the way Plato added to Parmenides' four elements cosmos as the fifth one (Genz 1999, 72). However, any study of the meaningful structures of communication reveals not another structure, but its lack, a gap (Eco 1997).

The quintessential element of the overall communication universe, then, is nothing but nothing, which, as the most potent source of meaning, gives rise to everything. As mentioned earlier, communication can be considered perfect only *in potentia*. In this sense, the expression "Nothing is perfect" reveals its profound meaning once the emphasis is placed on the link verb "is" linking or connecting nothing with—the perfect—everything, so to speak. By the same token, the expression "Nothing matters" receives a similar interpretation: "The nature of existence is the nature of the immaterial idea: Words do not matter . . . , but then again, nothing matters. . . . The irony here is quite layered: Nothing matters; communication, in modernity, is nothing (*Nullius in Verba*); therefore communication, in this ironic postmodern sense, matters (as the nothing, it is the only thing that can matter" (Shepherd 1993, 89); cf. the following words by Aristotle: "[The activity of *theoria*] seems to be the only one which is loved for its own sake; *for nothing comes into being from it*" (Aristotle, 1177b, 1–15; emphasis added).

It is not easy to come to terms with nothing as the quintessential element of communication, especially considering the significance of presence associated with various technologies (Gumbrecht 2004, 139; Riva et al. 2006). For example, logocentrism's search for presence unfolded "in the void left by the absence of the god" (Vivian 2004, 49). It is not easy yet essential to accept the fact, re-signing (to) it, that the nature of communication constantly comes into being from nothing.

Figuring It All Out

Emphases

At every staging, a certain aspect of communication is emphasized, associated with the key moving factor (agency) of communication as a spatio-temporal continuum of meaningful experience. At each staging, a certain aspect of communication is brought into focus (unfolds), while all the other aspects remain enfolded in the background. Communication at each staging, of course, remains one indivisible whole. At the staging of invocation, the nature of communication is highlighted in the form of what is "naturally given," cf. "nature," or objects that can be invoked yet call out for more attention. At the staging of conversation, objects start to move in different ways, and so attention shifts to the Other. At the staging of construction, a certain world order, built in the process of communication as discourse, comes into view. At the staging of resignation, the role of Self is emphasized, moving communication further in the creative act. By the staging of transformation, communication makes a complete turn; now the emphasis is placed on the entire universe of communication as (trans) culture. Similar to the staging of invocation, communication here appears natural, only it is not "naturally given" but "(trans)culturally" re-created; by the same token, what is "naturally given" at the staging of invocation is still culturally conditioned. In other words, the connections between these stagings are not clear-cut; hence both "nature" and "culture" are put in quotes, i.e., "nature" is what is "cultivated," while "culture" is what is "naturalized." We should not forget, of course, that the strategic, constitutive, or transcendental illusion underlies communication. As L. Wittgenstein put it, "the whole modern conception of the world is founded on the illusion that the so-called laws of nature are the explanations of natural phenomena" (*Tractatus*, 6.371).

Goals of Communication

At the staging of invocation, the goal of communication consists in the recognition of what is "naturally given," or finding out the supposedly timeless meanings of objects. At the staging of conversation, the goal of communication is to understand the Other; in the process of the interpretation of the Other's meanings, one begins to understand oneself. At the staging of construction, the goal of communication is to build a certain world order—a consciousness shared by (ideally all) its participants. At the staging of resignation, the goal of communication is self-awareness; one becomes aware of one's role in the process of communication as an act of creation. Finally, at the staging of transformation, the goal of communication is the recognition of objects, not as "naturally given," but "(trans)culturally" re-created things. Here recognizing is understood not as finding meaning(ful) things out, but acknowledging, reviving them, i.e., bringing them back to life in every act of their ritual reunification.

Modality of Communication

At the staging of invocation, communication can be conceptualized as materiality; here communication exists in the form of "naturally given" objects. As mentioned earlier, this form of existence includes not only verbal experiences, but also "all others, including those at the molecular level, where the odor of freshly baked foods communicates in much the same way as speech" (Jordan 2002, 380). At the staging of conversation, communication exists as actuality; here each situation of communication is significant *hic et nunc*. At the staging of construction, communication exists as reality or in the form of a certain sociocultural world order that is built on the basis of what is "naturally given," hence the difference between materiality and reality. At the staging of resignation, communication exists as virtuality, and, at the staging of transformation—as potentiality. These aspects of existence of communication can be correlated with the states of semiotic existence of any entity proposed by A. Greimas and J. Courtés (1982) and further developed by A. Greimas and J. Fontanille (1993): the potential, the virtualized, the actualized, and the realized. According to their views, any action can be described as a process of signification going through the states of potentialization, virtualization, actualization, and realization of meaning. According to the approach developed in the present book, the (trans)formation of the communication universe goes through the stagings of materiality, actuality, reality, virtuality, and potentiality.

Intellectual Virtues

Communication can be viewed as a constant search for the common good conducted with the help of several intellectual virtues and based upon certain kinds of knowledge. The virtue activated at the staging of communication as invocation is *nous* as the faculty that has a non-discursive nature, grasping the first principles intuitively; "*nous* is . . . present in the other intellectual virtues" (Mailloux 2004, 464). At the staging of conversation, where technical skills are produced as something separate from the activity of making, communication is based on the virtue of *techné*. The virtue that lies at the basis of the staging of communication as construction is *Epistêmê*, i.e., scientific knowledge of the order of things in the universe; *Epistêmê* provides a comprehensive account of a world order that is derived from indisputable principles and can be demonstrated. At the staging of resignation, communication can be identified with *phrónêsis*, which, unlike a crafty procedure toward achieving a certain end, is the ability to reflect upon and decide that end by acting on it. Finally, communication at the staging of transformation can be related to the virtue of *sophia* as a self-contained and intrinsically valuable activity not motivated by any direct instrumental external goals. Only wisdom can bring eternal and divine bliss.

Forms of Similitude

At the staging of invocation, communication can be viewed in terms of *convenientia* as one of four similitudes; *convenientia* refers to the universal "convenience" of things and is connected with space. *Aemulatio* that lies at the basis of the staging of communication as conversation can be viewed as the means by which things scattered through the universe can look like one another; *aemulatio* thus brings to mind the concept of the looking-glass self. At the staging of communication as construction, the form of similitude is *analogy* in which *convenientia* and *aemulatio* are superimposed; as a result, *analogy* refers to adjacencies and the fitting of resemblances across space. Communication at the staging of resignation can be viewed in terms of *sympathy*, which excites things to movement by drawing them together no matter how distant those may be; through *sympathy*, communication is transformed toward identity. To these four forms, the fifth one is added in the present book, called *pleroma*; *pleroma* is found at the staging of communication as transformation where/when everything is reunited with itself and everything else. This form of order of things is similar to J. Gebser's "integral," which is "*a space-and-time free* a perspectival world where the free (or freed) consciousness has at its disposal all latent as well as actual forms of space and time, without having either to deny them or to be fully subject to them" (Gebser 1985, 117).

The key moments of the discussion above are represented in the figure below.

Communication as a Universe

Stagings / Features	Invocation	Conversation	Construction	Resignation	Transformation
Emphases	"Nature"	Other	World Order	Self	"(Trans)culture"
Goals	Recognition	Understanding	Realization	Awareness	Revival
Modalities	Materiality	Actuality	Reality	Virtuality	Potentiality
Intellectual Virtues	Nous	Techné	Epistêmê	Phrónêsis	Sophia
Forms of Similitude	Convenientia	Aemulatio	Analogy	Sympathy	Pleroma

The staging of communication as invocation can be conceptualized best of all in terms of ontology, the staging of communication as conversation—praxeology, the staging of communication as construction—epistemology, the staging of communication as resignation—aesthetics, and the staging of communication as transformation—ethics (axiology). The main question raised at the staging of invocation is, "What is (the nature of objects that exist)?"; hence the ontological aspects of communication (being) are addressed most directly. At the staging of conversation, the main question raised is, "How (can an action be technically produced)?"; hence the aspects of communication as praxis (praxeology) are addressed most directly. At the staging of construction, the main question raised is, "Why (is the world order constructed and claimed to be the most rational one)?"; hence knowledge claims and their verifiability are addressed most directly. At the staging of resignation, the main question raised is, "What for?", which, although similar to "Why?," places less emphasis on epistêmê and focuses more on the creative activity of re-signation, cf. phrónêsis; hence the aesthetic aspects of creating (beautiful) meanings are addressed most directly. It is interesting to note that, in Russian, the question "Why?" has two variants—"Pochemu?" ("Почему?") and "Zachem?" ("Зачем"); if the syllables in the latter are separated with but one space (a gap), cf. "Za chem?" ("За чем?"), it comes to mean "What follows what?," which nicely captures the essence of resignation. The question raised at the staging of transformation coincides with that of the staging of invocation, but takes the essence of communication further, cf. "What is (proper)?" In other words, ontology and ethics (axiology) go hand-in-hand; sometimes the latter is considered more significant than the former because "ethics does not have an essence. . . . Its 'essence' is precisely to unsettle essences, and its 'identity' is not to have an identity" (Pinchevski 2005). Clearly, ethics cannot not be ontological just as ontology cannot not be ethical.

Most of the studies of communication seem to deal with the aspects of praxeology and epistemology; it is such studies that, as a rule, are considered foundational (Anderson and Baym 2004). Apparently, this way, our desire to be skillful is revealed, i.e., our desire to be able to know how to behave in various situations of communication, and to be well-versed in the worldly affairs, or knowing why something is constructed/takes place. Meanwhile, the study of communication as an aesthetic, beautifully rhythmic process is of great importance, too. The aesthetic study of communication is usually conducted as an analysis of strategic use of symbolic means toward a certain end, cf. techné. Of greater interest, however, is the study of communication as a creative process of passibilité, in which meaning passes through the subject (Self), i.e., the study of "what (communication is) for" or "what follows what."

It is difficult to study communication in this light because of the tacit—and partly illusionary—nature of knowledge. It can be noted that the expressions "ontology of communication," "praxeology of communication," and "epistemology of communication" are quite common, while the expression "aesthetics of communication" is much more rare (cf. Parret 1993); this testifies to how much—or little—importance is given to the study of communication from a certain philosophical point of view. However, most important and most difficult is the study of "ethics of communication," or its analysis as a ritual revival of meanings, in other words, the study of "what is (proper)." The difficulty of such study can be explained by the fact that—especially—at the staging of transformation, one cannot be separated from communication at this staging; it must be reminded, communication is a process where/when one is one with communication. One cannot look at communication objectively being a subjective part of this being. And yet, the importance of understanding of "what is (proper) communication?" cannot be emphasized enough.

It is interesting to see how different philosophical views of communication are reflected in the frequency of its common definitions. Most often, communication is defined as a process of message transmission, cf. the staging of invocation/ontology; next, communication is defined as a skillful exchange of information, cf. the staging of conversation/praxeology; next, communication is defined as a process of constructing something common based on the knowledge of rules, cf. the staging of construction/epistemology. Very rarely is communication defined as a creative process of resignation, cf. the staging of resignation/aesthetics, or as a ritual process of constant transformation where/when sacred, proper meanings are maintained (returned), cf. the staging of transformation/ethics. The less common the definition, the more attention must be paid to the study of communication from that respective point of view.

The Dialectics of (the Study of) Communication

The main stagings of communication, identified in the present book, are not mutually exclusive; on the contrary, each staging can be viewed as contained (enfolded) within the previous one(s); in this sense, communication unfolds as a living being. Thus, the nature of communication is holographic, and one can see in/through each of its smallest parts the entire universe of communication. By the same token, the theoretical view of communication has a perspectival character; in this respect, "each perspective is certainly an epistemology that guides our theorizing, our inquiry, our thinking into the process of communication" (Fisher 1978, 322). Also, as mentioned earlier, "perspective" means not only "a view of/on something," but also "a relative significance of something" (Morris 1982, 979). In other words, each perspective of a certain staging of communication, presented in the respective chapter, is significant, and the entire universe of communication must be viewed from all these perspectives at once; after all, communication is one whole indivisible being. Similar to (ontologically speaking) each staging of communication connected to the other stagings, each theoretical perspective (epistemologically speaking) is connected to the other perspectives; the further such stagings/perspectives are apart, the more difficult it is to see connections between them.

Ontologically speaking, each staging of communication is further developed by/in the next one, which can be viewed as its antithesis. For this reason, the stagings that are not next to each other, but across each other, have more in common; in a way, each staging looks into the eyes of the other one and sees itself there, as if in a mirror, only somewhat different(ly developed). Thus, each staging goes through the one next to it, as its antithesis, and can be viewed as one of the second order, so to speak. For example, the staging of construction, focused on a world order ("culture"), is the more developed staging of invocation ("nature"); the staging of resignation where the focus of attention is the subject (Self) is the more developed staging of conversation, i.e., Self is a different(ly developed) Other; the staging of transformation where/when the focus of attention is "(trans)culture" is the staging of construction in the second order; and the Other at the staging of conversation is the differently developed Self from the staging of resignation.

So, each staging can be viewed as re-signation of the staging with which it is in oblique or indirect relations; the new meanings that appear as a result of such re-signation are due to what is experienced during the previous—intermediary, antithetical—staging. For example, a certain world order is the materiality in its potentiality, experienced differently, i.e., in (an) Other way; the subject (Self) is the Other that experienced a certain world order; the potentiality of "(trans)culture" is the reality of the world order experienced and re-signed by the subject; and the Other is the subject (Self) that actualizes the meaningful experience for which Self was invigorated through ritual transformation.

Overall, communication being is as a process of spatiotemporal experience constantly returning to itself; one complete turn means all the main stagings are traversed, i.e., one complete turn of the Moebius strip. Communication being returns to itself as a result of two triads (thesis-antithesis-synthesis); one such triad is only one half of the way. It was noted earlier that the triadic conceptual frameworks in the history of culture are preceded by the binary ones and also the fourfold frameworks, based upon the binary ones. In this light, it is possible to say that the cultures where the triadic frameworks are dominant, for example, the Russian culture (Vladimirova 2007, 340–344), are only halfway returning to themselves. In other words, their communicative experience is still mostly at the staging of conversation with the Other (as a synthesis); that is why, perhaps, such cultures are never satisfied, always looking at the Other and trying to do everything in (an)Other way without finishing what they started themselves. One might say that their view of life is more revolutionary than evolutionary. If that is, indeed, the case, the second half of the way must be traversed; as a result, the culture can return to itself and learn what one's true self is, thus becoming more stable, balanced, healed—whole.

Epistemologically speaking, each perspective is also further developed by the next one, which can be viewed as its antithesis, and appears as one of the second order. For example, traditional rhetorical theories turn into normative theories; traditional interpersonal communication theories such as symbolic interactionism turn into critical, i.e., in essence, intrapersonal theories; normative theories appear as performative theories; and critical or deconstructive theories turn back into interactional theories.

It is crucial that we focus on the intermediate—antithetical—staging because every staging can be viewed as intermediate, connecting the two oblique or indirect stagings. Thus, communication overall can be viewed as one intermediate interval, one staging of significance, one manifestation of meaning. Overall, this interval is where/when communication being constantly unfolds/enfolds as a spatiotemporal continuum of meaningful experience. An interval is a gap that equally relates to space and time; communication as interval is spacetime or timespace, or rather a meaningful gap between them, constantly (attempted to be) bridged and also maintained as a gap.

The intermediate staging (interval) falls out of our attention because, to us, a beginning and an end of something are more important, cf. thesis and synthesis rather than what lies between them ("the way"). And yet, the intermediate staging should be viewed as that test that falls to one's lot, or that befalls one; it is out of this staging that the meaningful experience of all participants of/in communication grows. The intermediate staging as antithesis is where/when the very dynamics of communication occurs or rather what communication is. The dialectic of communication, then, lies in its intermediate/interval character; the intermediate staging is always a question that is more important than an answer because one (and only) answer is impossible just as one (and only) spacetime/timespace is impossible. Communication as a spatiotemporal continuum of meaning is always a gap, an interval, a line drawn between something and something else.

One might say that we feel more comfortable with answers given rather than questions posed, i.e., with sameness or experience (seemingly) returned to itself. The intermediate staging, as antithesis, seems to be directed against communication, cf. "anti"; it seems to have a destructive, "negative" character. However, in reality the character of the intermediate staging can be best expressed by the following words of Mephistopheles from Goethe's *Faust*: asked who he/she it is, the devil of the romantic imagination answers: "Part of that force which would / Do evil evermore, and yet creates good . . . / I am the spirit that negates" (lines 168–170).

In other words, the seeming "negativity" of the intermediate staging is a crucial constitutive factor of communication as meaningful interval. It is this very constitutive factor that is found in the ideas of the "negative dialectics," or T. Adorno's dialectical critique of dialectics (in a way, the negative dialectics can be viewed as dialectics of the second order). Using the concept of constellation as one of T. Adorno's favorite concepts, every act of communication can be viewed as "a juxtaposed rather than integrated cluster of changing elements that resist reduction to a common denominator, essential core, or generative first principle" (Jay 1984, 14–15). Following T. Adorno's ideas, it is crucial to emphasize the always transformative character of the negative dialectics because "the dialectic, when it ceases to be negative, immediately and unavoidably replaces that which it would criticize" (Wolfe 1991, 80). Clear parallels exist between these ideas and those of J. Derrida (cf. Jay 1984, 21). In this light, as H. de Vries reminds us, the negative or seemingly destructive thrust of such ideas should not allow the reader to "forget that deconstruction involves in the first place an *affirmative* act" (de Vries 2005, 632). At the same time, it can be argued that "Adorno's negative dialectics constantly undermines the dream of reconciliation between people—in the name of that dream. Removing a false hope is a fine service so long as it does not damage our animal faith, since *all action rests on strategic illusion*" (Peters 1999, 224; emphasis added). In one of the earlier chapters, it was discussed how the critics of J. Habermas could themselves be criticized for their unwillingness to admit important metaphysical underpinnings in his work; after all, J. Habermas clearly states that "for every possible communication, the anticipation of the ideal speech situation has the significance of a *constitutive illusion* that is at the same time a prefiguration [*Vorschein*] of a form of life" (quoted by: Craig and Muller 2007, 455; emphasis mine). Elsewhere, he notes that his theory of universal pragmatics "is still accompanied by the shadow of *a transcendental illusion*" (Habermas

1993, 144; emphasis mine). To admit the significance of a constitutive or transcendental illusion in(to) the process of communication seems to be the only way of dealing with the performative contradiction, which occurs when one criticizes rationality using language as a tool of reason (Jay 1993, 25–37), or—more broadly—when one communicates about the impossibility of communication. In fact, communication can be conceptualized as "*a stand-in for an impossible presence*, enveloping the central void" (Dolar 2006, 53). This way, as one tries to understand the nature of communication, one can have it both ways, so to speak, seeing communication as a real, physically inscribed process of meaning (trans)formation and as a process of imagination when meaning borders on the illusionary, always a prefiguration, always existing "as if," i.e., as if existing. In this sense, the nature of communication can be identified as *seemeangness*, i.e., seeming meaningfulness or meaningful seemingness.

Thus, communication can be conceptualized as the dialectics of two parts, two forces, which constantly try to become one and are simultaneously kept apart. These two forces can be labeled in a number of different ways, e.g., space and time, question and answer, thesis and antithesis, denotation and signification, analogic communication and digital communication, speech and writing, dialogue and dissemination, etc. The dialectics of communication consist in a simultaneous motion of these two forces toward, and away from, each other. Their synthesis is (or rather seems to be) achieved at every point of their unification, while leaving a gap for new meanings to appear *then and there*. A gap is an inherent part of communication being because "every relation with being is simultaneously a taking and a being taken, the hold is held, it is inscribed and inscribed in the same being that it takes hold of" (Merleau-Ponty 1968, 266).

Communication, therefore, is a dialectical process of filling gaps with meaning at different levels. It is possible to speak about communication between one and the Other (cf. the staging of conversation), one and many (cf. the staging of construction), one(Self) and one(Self) (cf. the staging of resignation), and one and all (cf. the stagings of invocation and transformation). These levels can be viewed as parallel to the communication domains identified by J. Ruesch and G. Bateson (Ruesch and Bateson 1951; cf. Lanigan 2008), cf. the interpersonal level or social domain corresponds to the staging of communication as conversation, the group level or cultural domain corresponds to the staging of communication as construction, the intrapersonal level or psychiatric/aesthetic domain corresponds to the staging of communication as resignation, and the intergroup level or (trans)cultural domain corresponds to the staging of communication as transformation.

It is important to study the degree of correspondence between the two parts of communication as a dialectical process because it is important to see to/in what degree one part of communication corresponds to the other. The study of every situation/level of communication, therefore, can be brought down to a number, representing a degree of correspondence between two parts of communication. In the present book, the most harmonious degree of correspondence is identified with 1.6180319 . . .—the Golden ratio, the number that never repeats itself and never ends, generating new meanings and thus making it possible for communication to continue. Communication as correspondence, the degree of which can be expressed by this number, is as close to the ideal as can possibly be. It should be noted that the root "ar" in the word "harmony" means "number," cf. "arithmos" (Morris 1982, 602, 1506).

Thus, ontologically speaking, harmonious communication—to/in various degrees of correspondence between its parts—is constantly created and disrupted, never reaching the ideal. By the same token, epistemologically speaking, a theoretical distinction is made between something and something else in its nature, and a certain degree of their correspondence is established. In the present book, such a line is drawn, and a degree of correspondence suggested, on the basis of a discursive analysis and intuition. It would be interesting to see how these ideas fare in the light of quantitative data, based, for example, on a simple content analysis of the books and articles in which the main stagings of communication are discussed; the key words from each staging could be taken as the terms for coding. This way, it would become possible to establish a degree of correspondence between word and number, analysis and synthesis. To put it differently, word will look into number, as if into the mirror; and so it will become possible to see to/in what degree the study of communication is a harmonious process.

Communication Being Successful

Thus, communication is a process in which a meaningful connection between something and something else is established, a gap between them filled with common experience. In this sense, it can be said that "communication offers itself as . . . connectivity" (Rasch 2000, 148). It would be even more accurate to say that communication *is* connectivity. At the same time, so labeled, communication appears as a somewhat mechanistic process; communication can be conceptualized more adequately as a process of (re)unification of something and something else into one whole—one communication being that is constantly (trans)formed, i.e., is different, yet remains itself, i.e., is the same. At various points, communication can be conceptualized as invocation, conversation, construction, resignation, or transformation. Overall, communication must be viewed as a process of unification of all these stagings—all these "-tions"—into one being, one indivisible and whole communication. Communication as unification is a process in which common meaningful experience can be seen as *what* is, *how* what is is technically produced, *why* it is constructed, *what* it exists *for*, and *what is proper*. In other words, communication can be viewed as one's reaction to/recognition of the materiality of what is naturally given; the actuality of skillful techniques in various empirical situations; the reality of a discoursively constructed world order; the virtuality of actions by which meaning is resigned; and the potentiality of everything that is sanctified (proper). To be more exact, communication is a process of unification of all these modalities into one (whole) being.

It is noted that the essence of something is found if no predicate about this subject can be expressed (Losev 1994). Indeed, the meaning of any thing is found at the point where/when the thing returns to itself, filled with the experience made meaningful along the way of its transformation/s. At this point, the predicate becomes the same as (equal to) the subject itself, . . . "a flower flowers," "a photographer photographs," "communication communicates." Such expressions as facts of communication are considered pointless, i.e., "speech mistakes"; there is no need for such expressions from a practical point of view. However, the closer communication gets to the staging of transformation, i.e., the staging of its end/beginning, the clearer it becomes that, perhaps, it is a mistake not to recognize the sacred uniqueness of every thing; perhaps it is a mistake not to see that "a flower" is what "flowers" and not simply what is sold at flower shops, given as a gift, or put into a vase. It is the meanings of such tautalogical expressions, considered senseless from a practical point of view, that turn out to be the most sacred ones and endure in/as communication, making its most significant, most pure sense.

Every thing is not only a self-sufficient part of communication in which the subject and the predicate are one and the same—every thing also corresponds to/with everything else. In principle, any thing can be predicated to anything else. In this light, it is possible to say "a flower communicates" or "communication flowers"; all such expressions make sense up to a point. By the staging of transformation, where/when the universe of communication is formed, communication being has undergone all the analytical breaks, cuts and ruptures; it has stood the tests of time (and space), and now all meanings are reunited in the dynamic state of their synthesis. In this process of reunification, communication communicates, healing itself.

Some expressions, as correspondences, make more sense than others, of course. To put it differently, some expressions are found more natural, which is determined by the frequency of their use. For example, in the so-called free association test, the Russian word "derevo" ("дерево")—("tree"), as a stimulus, is most often related to (corresponds to/with) the word "bereza" ("береза")—("birch tree"), while the most frequent response to the word "pie" in the American culture is "apple pie." This test is called a free association test for a reason: it shows how freely meanings move within a certain culture. It is interesting to mention that "the concept of association can be traced back to Aristotle. . . . Some of Aristotle's concepts such as contiguity, similarity, and sequence effects anticipated a variety of associationist and connectionist models of the last century and today" (Stacy et al. 2006, 75–76).

So, what is communication? Phrased this way, the question is more likely to lead to the dangers of reification and essentialization of communication, discussed earlier. It is more appropriate to ask "What is communication being?" or "What is the being of communication?" In this respect, communication must be treated not so much as a thing, but rather as a living being, cf. the dynamic connotations of "being" as a gerund. Communication being can be conceptualized in many different ways; for example, in the present book, communication is viewed as invocation, reflection, construction, resignation, and transformation. Overall, communication is presented as a universe of meaningful experiences existing in the gap between space and time. Hence communication is a constant attempt to bridge this gap so that space and time, and thus every meaning, could become one whole. At the end of one staging and beginning of the next one, it seems as if this gap is filled with—one and only—meaning, and the motion of communication as a spatiotemporal continuum seems to stop. And yet, it only seems so for, as a continuous process of (trans)formation of meaning, communication is but *seemeangness*.

Because the gap in (as) communication cannot be eliminated, it may be tempting to view communication as failure (cf. St. John 2006), i.e., not successful. However, this is not the case; on the contrary, communication is always successful. It can be argued, of course, that there is no well-defined concept of communicative success (cf. Pagin 2008). However, communication is always successful insofar as it is one meaningful experience succeeding another. Communication is successful as long as a meaningful connection between something and something else is (seems to be) established. How long must it take, i.e., how much space and time is needed for such a connection to be established? As long/much as necessary for the meaningful interval to appear bridged, i.e., to be (to seem) as natural as possible, reaching (for) the staging of *singlarity* where/when communication being appears as one and all is/are the same.

Each moment where/when a meaningful connection between something and something else is established and a gap between space and time momentarily bridged, is a moment of wonderment. The moment an object responds to one's invocation, or the Other understood, or a certain world order constructed, or an experience re-signed, or a sacred meaning revived—all these moments are full of wonder because it all seems to happen so naturally. If this is not the case, a feeling of puzzlement sets in. The exclamation "How can this be?!" equally applies to wonder and puzzlement, cf. "How can this (not) be the case?!" or how can a meaningful connection (not) be established?! One is puzzled if something is done "against nature," trying to find a shortcut to meaning, so to speak. As a result, a search for meaning turns into a contest, a battle that one always "loses" because one feels "lost" or rather "not found": one never finds one's true self, never returns to oneself. A feeling of wonderment, on the contrary, is experienced if one acts "together with" someone or something; time simply passes, and things simply take place, and the meaning unfolds as if by itself, and so communication succeeds. Thus, in communication one should not look for a better place and spur up the time, trying to stage a(nother) revolution; one must just do what one does, and do it creatively—with love and devotion. Then, communication will continue, full of beauty and wonder—as life itself continues. Communication is one meaningful and wonderful experience after another, and one cannot escape communication because one cannot escape one's lot. In fact, one should not even try to escape communication; on the contrary, one should live one's life in order to become one with communication—become communication being.

For the Time and Space Being

There are always two sides to communication; for example, it can be viewed at once as a bridge and as a chasm (Peters 1999, 5). Communication is a dialectical process in which two parts always try to yet never completely unite into one (whole). One can conceptualize communication as "constituted by material objects that display discernable boundaries and exist within relatively stable and observable patterns of relationships," and also as meanings that "make their appearance within localized patterns of human practice, language, and discourse" (Anderson and Baym 2004, 590).

A communication message is, therefore, made up of two parts: on the one hand, it exists as physical material, and, on the other hand, as formal content (roughly, a signifier and a signified). Of course, not everything that is physically material is equally significant; and not everything that has formal content is equally physically real. Overall, however, these two parts of communication cannot be denied; taken to their extremes, they can be—quite broadly and loosely—identified with physics and metaphysics, cf. the

> division of all the sciences is into the real and the formal, where the first represent in thought the existent as standing independently over against thought, and have their truth in the correspondence of thought with that existent. The formal sciences, on the other hand, have as their object that which is posited through thought itself and have their truth in the correspondence of the reasoning processes among themselves. (Lewis 2004, 8)

One can find physically real traces even in the most abstract (formal) constructions of thought; for example, the public sphere, conceptualized as (an) ideal, still takes place (and time) in coffee-houses, on the radio air-waves, in the electrical wires, etc. Any act of communication, no matter how "transparent" or "ghostly" it may seem, is physically mediated, inscribed in/by the reality of our instruments. In this sense, "like Derrida, laboratory studies observe the striking congruence between literary inscriptions and 'facts': discussions about facts are inseparable from their inscriptions; the acceptance of a scientific fact is tied to the strength of its links to layers of text; the ostensibly factual nature of a statement can be undermined by drawing attention to the process of its inscription" (Lenoir 1998, 8). At the same time, every instrument as a physically real tool of mediation is created on the basis of acts of communication that have some formal content, i.e., it is infused with some "metaphysical" spirit. That is why the facts of the physical/natural sciences go hand-in-hand with the "metaphysical" discourse on every significant aspect of reality; how this discourse is conducted affects how the "reality as such" is discovered and changed. The communibiological theory, mentioned earlier, is a good illustration of that; while undoubtedly a (neuro)biological process, communication still presupposes live interaction, for example, between scientists or a doctor and a patient, cf. the discussion of such metaphysical concepts as pain, suffering, or illness.

In this light, no sharp distinction can be made between the so-called physical/natural sciences and the so-called social sciences/humanities; the difference between them is one of degree. In an interesting twist, it can be argued that "the relationship between humanities and science (in Marcus's terms, the hermeneutic and the empirical) in the West is . . . arbitrary and ideological—arbitrary in the sense that we are largely unconscious of the fact that it is socially reproduced; ideological in the sense that we are largely unconscious of the fact of its social reproduction. The legitimacy of social institutions, in particular the academic division of science from humanities, is sustained only by denying this arbitrariness" (Sangren 1988, 293). It should be mentioned that the representatives of the former—"the physicists"—are often, in some measure, methodologists and philosophers—"the metaphysics," while the representatives of the latter are seldom, even in small measure, "the physicists," usually staying away from that (real) world. Whatever the case may be, each side does not venture very often on the territory of the other. The study of communication, by definition, can provide a bridge between these two (supposedly rival) realms, showing how the gap can be meaningfully filled between the so-called inanimate (material) objects and the live world of (animate) human beings with their ideas (formal content). In a way, the study of communication can be seen as a universal science/discipline/area—a sort of Theory of Everything. Thus, the study of communication can be viewed as a search for the point where/when "physics" and "metaphysics" are one, (re)united in one—universal view of—being. In other words, the study of communication can be seen "as the ontological force . . . where communication rather than cellular structure, energy or mass, aesthetic quality or commodiousness, is the foundation for Being" (Shepherd 1993, 90).

Every science/discipline exists insofar as its ontology can be identified. It is the inability of communication study to articulate its own ontology that is considered its main problem (Shepherd 1993, 84), leading to its "epistemological erosion" (Donsbach 2006, 444). In this respect, one "can well imagine the physicist, the biologist, the artist, and the economist speaking in turn to me of the chair in my room: 'How sturdy!,' 'How natural!,' 'How handsome!,' 'How much?'" (Shepherd 1993, 84). The communicologist in this situation—or any other, for that matter—it seems, has nothing to say. However, communication being is the foundation of Being; "to be means to communicate" (Bakhtin 1984, 287). So, the communicologist in this situation—or any other, for that matter—could say "How universal!" i.e., how connected materially, actually, really, virtually, and most importantly potentially—with everything else. It is this process of connectedness or unification that constitutes—ontologically—the nature of communication and—epistemologically—the nature of its study.

Thus, communication can be seen as "a concept able to unify the natural sciences (DNA as the great code), the liberal arts (language as communication), and the social sciences (communication as the basic social process)" (Peters 1999, 25). Communication is a constant attempt to bring together into one being space and time, subject and object, object and thing, existence and essence, sense and meaning, observer and observed, explanation and understanding, physics and metaphysics, Plato and Aristotle, Self and Other/s, or Self and Self. The gap between these parts or "constituents" of communication is always filled with meaning yet never completely disappears; it is in this gap that communication becomes possible as a spatiotemporal transformation of meaningful experience. By the same token, the science/discipline/area of communication study is always "in crisis." As S. Hall notes, "communication research is constantly breaking apart and coming to the end of the road, arriving at terminal points beyond which it cannot survive, and so on. Yet, it does not disappear" (Hall 1989, 46). It is now clear that (the crisis of) communication research can disappear only with the disappearance of communication itself. For the time and space being, though, the study of communication will face the most important and impossible task, i.e., explaining/understanding and thus uniting or reconciling the nature of communication and the communication of nature.

Every study of communication is a communication itself. The self-reflexive character of studies of "real phenomena" is less apparent although a chemist's study involves chemical reactions and a physicist's study involves physical processes of/in the chemist/physicist him/herself. Meanwhile, a book about communication is clearly a communication. In other words, what is studied and what constitutes what is studied is one and the same. This fact, in spite of, or perhaps because of, being so apparent, is usually not given any attention. Self-reflexivity is demanding and can be a risky undertaking; indeed, "it is a subversive concept" (Hayles 1999, 9–10), and so it is not surprising that "good intentions are rarely applied to themselves" (Krippendorff 2009, 131). An interesting example of a component of reflexivity is found in the Macy conference transcripts where it

> surfaced most distinctly in terms of psychoanalysis, which was threatening to the physical scientists . . . because it seemed to reduce scientific debate to a morass of language. When they would object to Lawrence Kubie who was the psychoanalyst there, he would answer with things like "Oh, you're showing a lot of hostility, aren't you?" To them, that was almost a debasement of scientific debate because it kept involving them as people in what the conference was trying to do. (Hayles 1999, 172)

The scientists were clearly shying away from reflexivity, trying to bring the debate to more serious cybernetic issues where they felt more comfortable; in other words, they were clearly reluctant to take reflexivity that far, in essence—back to themselves.

However, everyone who conducts a study must ask how the very process of doing it makes one feel, i.e., one must try to establish a connection between one's object of study and one's subjective life. In other words, there is a connection between how one practically lives in the world and how one theoretically conceptualizes this world. Thus, no sharp distinction can be made between what is called "practice" and what is called "theory." In reality, no theory of communication exists in isolation from communication as practice. All theories *of* communication are, by the same token, theories *for* communication because "they must prove themselves viable in the communication practices they engender" (Krippendorf 1994, 102). Thus, any viable theory of communication must, at the same time (and space), be livable, existing not only as its explanation/understanding, but also its living part. As Aristotle says, "for we are inquiring not in order to know what virtue is, but in order to become good, since otherwise our inquiry would have been of no use" (Aristotle 1947, 1103, 25).

It must be emphasized that people do not simply develop or study communication theories; they live in/by them. The science (or discipline or area) of communication, therefore, as communication, tries to bridge the gap between theory and practice, to unite them. From this perspective, the main criteria of evaluating theories can be seen as corresponding to the stagings of communication, identified earlier. The staging of invocation can be best understood in terms of reliability: here one relies on communication as always reaching the same end. The staging of conversation can be best understood in terms of testability; here every skill is tested against a concrete empirical situation. The staging of construction can be best understood in terms of verifiability; here claims are made and defended in the process of discourse (as a result, something may not necessarily be testable yet can be rationally proven and thus trusted). The staging of resignation can be best understood in terms of validity; here every act of resignation must be seen as efficacious, binding one to one's reality. Finally, the staging of transformation can be best understood in terms of parsimony. Although in everyday usage it means unusual or excessive frugality or even stinginess, parsimony as a criterion of theory evaluation is identified with the meaning of economy or simplicity of assumptions in formulations (Morris 1982, 955). When a communication theory is said to be parsimonious, it means that "it can be briefly and succinctly stated" (Heath and Bryant 2000, 15). As the etymology of the word reminds us, "parsimony" is derived from "parcere," meaning "to spare," "to save" (Morris 1982, 955). This is exactly what occurs at the staging of transformation; here communication is revived, brought back to itself again and again, i.e., saved and protected.

To study communication does not mean to look for and discover its nature; to study communication means to open its nature the way a wound is opened (revealed) in the live flesh. (That is why it is so difficult to separate the ontology of communication from its axiology.) It is convenient to think that one studies communication by looking at/for its nature. In reality, however, one opens communication by cutting the quick, tearing apart space and time, and—it is hoped—feeling the pain from each open cut.

A researcher must be able not only to look at communication, but also listen to it, touch, smell and taste it. In a word, one must do one's best in order to (re)unite with communication, be(com)ing one with it—one communication being. Only then will one be able to explain/understand the nature of communication for each time one discovers something in communication, one discovers, opens up, cuts oneself.

So, the main criterion in (the study of) communication is parsimony as a careful, loving, simple, sparing attitude to everything one is connected to/with, forming one whole. A revolutionary approach to communication does not spare time (and space)—the very gaps that communication, as the Dreaming, is made of. A more evolutionary approach is less intrusive; it does less harm, willing to wait for as long as it is necessary for any gap to be naturally bridged, any wound to heal, and thus for communication being to reveal itself.

The criterion of parsimony is usually put at the end of the list of all criteria of theory evaluation—something desirable, but unnecessary. In reality, however, this criterion should be put on top of the list as the decisive one; while comparing different theoretical views on communication, with all the other criteria being equal(ly present), the last word remains with that of parsimony—the simplicity that spares and saves. The "secret" to successful communication, or the study of communication, is captured well by the old Latin phrase *Primum non nocere*—"First, do no harm."

To arrive at such simplicity, one must go through all the stagings of communication and find oneself at the staging where/when communication is constantly transformed. In other words, such simplicity requires a lot of space and time. Such is one's lot, however, because only this way is the universe of communication (trans)formed, and only this way can one's study of communication become viable and one's life livable. Then, it no longer matters what theory is—as something supposedly speculative and separate/d from practice—and what practice is—as something supposedly having nothing in common with theory. It no longer matters if one is the author of these lines or a work of communication written by the hand of Fate. It all no longer matters because it is all the same. It is all the same as long as communication being—this wonderful experience, this ever-lasting and ever-changing interval—re-turns like Odysseus returns home, "filled with space and time" (Osip Mandel'shtam).

Bibliography

Aboulafia, Mitchell. 1991. "Self-Consciousness and the Quasi-Epic of the Master." In *Philosophy, Social Theory, and the Thought of George Herbert Mead*, edited by Mitchell Aboulafia, 223–248. Albany: State University of New York Press.

Adam, Barbara. 2000. "The Temporal Gaze: The Challenge for Social Theory in the Context of GM Food." *British Journal of Sociology* 51, no. 1: 125–142.

Adams, Glenn, and Hazel Markus. 2004. "Toward a Conception of Culture Suitable for a Social Psychology of Culture." In *The Psychological Foundations of Culture*, edited by Mark Shaller and Christian Crandall, 335–359. Muhwah, NJ: Lawrence Erlbaum Associates.

Aderounmu, Ganiyn A., et al. 2006. "Remote Method Invocation and Mobil Agent: A Comparative Analysis." *Issues in Informing Science and Information Technology* 3: 1–11.

Adorno, Theodor. 1973. *Negative Dialectics*. New York: Continuum.

Albion, Robert. 1932. "The Communications Revolution." *American Historical Review* 32: 718–720.

Allison, David. 1973. "Translator's Introduction." In Jacques Derrida, *Speech and Phenomena: And Other Essays on Husserl's Theory of Signs*, translated by David Allison, xxxi–xlii. Evanston, IL: Northwestern University.

Anderson, James. 1996. *Communication Theory: Epistemological Foundations*. New York: Guilford Press.

Anderson, James, and Geoffrey Baym. 2004. "Philosophies and Philosophic Issues in Communication, 1995–2004." *Journal of Communication* 54, no. 1: 589–615.

Anderson, Rob, and Veronica Ross. 2002. *Questions of Communication: A Practical Introduction to Theory*. Boston and New York: Bedford / St. Martin's.

Angus, Ian. 1998. "The Materiality of Expression: Harold Innis' Communication Theory and the Discursive Turn in the Human Sciences." *Canadian Journal of Communication* 23, no. 1: 9–29.

Anton, Cory. 2002. "Discourse as Care: A Phenomenological Consideration of Spatiality and Temporality." *Human Studies* 25: 185–205.

Apel, Karl-Otto. 1972. "The A Priori of Communication and the Foundation of the Humanities." *Man and the World* 5, no. 1: 3–37.

Aristotle. 1947. "Ethica Nicomachea (Nicomachean Ethics)." In *Introduction to Aristotle*, edited by Richard McKeon, 308–545. New York: Modern Library.

———. 1961. *Physics*. Newly translated by Richard Hope. Lincoln: University of Nebraska Press.

Arneson, Pat. 2007. "Jean Gebser's Cosmology: Poetic Openings and Dialogic Possibilities." In *Perspectives on Philosophy of Communication*, edited by Pat Anderson, 95–212. West Lafayette, IN: Purdue University Press.

Arutyunova, Nataliya, and Irina Levotina, eds. (Арутюнова, Наталия, и Ирина Левотина). 2000. *Logical Analysis of Language: Language and Time* (Логический Анализ Языка: Язык и Время). Moscow: Yazyki Russkoi kul'tury.

Austin, John. 1962. *How to Do Things with Words*. Cambridge, MA: Harvard University Press.

Averbeck, Stephanie. 2008. "Comparative History of Communication Studies: France and Germany." *Open Communication Journal* 2: 1–13.

Aydede, Murat. 1998. "Aristotle on Epistêmê and Nous: The Posterior Analytics." *Southern Journal of Philosophy* 36, no. 1: 15–46.

Ayish, Muhammad I. 2003. "Beyond Western-Oriented Communication Theories: A Normative Arab-Islamic Perspective." *Public* 10, no. 2: 79–92.

Babe, Robert. 2000. *Canadian Communication Thought: Ten Foundational Writers*. Toronto: University of Toronto Press.

Babrow, Austin. 2005. "Point, Counterpoint, to the Side of the Point, and Other Points of Interest in the Latest Debate about Communibiological Theory: A Response to Nelson, McCroskey, and Beatty." *Communication Theory* 15, no. 4: 475.

Baldwin, James, et al., eds. 2006. *Redefining Culture: Conceptualizing Culture across Disciplines*. Mahwah, NJ: Lawrence Erlbaum Associates.

Bakhtin, Mikhail (Бахтин, Михаил). 1972. *Problems of Dostoyevsky's Poetics* (Проблемы Поэтики Достоевского). Moscow: Sovetskĭ Pisatel'.

———. 1981. *The Dialogic Imagination: Four Essays*. Edited by Michael Holquist, translated by Caryl Emerson and Michael Holquist. Austin and London: University of Texas Press.

———. 1984. *Problems of Dostoevsky's Poetics*. Edited and translated by Caryl Emerson. Manchester: Manchester University Press.

———. 1986a. "The Problem of the Text in Linguistics, Philology, and the Human Sciences: An Experiment in Philosophical Analysis." In *Speech Genres and Other Late Essays*, translated by Vern W. McGee, edited by Caryl Emerson and Michael Holquist, 103–131. Slavic Series 8. Austin: University of Texas Press.

———. 1986b. *Speech Genres and Other Late Essays*. Translated by Vern W. McGee, edited by Caryl Emerson and Michael Holquist. Slavic Series 8. Austin: University of Texas Press.

———. 1993. *Toward a Philosophy of the Act*. Translated by Vadim Liapunov, edited by Vadim Liapunov and Michael Holquist. Austin: University of Texas Press.

Barthes, Roland. 1972. *Mythologies*. Translated by Annette Lavers. New York: Noonday Press.

Bateson, Gregory. 1972. *Steps to an Ecology of Mind: Collected Essays in Anthropology, Psychiatry, Evolution, and Epistemology*. Chicago: University of Chicago Press.

———. 1979. *Mind and Nature: A Necessary Unity*. Toronto: Bantam Books.

Bateson, Gregory, and Mary Catherine Bateson. 1987. *Angels Fear: Towards an Epistemology of the Sacred*. New York: Bantam Books.

Baudrilliard, Jean. 1988. *The Ecstasy of Communication*. Translated by Bernard and Caroline Schutze. Foreign Agents Series. New York: Semiotext(e).

Bauman, Zygmunt. 2008. *The Art of Life*. Cambridge and Malden, MA: Polity.

Baxter, Leslie, and Earl Babbie. 2004. *Communication Research*. Elmont, CA: Wadsworth / Thomson Learning.

Beatty, Michael, and James McCroskey. 2000. "Theory, Scientific Evidence, and the Communibiological Paradigm: Reflections on Misguided Criticism." *Communication Education* 49, no. 1: 36–44.

Beatty, Michael, James McCroskey, and Kory Floyd, eds. 2009. *Biological Dimensions of Communication: Perspectives, Models and Research*. Cresskill, NJ: Hampton Press.

Beatty, Michael, James McCroskey, and Kristin Valencic. 2001. *The Biology of Communication: A Communibiological Perspective*. Cresskill, NJ: Hampton Press.

Behringer, Wolfgang. 2006. "Communications Revolutions: A Historiographical Concept." *German History* 24, no. 3: 333–74.

Beiner, Ronald. 1984. *Political Judgment*. Chicago: University of Chicago Press.

Beniger, James, and Jodi Gusek. 1995. "The Cognitive Revolution in Public Opinion and Communication Research." In *Public Opinion and the Communication of Consent*, edited by Theodore Glasser and Charles Salmon, 217–248. New York: Guilford.

Berdyaev, Nikolai (Бердяев, Николай). 1990. *The Meaning of History* (Смысл Истории). Moscow: Mysl'.

Berlin, Isaiah. 1958. *Two Concepts of Liberty*. Oxford: Oxford University Press.

Berlo, David. 1960. *The Process of Communication*. New York: Holt, Rinehart, and Winston.

Berman, Marshall. 1983. *All That Is Solid Melts into Air*. London and New York: Verso.

Bernstein, Richard. 1992. *The New Constellation: The Ethical-Political Horizons of Modernity/Postmodernity*. Cambridge, MA: MIT Press.

Bertalanffy, Ludwig von. 1962. "General System Theory—a Critical Review." *General Systems* 7: 1–20.

Bhabha, Homi. 1994. *The Location of Culture*. New York: Routledge.

Bialostosky, D. 2003. "Aristotle's Rhetoric and Bakhtin's Discourse Theory." In *A Companion to Rhetoric and Rhetorical Criticism*, edited by Walter Jost and Wendy Olmsted, 393–408. Malden, MA: Blackwell Publishing.

Bińczyk, Kögler Ewa. 2007. "Language in Archaic, Pre-referential Cultures: The Emergence of Dualism." *Publications: Austrian Ludwig Wittgenstein Society New Series* 3: 101–110.

Binding, Linda, and Dianne Tapp. 2008. "Human Understanding in Dialogue: Gadamer's Recovery of the Genuine." *Nursing Philosophy* 9, no. 2: 121–130.

Bitzer, Lloyd. 1968. "The Rhetorical Situation." *Philosophy and Rhetoric* 1: 1–14.

Bloom, Harold. 1999. *Shakespeare: The Invention of Human*. New York: Riverhead Books.

Blumer, Herbert. 1969. *Symbolic Interactionism: Perspective and Method*. Englewood Cliffs, NJ: Prentice-Hall.

Bondanella, Peter. 1997. *Umberto Eco and the Open Text: Semiotics, Fiction, Popular Culture*. Cambridge, MA: Cambridge University Press.

Bonnell, Victoria E., and Lynn Avery Hunt, eds. 1999. *Beyond the Cultural Turn: New Directions in the Study of Society and Culture*. Berkeley: University of California Press.

Boothroyd, Dave. 2009. "Touch, Time and Technics: Levinas and the Ethics of Haptic Communications." *Theory, Culture & Society* 26, nos. 2–3: 330–345.

Bormann, Ernest G. 1985. "Symbolic Convergence Theory: A Communication Formulation." *Journal of Communication* 35: 128–138.

Bostrom, Robert. 2003. "Theories, Data and Communication Research." *Communication Monographs* 70: 275–294.

Bouchard, Gianna. 2005. "The Revelation of Techné: An Anatomical Theatre." *Performance Research* 10, no. 4: 24–32.

Bowers, John, and James Bradac. 1982. "Issues in Communication Theory: A Metatheoretical Analysis." In *Communication Yearbook 5*, edited by Michael Burgoon, 1–27. New Brunswick, NJ: Transaction.

Bradac, James. 2001. "Theory Comparison: Uncertainty Reduction, Problematic Integration, Uncertainty Management, and Other Curious Constructs." *Journal of Communication* 51, no. 3: 456–477.

Braman, Sandra. 1994. "Commodities as Sign Systems: Commentary." In *Information and Communication in Economics*, edited by Robert Babe, 92–103. Boston: Kluwer Academic.

Brittain, Nathanael. 1984. "Shannon's General Theory of Communication." *Proceedings of the IEEE* 72, no. 9: 1191.

Brown, Penelope, and Stephen Levinson. 1987. *Politeness*. Cambridge: Cambridge University Press.

Bruneau, Thomas. 2007. "Time, Change, and Sociocultural Communication: A Chronemic Perspective." *Sign Systems Studies* 35, no. 1–2: 89–117.

Bryant, Jennings, and Dorina Miron. 2007. "Historical Contexts and Trends in Development of Communication Theory." In *Explaining Communication: Contempo-*

rary Theories and Exemplars, edited by Brian Whaley and Wendy Samter, 403–432. Mahwah, NJ: Lawrence Erlbaum Associates.

Bühler, Karl. 1990. *Theory of Language: The Representational Function of Language.* Amsterdam and Philadelphia: John Benjamins.

Burger, Charles. 1987. "Communicating Under Uncertainty." In *Interpersonal Processes: New Directions in Communication Research*, edited by Michael E. Roloff and Gerald R. Miller, 39–62. Newbury Park, CA: Sage Publications.

Burke, Kenneth. 1941. *The Philosophy of Literary Form: Studies in Symbolic Action.* Baton Rouge: Louisiana State University Press.

———. 1965. *Language as Symbolic Action.* Berkeley: University of California at Berkeley Press.

Burleson, Brant R. 1992. "Chautauqua: A Reprise of 'Why Are There So Few Communication Theories?' Taking Communication Seriously." *Communication Monographs* 59, no. 1: 79–86.

Butler, Judith. 1995. "For a Careful Reading." In *Feminist Contentions: A Philosophical Exchange*, edited by Benhabib Seyla et al., 127–144. New York, London: Routledge.

Buzzanell, Patricia, and Donal Carbaugh, eds. 2009. *Distinctive Qualities in Communication Research.* London and New York: Routledge.

Čapek, Milič. 1961. *The Philosophical Impact of Contemporary Physics.* Princeton, NJ: D. Van Hostr and Company.

Caputo, John. 2005. "In Praise of Ambiguity." In *Ambiguity in the Western Mind*, edited by Craig J. N. De Paulo, 15–34. New York: Peter Lang Publishing.

Carey, James. 1992. *Communication as Culture: Essays on Media and Society.* New York, London: Routledge.

———. 1995. "The Press, Public Opinion, and Public Discourse." In *Public Opinion and the Communication Consent*, edited by Theodore Glasser and Charles Salmon, 373–402. New York: Guilford.

Carter, M. 1988. "Stasis and Kairos: Principles of Social Construction in Classical Rhetoric." *Rhetoric Review* 7, no. 1: 97–112.

Cartmill, Matt. 1999. "Revolution, Evolution, and Kuhn: A Response to Chamberlain and Hartwig." *Evolutionary Anthropology* 8: 45–47.

Catt, Isaac. 2003. "Gregory Bateson's 'New Science' in the Context of Communicology." *American Journal of Semiotics* 19, nos. 1–4: 153–172.

———. 2006. "Pierre Bourdieu's Semiotic Legacy: A Theory of Communicative Agency." *American Journal of Semiotics* 22, no.104: 31–54.

Catt, Isaac, and Deborah Eicher-Catt, eds. 2010 (in press). *Communicology: The New Science of Embodie Discourse.* Madison, NJ: Fairleigh Dickinson University Press.

Cavell, Richard. 1999. "McLuhan and Spatial Communication." *Western Journal of Communication* 63, no.3: 348–363.

Cavell, Richard. 2002. *McLuhan in Space: A Cultural Geography.* Toronto: University of Toronto Press.

Chang, Breanke. 1996. *Deconstructing Communication: Representation, Subject, and Economies of Exchange*. Minneapolis: University of Minnesota Press.

Cheal, David. 1992. "Ritual: Communication in Action." *Sociological Analysis* 53, no. 4: 363–374.

Chen, Xiang. 1997. "Thomas Kuhn's Latest Notion of Incommensurability." *Journal for General Philosophy of Science* 28: 257–73.

Chernyakov, Alexei. 2002. *The Ontology of Time: Being and Time in the Philosophies of Aristotle, Husserl and Heidegger*. Dordrecht: Klüwer Academic Publishers.

Chertkova, Elena (Черткова, Елена). 2005. "Science as an Axiological Problem" (Наука и Научность как Аксиологическая Проблема). In *Science through the Eyes of Humanitarian* (Наука Глазами Гуманитария), 113–134. Moscow: Progress-Traditsiya.

Chou, Chien, et al. 2005. "A Review of the Research on Internet Addiction." *Educational Psychology Review* 17, no. 4: 363–388.

Cobley, Paul. 1996. *The Communication Theory Reader*. London: Routledge.

Cohen, Richard. 2001. *Ethics, Exegesis and Philosophy: Interpretation after Levinas*. Cambridge: Cambridge University Press.

Colapietro, Vincent. 1989. *Peirce's Approach to the Self: A Semiotic Perspective on Human Subjectivity*. Albany: State University of New York Press.

Cooley, Charles. 1968. *Human Nature and the Social Order: The Self in Social Interaction*. Vol. 1, *Classic and Contemporary Perspectives*. New York: Wiley & Sons. (Original work published in 1902.)

Combs, Steven. 2005. *The Dao of Rhetoric*. Albany: State University of New York Press.

Corcoran, John. 2009. "Aristotle's Demonstrative Logic." *History and Philosophy of Logic* 30, no. 1: 1–20.

Cornell, Drucilla. 1992. *The Philosophy of the Limit*. New York: Routledge.

Craig, Robert. 1993. "Why Are There So Many Communication Theories?" *Journal of Communication* 43, no. 3: 26–33.

———. 1999. "Communication Theory as a Field." *Communication Theory* 9, no. 2: 119–161.

———. 2001. "Minding My Metamodel, Mending Myers." *Communication Theory* 11, no. 2: 231–240.

———. 2005. "How We Talk about How We Talk: Communication Theory in the Public Interest." *Journal of Communication* 55, no. 4: 659–667.

———. 2007. "Issue Forum Introduction: Cultural Bias in Communication Theory." *Communication Monographs* 74, no. 2: 256–258.

———. 2008. "Communication in the Conversation of Disciplines." *Russian Journal of Communication* 1, no. 1: 7–23.

Craig, Robert, and Heidi Muller. 2007. *Theorizing Communication: Readings across Traditions*. Thousand Oaks, CA: Sage Publications.

Cragan, John, and Donald Shields. 1998. *Understanding Communication Theory: The Communicative Forces for Human Action*. Boston: Allyn & Bacon.

Cresswell, Tim. 2009. "Place." www.elsevierdirect.com/brochures/hugy/SampleContent/Place.pdf (accessed October 3, 2009).

Cronen, Vernon. 2001. "Practical Theory, Practical Art, and the Pragmatic-Systemic Account of Inquiry." *Communication Theory* 11, no. 1: 14–35.

Cronen, Vernon, and Barnett W. Pearce. 1982. "The Coordinated Management of Meaning: A Theory of Communication." In *Human Communication Theory*, edited by Frank E. X. Dance, 61–89. New York: Harper & Row.

Crosby, Joy. 2009. "Liminality and the Sacred: Discipline Building and Speaking with the Other." *Liminalities: A Journal of Performance Studies* 5, no. 1: 1–19.

Crowley, Sharon, and Debra Hawhee. 1999. *Ancient Rhetoric for Contemporary Students*. Boston: Allyn and Bacon.

Crusius, Timothy. 1999. *Kenneth Burke and the Conversation after Philosophy*. Carbondale and Edwardsville: Southern Illinois University Press.

Csikszentmihalyi, Mihaly. 1990. *Flow: The Psychology of Optimal Experience*. New York: Harper and Row.

Curry, Michael. 2000. "Wittgenstein and the Fabric of Everyday Life." In *Thinking Space*, edited by Mike Crang and Nigel Thrift, 89–114. London and New York: Routledge.

Dale, Jacquette. 2004. *Pathways in Philosophy: An Introductory Guide with Readings*. Oxford University Press.

Dauenhauer, Bernard. 1980. *Silence: The Phenomenon and Its Ontological Significance*. Bloomington: Indiana University Press.

De Kerckhove, Derrick. 1981. "Understanding McLuhan." *Canadian Forum* 51 (May): 8–9.

Delia, Jesse. 1987. "Communication Research: A History." In *Handbook of Communication Science*, edited by Charles R. Berger and Steven H. Chaffee, 20–98. Newbury Park, CA: Sage Publications.

Demers, David. 2000. "Communication Theory in the 21st Century: Differentiation and Convergence." *Mass Communication and Society* 3, no. 1: 1–2.

Derrida, Jacques. 1973. *Speech and Phenomena: And Other Essays on Husser's Theory of Signs*. Evanston: Northwestern University Press.

———. 1997. "The Villanova Roundtable: A Conversation with Jacques Derrida." In *Deconstruction in a Nutshell: A Conversation with Jacques Derrida*, edited by John Caputo, 3–28. New York: Fordham University Press.

———. 1998. *Of Grammatology*. Translated by Gayatri C. Spivak. Baltimore: John Hopkins University Press.

Deutscher, Guy. 2005. *The Unfolding of Language: An Evolutionary Tour of Mankind's Greatest Invention*. New York: Metropolitan Books.

DeVito, Joseph. 1978. *Communicology: An Introduction to the Study of Communication*. New York: Harper & Row.

De Vries, Hent. 2005. *Minimal Theologies: Critiques of Secular Reason in Adorno and Levinas*. Translated by Geoffrey Hale. Baltimore: Johns Hopkins University Press.

Dolar, Mladen. 2006. *A Voice and Nothing More*. Cambridge, MA, and London: MIT Press.

Donsbach, Wolfgang. 2006. "The Identity of Communication Research." *Journal of Communication* 56: 437–448.

Dresner, Eli. 2006. "Davidson's Philosophy of Communication," *Communication Theory* 16: 155–172.

Durig, Alex. 1995. "The Event Frame." *Studies in Symbolic Interactionsim* 17: 241–264.

Eco, Umberto. 1984. *The Role of the Reader: Explorations in the Semiotics of Texts.* Bloomington: Indiana University Press.

———. 1986. *Travels in Hyperreality: Essays.* San Diego, CA: Harcourt Brace Jovanovich.

Eicher-Catt, Deborah. 2001. "A Communicology of Female/Feminine Embodiment: The Case of Non-custodial Motherhood." *American Journal of Semiotics* 17, no. 4: 93–129.

Eikeland, Olav. 2006. "Phrónêsis, Aristotle, and Action Research." *International Journal of Action Research* 2, no. 1: 5–53.

Emauel, Richard. 2007. "Communication: Humanities' Core Discipline." *American Communication Journal* 9, no. 2. www.acjournal.org/holdings/vol9/summer/articles/discipline.html (accessed October 9, 2008).

The Encyclopædia Britannica: A Dictionary of Arts, Sciences, and General Literature. 1890. 9th ed. Vol. 14. New York: Henry G. Allen Company.

Encyclopædia Britanica Online. "Consubstantiation." www.britannica.com/EB-checked/topic/134483/consubstantiation (October 11, 2009).

Epshtein, Mikhail (Эпштейн, Михаил). 2001. *Philosophy of the Possible* (Философия Возможного). St. Petersburg: Aleteiya.

———. 2004. *Sign of Blank: On the Future of the Humanities* (Знак Пробела: О Будщем Гуманитарных Наук). Moscow: Novoe Literaturnoe Obozrenie.

———. 2006. *Philosophy of Body* (Философия Тела). St. Petersburg: Aleteiya.

Epstein, Mikhail. 1996. "The Phoenix of Philosophy: On the Meaning and Significance of Contemporary Russian Thought." *Symposion: A Journal of Russian Thought* 1: 35–74.

———. 2007. "Methods of Madness and Madness as a Method." In *Madness and the Mad in Russian Culture*, edited by Angela Brintlinger and Ilya Vinitsky, 263–282. Toronto: University of Toronto Press.

———. 2008. "Semiurgy: From Language Analysis to Language Synthesis." *Russian Journal of Communication* 1, no. 1: 24–41.

Evered, Mark, Axel Schmolitzky, and Michael Kölling. 1995. "A Flexible Object Invocation Language Based on Object-Oriented Language Definition." *Computer Journal* 38, no. 3: 181–192.

Farman, Inna (Фарман, Инна). 2005. "Communicative Paradigm in Social Cognition" (Коммуникативная Парадигма в Социальном Познании). In *Science through the Eyes of a Humanist* (Наука Глазами Гуманитария), 229–261. Moscow: Progress-Traditsiya.

Farrell, Thomas. 1987. "Beyond Science: Humanities Contributions to Communication Theory." In *Handbook of Communication Science*, edited by Charles R. Berger and Steven H. Chaffee, 123–142. Newbury Park, CA: Sage Publications.

Farriss, Nancy. 1986. "Foreword." In *The Social Life of Things: Commodities in Cultural Perspective*, edited by Arjun Appadurai, ix–xii. Cambridge: Cambridge University Press.

Farronato, Christina. 2003. *Eco's Chaosmos: From the Middle Ages to Postmodernity.* Toronto: University of Toronto Press.

Feldman, Stephen. 2005. "The Problem of Critique: Triangulating Habermas, Derrida, and Gadamer within Metamodernism." *Contemporary Political Theory* 4: 296–320.

Fisher, Aubrey. 1978. *Perspectives on Human Communication.* New York, London: Macmillan Publishing Co.

Fisher, Walter. 1989. *Human Communication as Narration: Toward a Philosophy of Reason, Value, and Action.* Columbia: University of South Carolina Press.

Flesch, William. 2002. "Ludwig Wittgenstein (1889–1951)." In *The Continuum Encyclopedia of Modern Criticism and Theory*, edited by Julian Wolfreys, 120–126. New York: Continuum.

Flichy, Patrice. 2007. *The Internet Imaginaire.* Cambridge, MA: MIT Press.

Floyd, Kory, Alan Mikkelson, and Colin Hesse. 2008. *The Biology of Human Communication.* Mason, OH: Thomson.

Foss, Sonia, and Cindy Griffin. 1995. "Beyond Persuasion: A Proposal for an Invitational Rhetoric." *Communication Monographs* 62: 2–18.

Foucault, Michel. 1970. *The Order of Things: An Archeology of the Human Sciences.* New York: Pantheon Books.

Freedman, Barbara. 1991. *Staging the Gaze: Postmodernism, Psychoanalysis, and Shakespearean Comedy.* Ithaca, NY, and London: Cornell University Press.

Gadamer, Hans-Georg. 1975. "Hermeneutics and Social Science." *Cultural Hermeneutics* 2, no. 4: 307–316.

———. 1989. *Truth and Method.* New York: Continuum.

Galison, Peter. 2000. "Einstein's Clocks: The Place of Time." *Critical Inquiry* 26, no. 2: 355–389.

Gallagher, Shaun. 1992. *Hermeneutics and Education.* Albany: State University of New York Press.

Gallant, Mary, and Sherryl Kleinman. 1983. "Symbolic Interactionsim vs. Ethnomethodology." *Symbolic Interaction* 6, no. 1: 1–18.

Gay, Volney. 2010. *Progress and Values in the Humanities: Comparing Culture and Society.* New York: Columbia University Press.

Gebser, Jean. 1985. *The Ever-Present Origin.* Translated by Noel Barstad and Algis Mickunas. Athens: Ohio University Press.

Genz, Henning. 1999. *Nothingness: The Science of Empty Space*. Cambridge, MA: Helix Books / Perseus Books.

Gerbner, George, et al. 2002. "Growing Up with Television: Cultivation Processes." In *Media Effects: Advances in Theory and Research*, edited by Jennings Bryant and Dolf Zillmann, 43–67. Mahwah, NJ: Lawrence Erlbaum Associates.

Giddens, Anthony. 1979. *Central Problems in Social Theory*. London: Macmillan.

———. 2004. *Runaway World: How Globalization Is Reshaping Our Lives*. London: Routledge.

Gillett, Grant, and John McMillan. 2001. *Consciousness and Intentionality: Advances in Consciousness Research*. Vol. 27. Amsterdam and Philadelphia: John Benjamins B.V.

Goffman, Erving. 1959. *The Presentation of Self in Everyday Life*. Garden City, NJ: Doubleday.

———. 2005. *Interaction Ritual: Essays in Face-to-Face Behavior*. New Brunswick, NJ: Transaction Publishers.

Goodman, Jeffrey. 2007. "A Critical Discussion of Talking Past One Another." *Philosophy and Rhetoric* 40, no. 3: 311–325.

Goldsmith, Daena. 2001. "A Normative Approach to the Study of Uncertainty and Communication." *Journal of Communication* 51, no. 3: 514–533.

Gordon, Ronald. 2007. "Beyond the Failures of Western Communication Theory." *Journal of Multicultural Discourses* 2, no. 2: 89–107.

Gottlieb, Anthony. 2007. "Take Five, and Call Me." *Book Review*, October 28, 2007, 16.

Grant, Colin. 2003a. "Destabilizing Social Communication Theory." *Theory, Culture & Society* 20, no. 6: 95–119.

———. 2003b. "Rethinking Communicative Interaction: An Interdisciplinary Programme." In *Rethinking Communicative Interaction: New Interdisciplinary Horizons*, edited by Colin Grant, 1–26. Amsterdam and Philadelphia: John Benjamins B.V.

Greenberg, Clement. 1993. *The Collected Essays and Criticism*. Vol. 3, *Affirmations and Refusals 1950–1956*. Chicago: University of Chicago Press.

Greene, Brian. 2004. *The Fabric of the Cosmos: Space, Time, and the Texture of Reality*. New York: Alfred A. Knopf.

Greene, Thomas. 2005. *Poetry, Signs, and Magic*. Cranbury, NJ: Rosemont Publishing & Printing Corp.

Greimas, Algirdas. 1987. *On Meaning*. Minneapolis: University of Minnesota Press.

Greimas, Algirdas, and Joseph Courtés. 1982. *Semiotics and Language*. Bloomington: Indiana University Press.

Greimas, Algirdas, and Jacques Fontanille. 1993. *The Semiotics of Passions: From States of Affairs to States of Feelings*. Translated by Paul Perron and Frank Collins. Minneapolis: University of Minnesota Press.

Grice, Herbert Paul. 1989. "Logic and Conversation." In *Studies in the Way of Words*, edited by Herbert Paul Grice, 22–40. Cambridge, MA: Harvard University Press.

Griffin, Em. 2002. *A First Look at Communication Theory.* Boston: McGraw-Hill.

Grois, Boris (Гройс, Борис). 1993. *Utopia and Exchange* (Утопия и Обмен). Moscow: Znak.

Gruber, Thomas. 1993. "A Translation Approach to Portable Ontology Specifications." *Knowledge Acquisition* 5, no. 2: 199–220.

Gumbrecht, Ulrich. 2004. *Production of Presence: What Meaning Cannot Convey.* Stanford, CA: Stanford University Press.

Habermas, Jürgen. 1979. *Communication and the Evolution of Society.* Toronto: Beacon Press.

———. 1989. *The Structural Transformation of the Public Sphere: An Inquiry into a Category of Bourgeois Society.* Cambridge, MA: MIT Press.

———. 1993. *Postmetaphysical Thinking: Philosophical Essays.* Translated by William Mark Hohengarten. Cambridge, MA: MIT Press.

———. 1994. "Three Models of Democracy." *Constellations* 1, no. 1: 1–10.

———. 2001. "Truth and Society: The Discursive Redemption of Factual Claims to Validity." In *On the Pragmatics of Social Interaction: Preliminary Studies in the Theory of Communicative Action,* translated by Barbara Fultner, 85–103. Cambridge, MA: MIT Press.

Hall, Stuart. 1989. "Ideology and Communication Theory." In *Rethinking Communication,* edited by Brenda Darwin, Lawrence Grossberg, Barbara O'Keefe, and Ellen Wartella, 40–52. Newbury Park, CA: Sage Publications.

Haney, David. 1999. "Aesthetics and Ethics in Gadamer, Levinas, and Romanticism: Problems of Phrónêsis and Techne." *PMLA* 111, no. 1: 32–45.

Hanke, Michael. 1990. "Socratic Pragmatics: Maieutic Dialogues." *Journal of Pragmatics* 14, no. 3: 459–465.

Hanna, Joseph. 1982. "Two Ideals of Scientific Theorizing." In *Communication Yearbook 5,* edited by Michael Burgoon, 29–47. New Brunswick, NJ, and London: Transaction Books.

Harbeck, James. 2001. "The Transcendent Function of Interculturalism." *Studies in the Literary Imagination* 34, no. 2: 13–29.

Harper, Nancy. 1979. *Human Communication Theory: The History of a Paradigm.* Rochelle Park, NJ: Hayden Book Company.

Harris, Amanda. 1999. "A Revolutionary View of Communication: Cheris Kramarae's Theory of Muted Groups." *Women and Language,* September.

Hay, James. 2006. "Between Cultural Materialism and Spatial Materialism: James Carey's Writing about Communication." In *Thinking with James Carey: Essays on Communication, Transportation, History,* edited by Jeremy Packer and Craig Robertson, 28–55. New York: Peter Lang.

Hayles, Katherine N. 1999. *How We Became Posthuman: Virtual Bodies in Cybernetics.* Chicago: University of Chicago Press.

Heath, Robert, and Jennings R. Bryant. 2000. *Human Communication Theory and Research: Concepts, Contexts, and Challenges.* Mahwah, NJ: Lawrence Erlbaum Associates.

Heidegger, Martin. 1962. *Being and Time*. Translated by John Macquarrie and Edward Robinson. New York: Harper & Row.

———. 1971. *Poetry, Language, Thought*. Translated by Albert Hofstadter. New York: Harper & Row.

———. 1977. "The Question Concerning Technology." In *The Question Concerning Technology and Other Essays*, edited by William Lovitt, 3-35. New York: Harper & Row.

———. 1982. *On the Way to Language*. Translated by Peter D. Hertz. New York: Harper & Row.

———. 1992. "Phenomenological Interpretations with Respect to Aristotle: Indication of the Hermeneutic Situation." Translated by M. Baur. *Man and Word* 25, nos. 3-4: 355-393.

———. 2005. *Sojourns: The Journey to Greece*. Albany: State University of New York Press.

Heisler, Jennifer, and Thomas Discenna. 2005. "Teaching Metatheoretical Beliefs in Communication Theory." *Communication Teacher* 19, no. 2: 44-47.

Herman, Edward S., and Noam Chomsky. 1988. *Manufacturing Consent: The Political Economy of the Mass Media*. New York: Pantheon.

Hesterly, William S., Julia Liebeskind, and Todd R. Zenger. 1990. "Organizational Economics: An Impending Revolution in Organization Theory?" *Academy of Management Review* 15: 402-420.

Ho, Wing-Chung. 2008. "Writing Experience: Does Ethnography Convey a Crisis of Representation, or an Ontological Break with the Everyday World?" *Canadian Review of Sociology* 45, no. 4: 343-365.

Honderich, Ted, ed. 1995. *The Oxford Companion to Philosophy*. Oxford and New York: Oxford University Press.

Hornsey, Matthew, et al. 2008. "The Intersection of Communication and Social Psychology: Points of Contact and Points of Difference." *Journal of Communication* 58: 749-766.

Horwitz, Betty. 2002. *Communication Apprehension: Origins and Management*. Florence, KY: Singular Publishing Group.

Hinchman, Lewis, and Sandra Hinchman. 1994. *Hannah Arendt: Critical Essays*. SUNY Series in Political Theory: Contemporary Issues. Albany: State University of New York Press.

Hoeppe, Götz. 2007. *Why the Sky Is Blue: Discovering the Color of Life*. Translated with John Stewart. Princeton, NJ: Princeton University Press.

Husserl, Edmund. 1960. *Cartesian Meditations: An Introduction to Phenomenology*. Translated by D. Cairns. The Hague: M. Nijhoff.

Hyde, Michael. 2007. "Searching for Perfection: Martin Heidegger (with Some Help from Kenneth Burke) on Language, Truth, and the Practice of Rhetoric." In *Perspectives on Philosophy of Communication*, edited by Pat Anderson, 23-44. West Lafayette, IN: Purdue University Press.

Illich, Ivan. 1985. *H2O and the Waters of Forgetfulness*. Dallas: Dallas Institute of Humanities and Culture.

Infante, Dominic A., et al. 2003. *Building Communication Theory*. Long Grove, IL: Waveland Press.

Innis, Harold. 1950. *Empires and Communications*. Oxford: Clarendon.

———. 1991. *The Bias of Communication*. Toronto: University of Toronto Press.

Irigaray, Luce. 1999. *The Forgetting of Air in Martin Heidegger*. Translated by Mary Beth Mader. Austin: University of Texas Press.

Ivanov, Vyacheslav (Иванов, Вячеслав). 1999. "Essays on the Prehistory and History of Semiotics" (Очерки по Предистории и Истории Семиотики). In *Selected Works on Semiotics and History of Culture* (Избранные Труды по Семиотике и Истории Культуры), vol. 1, 605–792. Moscow: Yazyki Russkoi kul'tury.

Jacoby, Russell. 2008. "Gone, and Being Forgotten: Why Are Some of the Greatest Thinkers Being Expelled from Their Disciplines?" *Chronicle Review*, July 25, 2008, B5–B6.

Jameson, Fredric. 1998. *The Cultural Turn: Selected Writings on the Postmodern, 1983–1998*. London and New York: Verso.

———. 2002. *A Singular Modernity: Essay on the Ontology of the Present*. London and New York: Verso.

Jay, Martin. 1984. *Adorno*. Cambridge, MA: Harvard University Press.

———. 1993. *Force Fields: Between Intellectual History and Cultural Critique*. New York and London: Routledge.

Jia, Wenshan, et al. 2002. *Chinese Communication Theory and Research: Reflections, New Frontiers, and New Directions*. Westport, CT: Ablex Publishing.

Johansen, Jørgen. 2002. *Literary Discourse: A Semiotic-Pragmatic Approach to Literature*. Toronto: University of Toronto Press.

Jordan, John. 2002. "Addressing Materiality in Communication Theory." *Review of Communication* 2, no. 4: 378–382.

Jost, Walter. 2003. "Epiphany and Epideictic: The Low Modernist Lyric." In *A Companion to Rhetoric and Rhetorical Criticism*, edited by Walter Jost and Wendy Olmsted, 311–324. Malden, MA: Blackwell Publishing.

Jung, Carl Gustav. 1993. *The Spirit in Man, Art and Literature*. London: Routledge.

Kalbfleisch, Pamela. 2002. "Communication-Based Theory Development: Building Theories for Communication Research." *Communication Theory* 12, no. 1: 5–7.

Kalmykov, Aleksandr (Калмыков, Александр). 2007. "Ontology of Communication as Socioanthropological Problem" (Онтология Коммуникации как Социально-антропологическая Проблема). *Vestnik RGGU* 1: 47–61.

Kasavin, Il'ya (Касавин, Илья). 2008. *Text. Discourse. Context: Introduction into Social Epistemology of Language* (Текст. Дискурс. Контекст: Введениие в Социальную Эпистемологию Языка). Moscow: "Kanon+" / ROOI "Reabilitatsiya."

Kashkin, Vyacheslav (Кашкин, Вячеслав). 2007. *Foundations of Communication Theory* (Основы Теории Коммуникации). Moscow: AST / Vostok-Zapad; Minsk: Kharvest.

Kauffman, Louis. 2001. "Virtual Logic—Reasoning and Playing with Imaginary Boolean Values." *Cybernetics & Human Knowing* 8, no. 3: 77–85.

Katayama, Errol. 1999. *Aristotle on Artifacts: A Metaphysical Puzzle.* Albany: State University of New York Press.

Kharitonov, Aleksandr (Харитонов, Александр). 2008. "Review of Communication and Cognition" (Общение и Познание). *Russian Journal of Communication* 1, no. 4: 476–481.

Khophmaister, Khaimo (Хофмайстер, Хаймо). 2006. *What It Means to Think Like a Philosopher* (Что Значит Мыслить Философски). St. Petersburg: St. Petersburg State University Press.

Kim, Min-Sun. 2002. *Non-Western Perspectives on Human Communication: Implications for Theory and Practice.* Thousand Oaks, CA: Sage Publications.

Kleinsasser, Joel. 2009. Podcast: "Social Media Leads Communication Revolution." www.wichita.edu/thisis/wsunews/news/?nid=731 (accessed October 10, 2009).

Klyagin, Sergei (Клягин, Сергей). 2008. "The Posesis of Time in the Space of an Event" (Поэзис Времени в Пространстве События). *Vestnik RGGU* 1: 49–65.

Kögler, Hans-Herbert. 2007. "Roots of Recognition—Cultural Identity and the Ethos of Hermeneutic Dialogue: The Emergence of Dualism." *Publications: Austrian Ludwig Wittgenstein Society New Series* 3: 353–371.

Korn, Charles, et al. 2000. "Defining the Field: Revisiting the ACA 1995 Definition of Communication Studies." *Journal of the Association for Communication Administration* 29: 40–52.

Korzybski, Alfred. 1980. *Science and Sanity: An Introduction to Non-Aristotelian Systems and General Semantics.* Lakeville, CT: Institute of General Semantics.

Kostetskiy, Viktor (Костецкий, Виктор). 2005. "Time as a Subject of Behavior" (Время как Субьект Поведения). In *Modalities of Time: Sociophilosophical Analysis* (Модусы Времени: Социально-философский Анализ), 108–114. St. Petersburg: St. Petersburg State University Press.

Kostina, Ol'ga (Костина, Ольга). 2004. *Ontology of Communication* (Онтология Коммуникации). Saratov, Russia: Saratov State University Press.

———. 2008. "The Ontological Dimension of Communication" (Онтолгическое Измерение Коммуникации). In *Mediaphilosophy: The Key Problems of Understanding* (Медиафилософия: Основные Проблемы и Понятия), 130–138. www.intelros.ru/intelros/biblio_intelros/2974-mediafilosofija.-osnovnye-problemy-i.html (accessed October 10, 2009).

Krippendorff, Klaus. 1989. "On the Ethics of Constructing Communication." In *Rethinking Communication: Paradigm Issues*, edited by Barbara Dervin, 66–96. Newbury Park, CA: Sage Publications.

———. 1994. "A Recursive Theory of Communication." In *Communication Theory Today*, edited by David Crowley and David Mitchell, 78–103. Stanford, CA: Stanford University Press.

———. 2009. *On Communicating: Otherness, Meaning, and Information*, edited by Fernando Bermejo. New York: Routledge.

Kristeva, Julia. 1991. *Strangers to Ourselves*. New York and Oxford: Columbia University Press.

Kudryashova, Tat'yana (Кудряшова, Татьяна). 2009. "Mediaphilosophy: Key problems and Concepts" (Медиафилософия: Основные Проблемы Понимания). www.intelros.ru/intelros/biblio_intelros/2974-mediafilosofija.-osnovnye-problemy-i.html (accessed October 10, 2009).

———. 2008. "The Experience of Time in the Conditions of Mediaspace" (Переживание Времени в Условиях Медиапространства). In *Mediaphilosophy: The Key Problems of Understanding* (Медиафилософия: Основные Проблемы и Понятия), 172–185. www.intelros.ru/intelros/biblio_intelros/2974-mediafilosofija.-osnovnye-problemy-i .html (accessed October 10, 2009).

Kuhn, Thomas. 1962. *The Structure of Scientific Revolutions*. Chicago: University of Chicago Press.

Lähteenmäki, Mika. 2008. "The Role of 'Sociology' in Lev Shcherba's Conception of Language." In *Festschrift in Honour of Professor Arto Mustajoki on the Occasion of His 60th Birthday*, edited by Jouko Lindstedt et al., 183–190. Helsinki: Department of Slavonic and Baltic Languages and Literatures.

Langer, Roy. 1999. "Towards a Constructivist Communication Theory?" *Nordicom Information* 21, nos. 1–2: 75–86.

Langsdorf, Lenore. 2007. "Callicles' Parlor. Revisiting the *Gorgias* after Dwelling with Gadamer." In *Perspectives on Philosophy of Communication*, edited by Pat Arneson, 47–59. West Lafayette, IN: Purdue University Press.

Langsdorf, Lenore, and Andrew Smith. 1995. *Recovering Pragmatism's Voice: The Classical Tradition, Rorty, and the Philosophy of Communication*. Albany: State University of New York Press.

Lanigan, Richard. 1995. "Embodiment: Signs of Life in the Self." A Paper Presented at the Symposium on "Musement to Meaning: Mind and Body" at the Twentieth Annual Meeting of the Semiotic Society of America, San Antonio, TX.

———. 2000. "The Self in Semiotic Phenomenology: Consciousness as the Conjunction of Perception and Expression in the Science of Communicology." *American Journal of Semiotics* 15–16, nos. 1–4: 91–111.

———. 2005. "Paradigm Shifts: Recalling the Early ICA and the Later PHILCOM." *Communication Review* 8: 377–382.

———. 2008. "Communicology." In *The International Encyclopedia of Communication*, edited by W. Donsbach, 10 vols. Oxford: Blackwell Publishing.

Latour, Bruno. 1988. "Mixing Humans and Non-Humans Together: The Sociology of a Door-Closer." *Social Problems* 35, no. 3: 298–310.

———. 2004. "Why Has Critique Run Out of Steam: From Matters of Fact to Matters of Concern." *Critical Inquiry* 30, no. 2: 225–248.

Lauf, Edmund. 2005. "National Diversity of Major International Journals in the Field of Communication." *Journal of Communication* 55, no. 1: 139–151.

LeBaron, Curtis, et al. 2003. "An Overview of Language and Social Interaction Research." In *Studies in Language and Social Interaction*, edited by Phillip J. Glenn et al., 1–39. Mahwah, NJ: Lawrence Erlbaum Associates.

Lenoir, Timothy, eds. 1998. *Inscribing Science: Scientific Texts and the Materiality of Communication*. Stanford, CA: Stanford University Press.

Lentz, Tony. 1983. "The Third Place from the Truth: Plato's Paradoxical Attack on Writing." *Communication Quarterly* 31, no. 4: 290–301.

Leydesdorff, Loet. 1994. "Uncertainty and the Communication of Time." *Systems Research* 11, no. 4: 31–51.

———. 2000. "Luhman, Habermas, and the Theory of Communication." *Systems Research and Behavioral Sciences* 17, no. 3: 273–288.

———. 2002. "The Communication Turn in the Theory of Social Systems." *Systems Research and Behavioral Science* 19: 129–136.

———. 2004. "Top-Down Decomposition of the *Journal Citation Report of the Social Science Citation Index*: Graph- and Factor-Analytical Approaches." *Scientomentrics* 60: 159–180.

Lewis, Albert. 2004. "The Unity of Logic, Pedagogy and Foundations in Grassmann's Mathematical Work." *History and Philosophy of Logic* 25: 15–36.

Levinas, Emmanuel. 1981. *Otherwise Than Being, or, Beyond Essence*. The Hague: Martinus Nijhoff.

Lingis, Alphonso. 1987. "Translator's Introduction." In Emmanuel Levinas, *Collected Philosophical Papers of Emmanuel Levinas*, vii–xxxi. Hingman, MA: Kluwer Academic Publishers.

———. 1994. *The Community of Those Who Have Nothing in Common*. Bloomington: Indiana University Press.

Liska, Jo R., and Gary Cronkhite. 1995. *An Ecological Perspective on Human Communication Theory*. Fort Worth, TX: Harcourt Brace College Publishers.

Littlejohn, Stephen. 2002. *Theories of Human Communication*. 7th ed. Belmont, CA: Wadsworth.

Littlejohn, Stephen, and Karen Foss. 2008. *Theories of Human Communication*. Belmont, CA: Thompson Wadsworth.

Losev, Aleksei (Лосев, Алексей). 1994. *Myth, Number, Essence* (Миф, Число, Сущность). Moscow: Mysl'.

Lotman, Yuriy (Лотман, Юрий). 1992. *Culture and Explosion* (Культура и Взрыв). Moscow: Gnozis.

Lyotard, Jean-François. 1984. *The Postmodern Condition: A Report on Knowledge*. Translated by Geoff Bennington and Brian Massumi. Minneapolis: University of Minnesota Press.

MacDonald, Michael. 2006. "Empire and Communication: The Media Wars of Marshall McLuhan." *Media, Culture & Society* 28, no. 4: 505–520.

Mah, Harold. 2000. "Phantasies of the Public Sphere: Rethinking the Habermas of Historians." *Journal of Modern History* 72, no. 1: 153–182.

Mailloux, Steven. 2004. "Rhetorical Hermeneutics Still Again: Or, on the Track of Phrōnēsis." In *A Companion to Rhetoric and Rhetorical Criticism*, edited by Walter Jost and Wendy Olmsted, 457–472. Malden, MA: Blackwell Publishing.

Makarov, Mikhail (Макаров, Михаил). 2003. *Foundations of Discourse Theory* (Основы Теории Дискурса). Moscow: Gnozis.

Malhotra, Valerie. 1987. "A Comparison of Mead's 'Self' and Heidegger's 'Dasein': Toward a Regrounding of Social Psychology." *Human Studies* 10: 357–382.

Mamardashvili, Merab (Мамардашвили, Мераб). 1997. *Arrow of Cognition: A Sketch of Natural Gnoseology* (Стрела Познания: Набросок Естественноистори-ческой Гносеологии). Moscow: Yazyki Russkoi kul'tury.

Mandel'shtam, Osip. 1991. *Selected Poems*. London: Penguin Books.

Mansell, Robin. 2002. *Inside the Communication Revolution: Evolving Patterns of Social and Technical Interaction*. Oxford, New York: Oxford University Press.

Marks, John. 2006. "Information and Resistance: Deleuze, the Virtual and Cyberspace." In *Deleuze and the Contemporary World*, edited by Adrian Parr and Ian Buchanan, 194–213. Edinburgh: Edinburgh University Press.

Marks-Tarlow, Terry. 2005. "Semiotic Seams: Fractal Dynamics of Reentry." *Cybernetics and Human Knowing* 11, no. 1: 49–62.

Martin, Alexander. 2008. "Review of Valerie Kivelson (2006): *Cartographies of Tsardom: The Land and Its Meanings in Seventeenth-Century Russia*." *Russian Journal of Communication* 1, nos. 3–4: 484–486.

Massey, Doreen. 1992. "Politics and Space/Time." *New Left Review* 196: 65–84.

Mattelart, Armand. 1996. *The Invention of Communication*. Minneapolis: University of Minnesota Press.

Mattelart, Armand, and Michele Mattelart. 1998. *Theories of Communication: A Short Introduction*. Thousand Oaks, CA: Sage.

Maturana, Humberto R. 1981. "Autopoiesis: Reproduction, Heredity and Evolution." In *Autopoiesis, Dissipative Structures and Spontaneous Social Order*, edited by Milan Zeleny, 48–89. Boulder, CO: Westview Press.

Humberto, R. Maturana, and Francisco J. Varela. 1980. *Autopoesis and Cognition: The Realization of the Living*. Dordrecht: D. Reidel.

McChesney, Robert. 2007. *Communication Revolution: Critical Junctures and the Future of Media*. New York and London: New Press.

McLuhan, Marshall. 1994. *Understanding Media: The Extensions of Man*. Cambridge, MA: MIT Press.

McPhee, Robert. 2006. "On Collective Mind and Conversational Analysis." *Management Communication Quarterly* 19, no. 3: 311–326.

Mead, George H. 1938. *The Philosophy of the Act*. Edited by Charles W. Morris with John M. Brewster, Albert M. Dunham, and David Miller. Chicago: University of Chicago.

———. 1967. *Mind, Self, and Society: From the Standpoint of a Social Behaviorist*. Chicago: University of Chicago Press.

Meadow, Charles. 2002. *Making Connections: Communication through the Ages*. Lanham, MD: Scarecrow Press.

Meltzer, Bernard, et al. 1975. *Symbolic Interactionism: Genesis, Varieties and Criticism*. London and Boston: Routledge & Kegan Paul.

Merleau-Ponty, Maurice. 1968. *Working Notes, 1959, The Visible and the Invisible, Followed by Working Notes*, edited by Claude Lefort, translated by Alphonso Lingis. Evanston, IL.: Northwestern University Press.

———. 2004. *Phenomenology of Perception*. Translated by Colin Smith. London and New York: Routledge.

Merrell, Floyd. 1995. *Semiosis in the Postmodern Age*. West Lafayette, IN: Purdue University Press.

———. 1996. *Signs Grow: Semiosis and Life Processes*. Toronto: University of Toronto Press.

———. 1997. *Peirce, Signs and Meaning*. Toronto: University of Toronto Press.

———. 2000. *Tasking Textuality: Literary and Cultural Theory*. Vol. 5. New York: Peter Lang Publishing.

Mickunas, Algis. 2007. "Maurice-Merleau Ponty: Communicative Practice." In *Perspectives on Philosophy of Communication*, edited by Pat Anderson, 139–158. West Lafayette, IN: Purdue University Press.

Miller, Katherine. 2002. *Communication Theories: Perspectives, Processes and Contexts*. New York: McGraw-Hill.

Monge, Peter. 1998. "Communication Theory for a Globalizing World." In *Communication: Views from the Helm for the 21st Century*, edited by Judith S. Trent, 3–7. Boston: Allyn & Bacon.

Morson, Gary, and Caryl Emerson. 199. *Mikhail Bakhtin: Creation of a Prosaic*. Stanford, CA: Stanford University Press.

Morris, Randa. 2009. *Instant Messenger and the Communication Revolution*. www.associatedcontent.com/article/223642/instant_messenger_and_the_communication.html?cat=12 (accessed November 2, 2009).

Morris, William, ed. 1982. *The American Heritage Dictionary of the English Language*. Boston: Houghton Mifflin Company.

Mowlana, Hamid. 2007. "Theoretical Perspectives on Islam and Communication." *China Media Research* 3, no. 4: 23–33.

Myers, David. 2001. "A Pox on All Compromises: Reply to Craig (1999)." *Communication Theory* 11, no. 2: 218–230.

Naddaf, Gérard. 2007. "The Role of the Poet in Plato's Idea of Callipolis and Magnesia." *Kriterion* 48, no. 116: 329–349.

Nancy, Jean-Luc. 1997. *The Gravity of Thought*. Atlantic Heights, NJ: Humanities Press International.

Nastasia, Diana I., and Lana F. Rakow. 2004. "Towards a Philosophy of Communication Theories: An Ontological, Epistemological and Ideological Approach." Paper presented at the annual meeting of the International Communication Association, New Orleans, LA. http://www.allacademic.com/meta/p113255_index (accessed October 17, 2009).

Neuliep, James W. 1996. *Human Communication Theory: Applications and Case Studies*. Boston: Allyn & Bacon.

Nightingale, Andrea W. 2006. *Spectacles of Truth in Classical Greek Philosophy: Theoria in Its Cultural Context*. Cambridge: Cambridge University Press.

Nordenstreng, Kaarle. 2007. "Discipline or Field?" *Nordicom Review*, Jubilee Issue: 211–222.

Nubiola, Jaime. 1994. "The Continuity of Continuity: A Theme in Leibniz, Peirce and Quine." In *Publicado en Leibniz und Europa, VI. Internationaler Leibniz-Kongress*, 361–371. Hannover: Gottfried-Wilhelm-Leibniz-Gesellschaft e. V.

Openkov, Mikhail (Опенков, Михаил). 1997. *Virtual Reality: Onto-dialogical Approach* (Виртуальная Реальность: Онто-диалогический Подход). Ph.D. Dissertation Abstract. Moscow.

Pagin, Peter. 2008. "What Is Communicative Success?" *Canadian Journal of Philosophy* 38, no. 1: 85–115.

Parret, Herman. 1993. *The Aesthetics of Communication: Pragmatics and Beyond*. New York: Springer-Verlag.

Pazienza, Maria T., et al. 2007. "Let's Talk about Our 'Being': A Linguistic-Based Ontology Framework for Coordinating Agents." *Applied Ontology* 2, nos. 3–4: 305–332.

Perlina, Nina. 1992. "Primeval and Modern Mythologies in the Life of Ol'ga Mikhailovna Freidenberg." *Russian Review* 51, no. 2: 188–197

Painter, Joe. 2000. "Pierre Bourdieu." In *Thinking Space*, edited by Mike Crang and Nigel Thrift, 239–259. London and New York: Routledge.

Pearce, Barnett. 1994. "Recovering Agency." In *Communication Yearbook 17*, edited by Stanley Deetz, 34–41. Thousand Oaks, CA: Sage Publications.

Peshkov, Igor' (Пешков, Игорь). 1998. *Introduction into a Rhetoric of Act* (Введение в Риторику Поступка). Moscow: Labirint.

Peters, John D. 1989. "John Locke, the Individual, and the Origin of Communication." *Quarterly Journal of Speech* 75: 387–399.

———. 1993. "Genealogical Notes on 'the Field.'" *Journal of Communication* 43, no. 4: 132–139.

———. 1999. *Speaking into the Air: A History of the Idea of Communication*. Chicago: University of Chicago Press.

———. 2003. "Space, Time, and Communication Theory." *Canadian Journal of Communication* 28: 397–411.

———. 2005. *Courting the Abyss: Free Speech and the Liberal Tradition*. Chicago: University of Chicago Press.

———. 2008. "Technology and Ideology: The Case of the Telegraph Revisited." In *Thinking with James Carey: Essays on Communication, Transportation, History*, edited by Jeremy Packer and Craig Robertson, 137–155. New York: Peter Lang.

Petrilli, Susan. 2008. "On Communication: Contributions to the Human Sciences and to Humanism from Semiotics Understood as Semioethics." *American Journal of Semiotics* 24, no. 4: 193–236.

Petrelli, Susan, and Augusto Ponzio. 2005. *Semiotics Unbounded: Interpretive Routes through the Open Network of Signs*. Toronto: University of Toronto Press.

Piaget, Jean. 2002. *Judgment and Reasoning in the Child.* Translated by Marjorie Warden. Taylor & Francis e-Library.

Pinchevski, Amit. 2005. *By Way of Interruption: Levinas and the Ethics of Communication.* Pittsburgh: Duquesne University Press.

Plato. 1804. *The Laws.* In *The Works of Plato.* Vol. 2. Translated by Fl. Sydenham and T. Taylor. London: T. Taylor.

Plummer, Ken. 2000. "Symbolic Interactionism in the Twentieth Century." In *The Blackwell Companion to Social Theory,* edited by Bryan S. Turner, 193–222. Malden, MA: Blackwell Publishers.

Polanyi, Michael. 1966. *The Tacit Dimension.* London: Routledge & Kegan Paul.

Pollock, Sheldon, et al. 2002. "Cosmopolitanism." In *Cosmopolitanism,* edited by Sheldon Pollock et al, 1–14. Durham, NC, and London: Duke University Press.

Ponzio, Augusto. 2004. "Modeling, Communication, and Dialogism." *American Journal of Semiotics* 20, nos. 1–4: 157–178.

Powers, John H. 1995. "On the Intellectual Structure of the Human Communication Discipline." *Communication Education* 44, no. 3: 191–222.

Prigogine, Ilya, and Isabelle Stengers. 1984. *Order Out of Chaos: Man's New Dialogue with Nature.* Toronto and New York: Bantam Books.

Prus, Robert. 1996. *Symbolic Interaction and Ethnographic Research: Intersubjectivity and the Study of Human Lived Experience.* Albany: State University of New York Press.

Psathas, George. 1995. *Conversation Analysis: The Study of Talk-in-Interaction.* Thousand Oaks, CA: Sage Publications.

Radford, Gary. 2005. *On the Philosophy of Communication.* Belmont, CA: Thomson Wadsworth.

Radnitzky, Gerard, and William W. Bartley, eds. 1987. *Evolutionary Epistemology, Rationality and the Sociology of Knowledge.* La Salle, IL: Open Court.

Raffoul, François. 1997. "Translator's Preface." In Jean-Luc Nancy, *The Gravity of Thought.* Atlantic Heights, NJ: Humanities Press International.

Raffoul, François, and Eric S. Nelson. "Introduction." In *Rethinking Facticity,* edited by François Raffoul and Eric S. Nelson, 1–24. Albany: State University of New York Press.

Rämö, Hans. 1999. "An Aristotelian Human Time-Space Manifold." *Time & Society* 8, no. 2: 309–328.

Rasch, William. 2000. *Niklas Luhman's Modernity: The Paradoxes of Differentiation.* Stanford, CA: Stanford University Press.

Reichenbach, Hans. 1958. *The Philosophy of Space and Time.* New York: Dover Publications.

Renckstorf, Karsten, ed. 2004. *Action Theory and Communicative Research: Recent Developments in Europe.* Berlin: Mouton de Gruyter.

Riva, Guiseppe, et al., eds. 2006. *From Communication to Presence: Cognition, Emotions and Culture: Towards the Ultimate Communicative Experience.* Amsterdam: IOS Press.

Roberts, Jeff. 2003. "Kairos, Chronos and Chaos." *Group Analysis* 36, no. 2: 202–217.

Roberts, Kathleen. 2004. "Texturing the Narrative Paradigm: Folklore and Communication." *Communication Quarterly* 52: 129–142.

Roche, Christophe. 2002. "From Information Society to Knowledge Society: The Ontology Issue." *Computing Anticipatory Systems: CASYS 2001—Fifth International Conference. AIP Conference Proceedings* 627, no. 1: 575–580.

Rogers, Everett. 1994. *A History of Communication Study: A Biographical Approach.* New York: Free Press.

Rogers, Richard. 2006. "From Cultural Exchange to Transculturation: A Review and Reconceptualization of Cultural Appropriation," *Communication Theory* 16: 474–503.

Rorty, Amélie. 1980. "The Place of Contemplation in Aristotle's *Nicomachean Ethics.*" In *Essays on Aristotle's Ethics,* edited by Amélie Rorty, 377–394. Berkeley: University of California Press.

Rorty, Richard. 1992. *The Linguistic Turn: Essays in Philosophical Method.* Chicago: University of Chicago Press.

Rosen, Steven. 2004. *Dimensions of Apeiron: A Topological Phenomenology of Space, Time, and Individuation.* Amsterdam and New York: Rodopi.

Rosengren, Karl. 1983. "Communication Research: One Paradigm, or Four?" *Journal of Communication* 33, no. 3: 185–207.

Rothenbuhler, Eric. 1998. *Ritual Communication: From Everyday Conversation to Mediated Ceremony.* Thousand Oaks, CA: Sage Publications.

Rotman, Brian. 1987. *Signifying Nothing: The Zemiotics of Zero.* New York: St. Martin's Press.

———. 2008. *Becoming Beside Ourselves: The Alphabet, Ghosts, and Distributed Human Being.* Durham, NC, and London: Duke University Press.

Roudaut, Jean. 2003. "A Grand Illusion." In *Magritte,* edited by Daniel Abadie, 23–37. New York: Distributed Art Publishers.

Ruben, Brent, and Lea Stewart. 2006. *Communication and Human Behavior.* Boston: Allyn & Bacon.

Ruesch, Jurgen, and Gregory Bateson. 1951. *Communication: The Social Matrix of Psychiatry.* New York. W. W. Norton & Company.

Russell, Jacoby. 2005. *Picture Imperfect: Utopian Thought for an Anti-utopian Age.* New York: Columbia University Press.

Russill, Chris. 2005. "The Road Not Taken: William James's Radical Empiricism and Communication Theory." *Communication Review* 8, no. 3: 277–305.

Salem, Philip. 2009. *The Complexity of Human Communication.* Cresskill, NJ: Hampton Press.

Sangren, Paul S. 1988. "Rhetoric and Authority of Ethnography: 'Postmodernism' and the Social Reproduction of Texts." In *Current Anthropology, Inquiry and Debate in the Human Sciences: Contributions from Current Anthropology, Celebrating the Fiftieth Anniversary of the Wenner-Gren Foundation for Anthropological Research,* edited by Sydel Silverman, 277–307. Chicago: University of Chicago Press.

Sarukkai, Sundar. 2002. *Translating the World: Science and Language*. Lanham, MD: University Press of America.

Scannell, Paddy. 2005. "Love and Communication: A Review Essay." *Media Development* 52, no. 4: 35–41.

Schiller, Dan. 1996. *Theorizing Communication: A History*. New York: Oxford University Press.

Schlegel, Friedrich. 1971. "On Incomprehensibility." In *Lucinde and the Fragments*, translated by Peter Firchow, 259–271. Minneapolis: University of Minnesota Press.

Schneider, Michael. 1995. *A Beginner's Guide to Constructing the Universe*. New York: HarperCollins Publishers.

Schramm, Wilbur. 1997. *The Beginnings of Communication Study in America: A Personal Memoir*. Thousand Oaks, CA: Sage.

Schrott, Angela. 1999. *"Que fais, Adam?* Questions and Seduction in the *Jeu d'Adam."* In *Historical Dialogue Analysis*, edited by Andreas Jucker et al., 331–370. Amsterdam and Philadelphia: John Benjamins B.V.

Schudson, Michael. 1997. "Why Conversation Is Not the Soul of Democracy." *Critical Studies in Mass Communication* 14: 297–309.

Schuller, Douglas. 2008. *Liberating Voices: A Pattern Language for Communication Revolution*. Cambridge, MA: MIT Press.

Schultz, Alfred. 1980. *The Phenomenology of the Social World*. Translated by George Walsh and Frederick Lehnert. Evanston, IL: Northwestern University Press.

Scollon, Ronald, and Suzie Scollon. 2004. *Nexus Analysis: Discourse and the Emerging Internet*. New York and London: Routledge.

Scott, Charles. 2007. *Living with Indifference*. Bloomington: Indiana University Press.

Sedda, Franciscu. 2009. *Reflections on Glocal on the Basis of the Semiotic Study of Culture*. www.usp.br/matrizes/img/03/eng/EmPauta2_FranciscuSedda_eng.pdf (accessed October 30, 2009).

Seifert, Josef. 1987. *Back to Things in Themselves: A Phenomenological Foundation for Classical Realism*. New York: Routldege & Kegan Paul.

Serres, Michel. 1982. *Hermes: Literature, Science, Philosophy*. Baltimore: John Hopkins University Press.

Shaikhitdinova, Svetlana (Шайхитдинова, Светлана). 2004. "On the Concept of Communication (К Понятию Коммуникация)." *Vestnik RGGU* 2: 162–168.

Shannon, Claude, and Warren Weaver. 1949. *The Mathematical Theory of Communication*. Urbana: University of Illinois Press.

Shcherba, Lev (Щерба, Лев). 2004. *Language System and Speech Activity* (Языковая Система и Речевая Деятельность). Moscow: URSS.

Sheldon, Kennon, and Maarten Vansteenkiste. 2005. "Personal Goals and Time Travel: How Are Future Places Visited, and Is It Worth It?" In *Understanding Behavior in the Context of Time: Theory, Research, and Application*, edited by Alan Strathman and Jeff Joireman, 143–163. Mahwah, NJ: Lawrence Erlbaum Associates.

Shepherd, Gregory. 1993. "Building a Discipline of Communication." *Journal of Communication* 43, no. 3: 83–91.

——. 1999. "Advances in Communication Theory: A Critical Review." *Journal of Communication* (Summer): 156–164.

——. 2001. "Pragmatism and Tragedy, Communication and Hope: A Summary Story." In *American Pragmatism and Communication Research*, edited by David Perry, 241–254. Mahwah, NJ: Lawrence Erlbaum Associates.

Shepherd, Gregory, et al., eds. 2006. *Communication as . . . Perspectives on Theory*. Thousand Oaks, CA: Sage Publications.

Shields, Rob. 2003. *The Virtual*. London: Routledge.

Shome, Raka. 2003. "The Power and Practice of Space." *Communication Theory* 13, no. 1: 39–56.

Simonson, Peter. 2001. "Varieties of Pragmatism and Communication: Visions and Revisions from Peirce to Peters." In *American Pragmatism and Communication Research*, edited by David Perry, 1–26. Mahwah, NJ: Lawrence Erlbaum Associates.

Simpson, Lorenzo. 1995. *Technology, Time, and the Conversations of Modernity*. New York and London: Routledge.

Sinekopova, Galina. 2006. "Building the Public Sphere: Bases and Biases." *Journal of Communication* 56, no. 3: 505–522.

Smith, Andrew. 1993. "Phenomenology of Intercultural Communication." In *Japanese and Western Phenomenology*, edited by P. Blasser et al., 235–247. Kluwer Academic Publishers.

——. 1997. "The Limits of Communication: Lyotard and Levinas on Otherness." In *Transgressing Discourses: Communication and the Voice of Other*, edited by Michael Huspek and Gary Radford, 329–352. Albany: State University of New York Press.

——. 2003. "Discord in Intercultural Negotiation. Toward an Ethic of Communicability." In *Ferment in the Intercultural Field: Axiology/Value/Praxis*, edited by William Starosta and Chen Guo-Ming, 91–127. Thousand Oaks, CA: Sage Publications.

——. 2008. "Dialogue in Agony: The Problem of Communication in Authoritarian Regimes." *Communication Theory* 18, no. 1: 160–185.

Smith, Dorothy. 1999. *Writing the Social: Critique, Theory, and Investigations*. Toronto: University of Toronto Press.

Smith, John. 2002. "Time and Qualitative Time." In *Rhetoric and Kairos: Essays in History, Theory, and Praxis*, edited by Phillip Sipiora and James Baumlin, 46–57. Albany: State University of New York Press.

Sonesson, Göran. 1996/1997. "Approaches to the Lifeworld Core of Pictorial Rhetoric (1)." *Visio: La Revue de l'association Internationale de Semiótique Visuelle* 1, no. 3: 49–76.

——. 2000. "Ego Meets Alter: The Meaning of Otherness in Cultural Semiotics." *Semiotics* 128, nos. 3–4: 537–559.

Spanos, William. 1976. "Heidegger, Kierkegaard, and the Hermeneutic Circle: Towards a Postmodern Theory of Interpretation as Dis-closure." *Boundary 2: A Journal of Postmodern Literature and Culture* 4, no. 2: 455–488.

Spencer-Brown, George. 1979. *Laws of Form*. New York: Dutton.

Stacks, Don, et al. 1991. *Introduction to Communication Theory*. Fort Worth, TX: Holt, Rinehart & Winston.

Stacy, Alan, et al. 2006. "Word Association Tests of Associative Memory and Implicit Processes: Theory and Assessment Issues." In *Handbook of Implicit Cognition and Addiction*, edited by Reinout Wiers and Alan Stacy, 75–90. Thousand Oaks, CA: Sage Publications.

Stanford Encyclopedia of Philosophy. 2009. http://plato.stanford.edu/info.html#c (accessed November 25, 2009).

Steelwater, Eliza. 1997. "Mead and Heidegger: Exploring the Ethics and Theory of Space, Place, and the Environment." In *Philosophy and Geography 1: Space, Place, and Environmental Ethics*, edited by Andrew Light and Jonathan Smith, 189–201. Lanham, MD: Rowman & Littlefield Publishers.

Stenning, Keith, et al. 2006. *Introduction to Cognition and Communication*. Cambridge, MA: MIT Press.

Stepanov, Yuriy (Степанов, Юрий). 1985. *In the Three-Dimensional Space of Language: Semiotic Problems of Linguistics, Philosophy, Art* (В Трехмерном Пространстве Языка: Семиотические Проблемы Линвиситики, Философии, Искусства). Moscow: Nauka.

———. 2004. *Constants: A Vocabulary of Russian Culture* (Константы: Словарь Русской Культуры). Moscow: Akademicheski Proekt.

———. 2005. *Proteus: Essays on Chaos Evolution* (Протей: Очерки Хаотической Эволюции). Moscow: Yazyki slavyanskoi kul'tury.

Stephenson, Hunter. 2009. "(Re)claiming the Ground: Image Events, Kairos, and Discourse." *Enculturation* 6, no. 2. http://enculturation.gmu.edu/6.2/stephenson (accessed October 21, 2009).

Sterne, Jonathan. 2006. "Techné." In *Communication as . . . Perspectives on Theory*. Edited by Gregory Shepherd et al., 91–98. Thousand Oaks, CA: Sage Publications.

Stewart, Ian. 2001. *Flatterland*. Cambridge, MA: Perseus Publishing.

Stewart, John. 1997. "Developing Communication Theories." In *Developing Communication Theories*, edited by Gerry Philipsen and Terrance Albrecht, 157–192. Albany: State University of New York Press.

Stewart, John, and Gerry Philipsen. 1984. "Communication as Situated Accomplishment: The Cases of Hermeneutics and Ethnography." In *Progress in Communication Sciences*, edited by Brenda Dervin and Melvin Voigt, 177–217. Norwood, NJ: Ablex Publishing Corporations.

St. John, Jeffrey. 2006. "Communication as Failure." In *Communication as . . . Perspectives on Theory*, edited by Gregory Shepherd et al., 249–266. Thousand Oaks: Sage Publications.

Stoker, Kevin, and Kati Tusinski. 2006. "Reconsidering Public Relations' Infatuation with Dialogue: Why Engagement and Reconciliation Can Be More Ethical Than Symmetry and Reciprocity." *Journal of Mass Media Ethics* 21, nos. 2–3: 156–176.

Stone, Gerald, et al. 1999. *Clarifying Communication Theories: A Hands-On Approach.* Ames: Iowa State University Press.

Struever, Nancy. 2004. "Rhetoric: Time, Memory, Memoir." In *A Companion to Rhetoric and Rhetorical Criticism*, edited by Walter Jost and Wendy Olmsted, 425–441. Malden, MA: Blackwell Publishing.

Swanson, Davis. 1993. "Fragmentation, the Field, and the Future." *Journal of Communication* 43, no. 4: 163–172.

Taylor, Charles. 1990. "Aristotle's Epistemology." In *Epistemology*, edited by S. Emerson, 116–142. Cambridge: Cambridge University Press.

TenHouten, Warren. 2005. *Time and Society*. Albany: State University of New York Press.

Teilhard de Chardin, Pierre. 1964. *The Future of Man*. Translated by Norman Denny. New York: Harper & Row.

Thayer, Lee. 1997. *Pieces: Toward a Revisioning of Communication/Life*. Greenwich, CT, and London: Ablex Publishing Corporation.

Thelwall, Mike. 2002. "Research Dissemination and Invocation on the Web." *Online Information Review* 26, no. 6: 413–420.

Tiupa, Valeriy (Тюпа, Валерий). 1998. "The Ontology of Communication" (Онтология Коммуникации). *Diskurs* 5–6: 5–17.

Todorov, Tzvetan. 1984. *Conquest of America: The Question of the Other*. New York: HarperCollins Publishers.

Turner, Victor. 1967. *The Forest of Symbols: Aspects of Ndembu Ritual*. Ithaca, NY, and London: Cornell University Press.

Uemov, Aleksandr (Уемов, Александр). 1975. "Afterword (Послесловие)." In L. Tondl (Л. Тондл), *Problems of Semantics* (Проблемы Семантики), 457–459. Moscow: Progress.

Vasilik, Mikhail, ed. (Василик, Михаил). 2006. *The Foundations of Communication Theory* (Основы Теории Коммуникации). Moscow: Gardariki.

Vivian, Bradford. 2004. *Being Made Strange: Rhetoric beyond Representation*. Albany: State University of New York Press.

Vladimirova, Tat'yana (Владимирова, Татьяна). 2007. "A Conception of Interpersonal Discourse of Representatives of Different Linguo-Cultural Communities (Концепция Межличностного Дискурса Представителей Различных Лингвокультурных Общностей)." In *Aspects of Cognition: Science, Philosophy, Culture in the XX Century* (Грани Познания: Наука, Философия, Культура в XX веке), 332–365. Moscow: Nauka.

Vroons, Erik. 2005. "Communication Studies in Europe: A Sketch of the Situation around 1955." *The International Communication Gazette* 67, no. 6: 495–522.

Vyvyan, Evans. 2003. *The Structure of Time: Language, Meaning and Temporal Cognition*. Amsterdam and Philadelphia: John Benjamins Publishing.

Wachterhauser, Brice, ed. 1986. *Hermeneutics and Modern Philosophy*. Albany: State University of New York Press.

Wagner, Roy. 1981. *The Invention of Culture*. Chicago: University of Chicago Press.

Walber, Daniel. 2009. "Facebook Creates a Communication Revolution." www
.convergemag.com/edtech/Facebook-Creates-a-Communication-Revolution.html
(accessed October 17, 2009).

Weaver, Warren. 1964. "Recent Contributions to the Mathematical Theory of Communication." In Claude Shannon and Warren Weaver, *The Mathematical Theory of
Communication*, 1–16. Urbana: University of Illinois Press.

West, Richard, and Lynn Turner. 2004. *Introducing Communication Theory: Analysis
and Application*. New York: McGraw-Hill.

Wexler, Bruce. 2006. *Brain and Culture: Neurobiology, Ideology, and Social Change*.
Cambridge, MA: MIT Press.

White, James M., and David M. Klein. 1996. *Family Theories: An Introduction*. Thousand Oaks, CA: Sage Publications.

Wiegmann, Hermann. 1990. "Plato's Critique of the Poets and the Misunderstanding
of His Epistemological Argumentation." *Philosophy and Rhetoric* 23, no. 2: 109–124.

Williams, Angie, and Jon Nussbaum. 2000. *Intergenerational Communication across the
Life Span*. Mahwah, NJ: Erlbaum.

Winston, Brian. 1998. *Media, Technology and Society: A History from the Telegraph to
the Internet*. London: Routledge.

Wittgenstein, Ludwig. 2009. *Philosophical Investigations*. Edited by Joachim Schulte
and P. M. S. Hacker. Hoboken, NJ: Wiley, John & Sons.

Wood, Julia. 2004. *Communication Theories in Action: An Introduction*. Belmont, CA:
Thomson Wadsworth.

Wolfe, Cary. 1991. "Nature as Critical Concept: Kenneth Burke, the Frankfurt
School, and 'Metabiology.'" *Cultural Critique* 18 (Spring): 65–96.

Wyschogrod, Edith. 1985. *Spirit in Ashes: Hegel, Heidegger, and Man-Made Mass
Death*. New Haven, CT, and London: Yale University Press.

Yampol'skiy, Mikhail (Ямпольский, Михаил). 2001. *On the Near: Essays on Non-
mimetic Sight* (О Близком: Очерки Немиметического Зрения). Moscow: Novoe
Literaturnoe Obozrenie.

Zaharna, R. S. 1989. "Self-Shock: The Double-Binding Challenge of Identity." *International Journal of Intercultural Relations* 13: 501–526.

Zeleny, Milan. 1996. *Human Systems Management: Integrating Knowledge, Management and Systems*. Toh Tuck Link, Singapore: World Scientific Publishing.

Zhuravlev, Ignatiy (Журавлев, Игнатий). 2006. "On the Non-classical Ontology of
Communication (К Неклсассической Онтологии Коммуникации)." In *Commu-
nication and Construction of Social Realities* (Коммуникация и Конструирования
Социальных Реальностей), 33–44. St. Petersburg: Roza Mira.

Zimmerman, Michael. 1981. *The Eclipse of Self*. Athens: Ohio University Press.

Index

5855

About the Author

Igor E. Klyukanov, Ph.D., is professor of communication studies at Eastern Washington University. He has authored numerous articles, book chapters, and books in communication theory, semiotics, translation studies, general linguistics, and intercultural communication. His works have been published in U. S., Russia, England, Spain, Costa Rica, Serbia, Bulgaria, India and Morocco. His works have appeared in such journals as *Studies in Humanities*, *The American Journal of Semiotics*, *The Atlantic Journal of Communication*, *Arob@ase: A Journal of Literature and Human Sciences*, *International Journal of Communication*, *International Journal of Applied Semiotics*, *Language*, *Individual & Society*, *Contrastes: Revista Interdisciplinar de Filosofía*, and *Discourse and Society*. He served as an associate editor of *The American Journal of Semiotics* and is the founding editor of *Russian Journal of Communication*.

Breinigsville, PA USA
27 August 2010
244359BV00002B/1/P

9 780739 137246